# DATE DUE

| | | | |
|---|---|---|---|
| AP 07 03 | | | |
| JE 6 03 | | | |
| | | | |
| | | | |
| | | | |
| | | | |
| | | | |
| | | | |
| | | | |
| | | | |
| | | | |
| | | | |
| | | | |
| | | | |
| | | | |
| | | | |
| | | | |

DEMCO 38-296

This book relates the history of Italian railways with special regard to their relation with the Italian state from the 1840s, when the first lines were constructed, until nationalization in 1905. It shows that while the Italian state interfered continuously in railway matters, it was nevertheless incapable of creating viable conditions for railway companies.

Throughout the nineteenth century the 'railway question' continued to have a pernicious and diverse influence on Italian political life; and because of the low quality of railway regulation, and other factors, the railways' contribution to the creation of a national market and the economic unification of the country was limited. The book also examines Italian regional social and economic statistics before and after political unification, in order to obtain a deeper insight into the continuing disparity between northern and southern Italy. Finally, the book places the development of the Italian railways in a European context, and compares their construction with those in Germany.

CAMBRIDGE STUDIES IN ITALIAN HISTORY AND CULTURE

# RAILWAYS AND THE FORMATION OF THE ITALIAN STATE IN THE NINETEENTH CENTURY

CAMBRIDGE STUDIES IN ITALIAN HISTORY AND CULTURE

Edited by GIGLIOLA FRAGNITO, Università degli Studi, Parma
CESARE MOZZARELLI, Università Cattolica del Sacro Cuore, Milan
ROBERT ORESKO, Institute of Historical Research, University of London
and GEOFFREY SYMCOX, University of California, Los Angeles

This series comprises monographs and a variety of collaborative volumes, including translated works, which will concentrate on the period of Italian history from late medieval times up to the Risorgimento. The editors aim to stimulate scholarly debate over a range of issues which have not hitherto received, in English, the attention they deserve. As it develops, the series will emphasize the interest and vigor of current international debates on this central period of Italian history and the persistent influence of Italian culture on the rest of Europe.

*For a list of titles in the series, see end of book*

R

# RAILWAYS AND THE FORMATION OF THE ITALIAN STATE IN THE NINETEENTH CENTURY

## ALBERT SCHRAM

*Universidad de Costa Rica*

**CAMBRIDGE**
UNIVERSITY PRESS

ΓE OF THE UNIVERSITY OF CAMBRIDGE
ιgton Street, Cambridge CB2 1RP

ΓNIVERSITY PRESS
The Edinburgh Building, Cambridge CB2 2RU, United Kingdom
40 West 20th Street, New York, NY 10011–4211, USA
10 Stamford Road, Oakleigh, Melbourne 3166, Australia

First published 1997

Printed in the United Kingdom at the University Press, Cambridge

Typeset in Bembo

*A catalogue record for this book is available from the British Library*

*Library of Congress cataloguing in publication data*
Schram, Albert.
Railways and the formation of the Italian state in the nineteenth century / Albert Schram.
p.   cm. – (Cambridge studies in Italian history and culture)
Based on the author's thesis (doctoral).
Includes bibliographical references and index.
ISBN 0 521 57159 6
1. Railroads and state – Italy – History – 19th century.
2. Railroads – Italy – History – 19th century.
3. Italy – Economic conditions – Regional disparities.
I. Title.   II. Series.
HE3097.S37   1997
385′.0945′09034–DC21   96–48555   CIP

ISBN 0521 57159 6 hardback

CE

TO TATHIANA, LAURA AND KEES

# CONTENTS

# ILLUSTRATIONS

# TABLES

# ACKNOWLEDGEMENTS

The financial aid of the Dutch Ministry of Education and the European University Institute for the completion of my Ph.D. thesis, on which this book is based, is gratefully acknowledged. I would also like to thank the Economic History Department of the London School of Economics, which, during three precious months, provided me with an excellent library and an ideal academic environment. The research grant from the Nederlands Instituut te Rome (Dutch Ministry of Culture) formed the starting point for this research.

My conversations with Dudley Baines, Carlo Bardini, Joerg Baten, Albert Carreras, Giovanni Federico, Stefano Fenoaltea, Tathiana Flores Acuña, James Foreman-Peck, Rainer Fremdling, Richard Griffiths, Michèle Merger, Jan Luyten van Zanden, Jeffrey Williamson and Vera Zamagni have always been greatly inspiring and I thank them all for their unconditional support. Since 1988, when I started doing research on Italian railways, many people have helped me in finding the necessary information. The help of the research librarian of the European University Institute, Michiel Tegelaars, has been invaluable. One of the most heroic librarians I have met is Sergio Barizza, who despite the appalling circumstances in the Archivio Communale of Venice, let me photocopy several documents free of charge.

# ABBREVIATIONS

## JOURNALS

| | |
|---|---|
| AEAPP | *American Economics Association Papers and Proceedings* |
| ASI | *Annali della Storia d'Impresa* |
| BHR | *Business History Review* |
| EDCC | *Economic Development and Cultural Change* |
| EEH | *Explorations in Economic History* |
| EHR | *Economic History Review* |
| HES | *Histoire, Economie et Société* |
| IC | *Italia Contemporanea* |
| IF | *Ingegneria Ferroviaria* |
| IP | *Il Politecnico* |
| JEEH | *Journal of European Economic History* |
| JEH | *Journal of Economic History* |
| JTH | *Journal of Transport History* |
| MC | *Moneta e Credito* |
| NRS | *Nuova Rivista Storica* |
| RHCF | *Revue d'Histoire des Chemins de Fer* |
| RSE | *Rivista di Storia Economica* |
| RSH | *Revue Suisse d'Histoire* |
| RSI | *Rivista Storica Italiana* |
| SJPE | *Scottish Journal of Political Economy* |
| SL | *Storia in Lombardia* |
| SU | *Storia Urbana* |
| TG | *Tijdschrift voor Geschiedenis* |
| VSW | *Vierteljahresschrift für Sozial- und Wirstschaftsgeschichte* |

## OTHER ABBREVIATIONS

| | |
|---|---|
| km | kilometre(s) |

PK            passengerkilometre(s)
TK            tonnekilometre(s)
TU            traffic unit(s) (1 TU is the sum of 1 PK + 1 TK)

# CHAPTER I

# THE HISTORY OF RAILWAYS

The history of technology demonstrates how, in the nineteenth century, progress in steam and transport technology led to a continuous increase in the speed and quality of railway transport. Only at the beginning of the twentieth century, with the introduction of electric traction and of the internal combustion engine, was a similar qualitative improvement in land transport achieved. In fact, during most of the nineteenth century, the only direct competitors of the railways were canal boats, horse-drawn coaches and wagons. The railways were so successful that the railway network expanded steadily to the remotest corners of the world. Nonetheless, the densest railway network was built in Europe, and this still remains the case today.

Traditional railway history is closely linked to the history of technology and frequently reads like a story of the triumph of man over nature, of breaking the centuries-old constraints of time and space, and of how the world was slowly made as small a place as it is today. Often, this kind of railway history is intended as a tribute to the touching dedication of men to their locomotives, to the personal heroism of railway engineers, and, last but not least, to the progress of humanity and the greatness of the nation.[1]

In the 1960s, a different kind of railway history emerged when Robert Fogel's book *Railroads and American Economic Growth. Essays in Econometric History* was published in 1964.[2] For the first time, a serious effort was made to measure the influence of the railways on the

---

[1] For a survey of traditional Italian railway history, see Erico Monti, *Il primo secolo di vita delle ferrovie italiane, 1839–1849* (Florence, 1939); L. Briano, *Storia delle ferrovie in Italia* (Milan, 1977); Livio Jannattoni, *Il treno in Italia* (Rome, 1980); Elvira Cantarella, 'Lo sviluppo delle ferrovie dalle origini alla statizazzione', in *Storia della società italiana*, 25 vols. (Milan, 1987); Andrea Giuntini, 'Le ferrovie nella storiografia italiana', *IC* (1990), pp. 327–32; and Andrea Giuntini, *Contributo alla formazione di una bibliografia storica sulle ferrovie in Italia* (Milan, 1991).

[2] In 1993 Robert Fogel was awarded the Nobel prize for economics for his work.

economy in a coherent way. In this paradigmatic study Fogel tried to determine how big the contribution of railways had been to the growth of national income in the United States of America during the nineteenth century. The results showed that the railways had contributed at most around 4 per cent of national income per year towards the end of the century, which seemed to contradict the suggestion of traditional railway histories that they had brought enormous benefits.

Since the publication of Fogel's book the methodological debate has never subsided. The main opponents to his methods argue that 4 per cent of national income per year, measured by Fogel's partial equilibrium model, amounts to a substantial amount when a general equilibrium model of the economy is applied.[3] This technical discussion must be left aside here, but it can be concluded that there is no full agreement among economic historians on how to measure the benefit of railways for an economy.

During the last decade, due to a wider acceptance of these advanced econometric methods by historians, however, the methodological gap between the 'traditional' and the 'econometric' schools of railway history has increased considerably.[4] Nevertheless, this book tries to steer a middle way between these two 'schools' of railway history by combining the merits of both. On the one hand, the importance of political factors and state intervention in determining the success or failure of the railways is stressed. On the other hand, by making comparisons with other European countries, a meaningful interpretation of those quantitative data available for Italian railways can be offered. No effort has been made to come up with a global measurement of the economic benefits of the railways, or their overall importance for the integration of the Italian market.

The creation of an appropriate statistical framework has presented a major challenge. Socio-economic data before Italian unification in 1860 are hard to harmonize and they are scarce or unreliable for the first decades after unification. The growth rates of gross domestic

---

See also Robert Fogel, 'Notes on the Social Savings Controversy', *JEH* 29 (1979), pp. 1–54.

[3] John James, 'The Use of General Equilibrium Analysis in Economic History', *EEH* 21 (1984), pp. 231–53; Jeffrey Williamson, 'Greasing the Wheels of Sputtering Export Engines: Midwestern Grains and American Growth', *EEH* 17 (1980), pp. 189–217; J. Foreman-Peck, 'Railways and Late Victorian Economic Growth', in James Foreman-Peck (ed.), *New Perspectives on the Late Victorian Economy. Essays in Quantitative Economic History 1860–1914* (Cambridge, 1991), pp. 73-95.

[4] Simon P. Ville, 'Transport and the Industrial Revolution', *JTH* 13 (1992), pp. 180–1; Terry Gourvish, 'What Kind of Railway History Did We Get? Forty Years of Research', *JTH* 14 (1993), pp. 111–25.

product, for example, estimated for the period from 1860 to 1890, are probably too low, but recent revisions have not produced significantly different results.[5] The data on railways, in particular those related to railway traffic, present problems of harmonization too, since until nationalization the companies which ran the network collected statistics according to different criteria. Not all of these problems could be solved and more research along these lines is needed.

For political reasons in the first decades after Italian unification, the role of the railways in the formation of the Italian state was considered to be very important. One minister of public works remarked in the 1860s that he was given the task of being the architect of Italian unity.[6] More than half of the state's spending on infrastructure in the 1860s and 1870s was on railways, and for the whole period between 1861 and 1913 the railways absorbed around 13 per cent of the total budget and around 75 per cent of the amount spent on public works.[7] Given these expenses, it is not surprising, therefore, that Italian politics devoted a substantial amount of time and effort to matters related to railways.

Around this false belief in the great importance of railways for the Italian state, a whole imagery and architecture was created, stressing elements like the speed, progress and 'Italianness' of the new transport system. It was not until after nationalization in 1905, however, that a truly Italian style came into being, and this was even more marked after the rise of fascism. Even a superficial glance at the architecture of the earlier nineteenth-century Italian stations reveals that they had been built by foreign railway companies and according to foreign tastes. These stations continued to dominate Italian railway architecture well into the twentieth century. The new station in Milan, for example, was only opened in 1931.

In the nineteenth century, it was generally thought that the railways were of the utmost importance for the economic and political development of a state. Consequently, all the effects of this technology tended to be regarded as immensely positive.[8] Moreover, after political unification in Italy it was believed that the railways would economically

[5] Angus Maddison, 'Una revisione della crescita economica italiana', MC 174 (1991), pp. 143–71; Giorgio Fuà and Mauro Gallegati, 'An Annual Chain Index of Italy's Real Product, 1861–1989' (working paper, Ancona, 1994).
[6] Stefano Jacini, quoted in Epicarmo Corbino, Annali dell'economia italiana, 1861–1870 (Città di Castello, 1931), p. 175.
[7] Vera Zamagni, Lo stato italiano e l'economia (Florence, 1981), pp. 9–10.
[8] Even in some contemporary writings the shadow of this unconditional optimism has lingered on; see P. M. Kalla Bishop, Italian Railroads (New York, 1972); M. Sereno Storia del paesaggio agrario italiano (Rome, 1982), p. 367.

Figure 1   Milan central railway station in the 1880s

Figure 2   Milan central railway station, 1931

unify and politically solidify the newly formed state and rapidly bring it to a level of development comparable to the northern European states. In economic terms this meant that the railways were expected to cause a general rise in income and that two types of integrational effects were hoped for: first, internal integration between the richer north and the poorer south of Italy, and second, the assimilation of Italy among Europe's major economic powers.

In reality, the economic impact of the railways was much more limited than contemporaries expected. First, this was because Italian governments did not follow a coherent railway policy, which led to insecurity for investors in Italian railways. Various mixed systems, the result of the compromises between proponents of the state versus those of a private railway system, were tried out with a limited degree of success. The responsibilities between the state and the railway companies were not clearly divided and consequently maintenance and new investments were sub-optimal. The overall performance and the quality of service of the Italian railways remained unsatisfactory. Second, because of the generally underdeveloped character of the economy, there was not enough demand for railway transport in the poorer regions. Particularly in the south, where most population centres had a harbour and access to cheap coastal transportation, traffic density on the railways was low. Eventually, in the twentieth century and particularly after the Second World War the income gap between rich and poor regions and between Italy and Europe would narrow, but certainly not exclusively because of the railways and certainly not as quickly as was hoped.

The history of railways from the viewpoint of business history remains largely an unexplored field. The virtual absence of company archives has probably been a major hindrance. Nevertheless, with the information available from official sources and periodicals, an attempt should be made to reconstruct the histories of the various Italian railway companies. Important themes would be, for instance, the functioning of railway management in Italy, its strategies and its responses to state policies.

Apart from the history of technology and various forms of railway history, the historiographical tradition concerning nineteenth-century Italy has had to be taken into account. At the Italian state universities nineteenth-century history was included in what was called Risorgimento history, or the history of the re-emergence of the Italian nation after the Renaissance, il Rinascimento. The formation of the Italian state was seen as the culmination of a long series of heroic struggles to liberate Italy from its foreign oppressors.

In fact, political unification of the Italian state in the nineteenth century was achieved in three phases, and was a relatively rapid and mainly a military and diplomatic affair. In 1860, almost the whole of Italy was unified under the king of Piedmont, with the exception of the regions of Venetia and Latium. The former territory was incorporated after the Third War of Independence (1866) between Italy and Austria, and the latter in 1870 when Rome became the capital. France's support during the Second War of Independence (1859) came at a price; Piedmont had to hand over to France the territories of Savoy and Nice, Giuseppe Garibaldi's native city. The various wars of independence and the subsequent border changes and disappearance of pre-unification states gave rise to a variety of legal and financial problems for the railway companies which saw border stations moving and their networks falling under different sovereigns.[9]

Time and again, historians have glorified the achievements of the founders of the Italian state and other 'great men' of the Italian nation. Some of these authors have maintained that 'the idea' of the Italian nation could be found in many writings long before the formation of the Italian state and a kind of competition between historians has taken place to push the beginning of this re-emergence of the Italian nation, or Risorgimento, further and further backwards.[10] For this purpose various texts were selected, canonized as fundamental Risorgimento literature, and subsequently declared compulsory reading for schoolchildren. In Italy, this Risorgimento history was heavily influenced by the idealistic philosophy of the famous historian–philosopher Benedetto Croce. For a long period of time Croce was a minister of education under the fascist dictatorship and, consequently, had the power to select textbooks and to nominate his followers to key positions.[11] One of the few British historians who were receptive to Croce's writings wrote in a review: 'I should find it easier to write of Croce's book if I had the least idea what it was all about', and 'much of it is the wallowing of the balloon among the clouds'.[12] In fact, Croce's aim was essentially to create a national political myth, not to write history.

Risorgimento history has more recently been put into a proper

---

[9]   A useful computer program for seeing the process of Italian political unification through a series of 'dynamic' maps is *Centennial,* by Clockwork Software Inc., P.O. Box 148036, Chicago.

[10]   For a brief introduction to Risorgimento historiography, see Umberto Marcelli, *Interpretazioni del Risorgimento* (Bologna, 1970). For a more extensive discussion, see Walter Venturi, *Interpretazioni del Risorgimento* (Turin, 1962).

[11]   In English, see Benedetto Croce, *A History of Italy* (Oxford, 1929).

[12]   Derek Beales, *The Risorgimento and the Unification of Italy* (London, 1971), p. 15.

perspective, first by several British historians who have unveiled some of its severest falsifications. Denis Mack Smith, for example, has contributed to the demystification of the actions of Risorgimento heroes such as King Victor Emmanuel, Camillo Cavour and Giuseppe Mazzini in various books.[13] James Stuart Woolf's textbook, which combines traditional Risorgimento history with other, more critical views, still figures prominently on reading lists for the period, particularly in Italy.[14] More recently, Marxist historians, such Antonio Gramsci, Giorgio Candeloro and Emilio Sereni have attacked the canons of Risorgimento history by offering an opposing, although sometimes similarly idealistic view of the Italian past.[15] Sereni, for example, argued that the railways had fulfilled the expectations of the Italian bourgeoisie of creating a unified market, although the costs of attaining this had been immense and had been borne chiefly by the masses. Regrettably, Sereni does not bother to find convincing empirical evidence for this thesis.

Last, economic historians have helped to shift the emphasis in nineteenth-century Italian history from the ideal to the real. In this book the great quantity of excellent research undertaken by Italian economic historians was gratefully used. The advantage of working with measurable data allows the economic historian, more strongly so than others, to compare Italy with other countries, and also to take a long-term view of developments when the time-series are homogeneous. This does not mean, however, that economic historians have been spared the ideological debate inspired by economic liberalism on the one hand and nationalism on the other. Despite the occurrence of similar arguments among economic historians, the use of statistics gives at least a solid framework in which arguments for and against can be clearly stated. The role of the state too can be assessed more precisely, since what it intended to achieve can be compared to the actual performance of the railways. A detailed analysis of the system of subsidies for railway companies, for example, can be gauged against their performance.

The debate on the economic history of Italy has a long and respected tradition, and has always been open to foreign participants. An early work by a North American historian, Kent Greenfield, is still

---

[13] Dennis Mack Smith, *Victor Emmanuel, Cavour and the Risorgimento* (Oxford, 1971).

[14] James Stuart Woolf, *A History of Italy, 1700–1860. The Social Constraints of Political Change* (London, 1979).

[15] Antonio Gramsci, *Il Risorgimento* (Rome, 1975); Giorgio Candeloro, *Storia dell'Italia moderna* (11 vols., Milan, 1955–86); Emilio Sereni, *Capitalismo e mercato nazionale in Italia* (Rome, 1966).

widely read, chiefly in its Italian translation.[16] In a series of studies which appeared in the 1950s and 1960s in the *Archivio Economico dell'Unificazione Italiana,* Italian and foreign historians published many fundamental studies and produced a substantial amount of useful data. Gino Luzzatto's 1963 book is still a hallmark in Italian economic history up to 1914, and is particularly strong on trade, banking and industrialization.[17]

Despite the formation of the Italian state between 1860 and 1870, the Italian economy continued to be characterized by great regional differences.[18] The explanation and measurement of these differences has been a fundamental theme in Italian history. The ambitious railway construction programmes of the 1860s and 1880s which led, as will be shown, to an even spread of the railway network over the whole of the territory, did little to diminish the great regional inequalities. In the 1960s, Rosario Romeo's study of the north–south problem helped to revive interest in Italian economic history worldwide. In this study an interesting interpretation of the role of railways is given for the first decades after unification, but regrettably it has too weak an empirical basis to be taken seriously today.[19] In the 1960s, several North American and Italian authors made important contributions to the understanding of the Italian north–south problem, often by making international comparisons.[20] Unfortunately, during the 1970s and 1980s research of the regional economies was not sufficiently developed, probably because of the difficulties in creating an appropriate statistical framework.[21]

The distinct political history and cultural identity of the Italian

---

[16] Kent Robert Greenfield, *Economics and Liberalism in the Risorgimento. A Study of Nationalism in Lombardy, 1815–1848* (Baltimore, 1934).

[17] Gino Luzzatto, *L'economia italiana dal 1861 al 1914* (Milan, 1963).

[18] Patrick McCarthy, *The Crisis of the Italian State: From the Origins of the Cold War to the Fall of Berlusconi* (London, 1995).

[19] Rosario Romeo, *Risorgimento e capitalismo* (Bari, 1963). For a critique, see Vera Zamagni, *Dalla periferia al centro. La seconda rinascita economica dell'Italia, 1861–1981* (Bologna, 1990), p. 82.

[20] Jeffrey Williamson, 'Regional Inequality and the Process of National Development. A Description of Patterns', *EDCC* 13 (1965), pp. 4–85; Shepard B. Clough and Carlo Livi, 'Economic Growth in Italy. An Analysis of the Uneven Development in North and South', *JEH* 19 (1959), pp. 334–49; Richard Eckhaus, 'The North-South Differential in Italian Economic Development', *JEH* 21 (1961), pp. 285–317; and more recently, Alfred G. Esposto, 'Italian Industrialization and the Gerschenkronian "Great Spurt". A Regional Analysis', *JEH* 52 (1992), pp. 353–400.

[21] With the exception of Zamagni's study which deals mainly with the 1911 industrial census, see Vera Zamagni, *Industrializzazione e squilibri regionali in Italia. Bilancio del'età giolittiana* (Bologna, 1978).

regions must be taken into account when examining the differences in the economic and social conditions between north and south found in 1860. It must be remembered that in 1860 Italian national identity still had to be 'invented' from quite a small common base. To begin with, the linguistic differences between regions impeded effective communication between northern and southern Italians. Even within regions, such as Apulia, for example, the difference in dialects with Greek or Arab influences created communication problems. And among the northern Italian elite, for instance, it was quite common for Italian to be a second language after French.[22] For Vittorio Alfieri, the famous poet, and for many others too, French was the first language and Alfieri learned Italian later in life.[23] When Italian unity came, the use of the Italian language, even as a lingua franca, had not spread sufficiently.

Apart from the north–south problem, the railways have formed another continuous point of debate among historians of Italy. Fascism, for its own military and propagandistic purposes, glorified the railways as symbols of the progress of the nation. Risorgimento historians took over this perspective and interpreted the building of the railway network in the nineteenth century as one among many heroic struggles to reach national unity and economic prosperity.

In the 1960s, this rosy view of railways and Italian economic success was put into a different perspective by a North American economic historian. Alexander Gerschenkron studied Italy as an example of a backward country which industrialized late, but rapidly, between 1896 and 1908. In his view, the Italian railways had not been able to create a unified national market and their performance continued to be poor. Moreover, the benefits of railway construction for Italian industry were to a great extent lost, since they occurred at a time when industrialization had barely begun. The first wave of investment in the 1860s mainly utilized imported products and the investment after nationalization in 1905 came too late to contribute to Italian industrialization. Thus Gerschenkron was the first prominent historian to cast doubt on the contribution of railways to economic growth and their capacity to integrate the national market. It must be noted, however, that he had no profound interest in regional aspects of growth.[24]

---

[22] Beales, *The Risorgimento*, p. 24.     [23] *Ibid.*, p. 97.

[24] Alexander Gerschenkron, *Economic Backwardness in Historical Perspective* (Cambridge, Mass., 1966). For a description of the reception of Gerschenkron in Italy, see Gianni Toniolo, 'Alexander Gerschenkron e l'Italia. Alcune osservazioni nel decimo anniversario della morte', *RSE* 5 (1988), pp. 397–404; Giovanni Federico and Gianni Toniolo, 'Italy', in Richard Sylla and Gianni Toniolo (eds.), *Patterns of European Industrialization. The Nineteenth Century* (London, 1991), pp. 197–217.

More recent research has largely confirmed Gerschenkron's main points. Carlo Bardini, Albert Carreras, Giovanni Federico, Stefano Fenoaltea and Gianni Toniolo, among others, have contributed to the refinement of Gerschenkron's index of industrial production and created a more complete quantitative framework of Italian economic growth and industrial production.[25] The meagre contribution of railway investment to the development of Italian industry has been studied extensively by Michèle Merger.[26] Vera Zamagni, moreover, has questioned the ability of railways to integrate the Italian market and has supported this thesis with data on internal trade.[27]

Since Gerschenkron's contributions, economic historians have concentrated on explaining the obstacles to and the problems of economic development and industrialization, rather than glorifying Italian achievements in the economic field. This has formed a healthy antidote to the sometimes bombastic Risorgimento history. In 1990, Vera Zamagni published the first comprehensive overview of Italian economic history since Gino Luzzatto's 1963 book, including the results of much recent research, a substantial amount of which she had undertaken herself.[28] This book takes a long-term perspective from the middle of the nineteenth century until the 1980s, and narrates how Italy, starting as a backward country, has today become one of the richest and largest industrial economies. This long-term view of Italian economic history allows for a more insightful interpretation than could be offered by those authors who do not fully realize the long-term implications of the historical processes which they describe. Given this significant long-term economic and social progress, it is no exaggeration to state, with Vera Zamagni, that the foundation for the

[25] For Giovanni Federico, Stefano Fenoaltea and Vera Zamagni's national account estimates for 1911, see Guido M. Rey (ed.), *I conti economici dell'Italia. Una stima del valore aggiunto per il 1911* (Milan, 1992); Gianni Toniolo, *An Economic History of Liberal Italy* (London, 1990); Carlo Bardini and Albert Carreras, 'The National Accounts for Italy, Spain, and Portugal, 1800–1990', conference paper, Groningen, 4–8 July 1994.

[26] Michèle Merger, 'L'industrie italienne de locomotives. Reflet d'une industrialisation tardive et difficile, 1850–1914', *HES* 8 (1989), pp. 336–70; Michèle Merger, 'Les chemins de fer italiens: leur construction et leurs effets amont, 1860–1915', *HES* 11 (1992), pp. 109–30; Michèle Merger, 'Chemins de fer et croissance économique en Italie au XIXème siècle et au début du XXème siècle. Etat de la question', *HES* 3 (1984), pp. 123–44.

[27] Vera Zamagni, 'Ferrovie e integrazione del mercato nazionale nell'Italia post-unitaria', in *Studi in onore di Gino Barbieri* (Salerno, 1983), pp. 1635–49.

[28] See Zamagni, *Dalla periferia al centro*, which has also appeared in an English translation: Vera Zamagni, *An Economic History of Italy, 1860–1990* (Oxford, 1993).

'second economic rebirth' of Italy in the twentieth century was laid in the nineteenth.

Thus, in the 1960s, the monolithic Risorgimento perspective was finally broken and a more pluriform and comparative historiography of Italy's nineteenth century came into being. In particularly, British, Marxist and economic historians proposed useful alternative interpretations to those offered by Risorgimento historians. Nevertheless, the confusion left behind after the period of large-scale falsification of history during fascism has left a deep imprint on Italian nineteenth-century historiography.

Given this change towards a more comparative perspective on Italian history and the increased use of quantitative methodology by historians, the role of railways in the political unification of Italy and the creation of a unified market deserves a serious re-examination.

# CHAPTER 2

# RAILWAYS AND THE ITALIAN STATE IN THE NINETEENTH CENTURY

## I INTRODUCTION

In the nineteenth century, private railways made up at least 60 per cent of total track length in continental Europe and, as a rule, within one state many different companies operated the railway network.[1] Even in 1910, roughly 180,000 km (60 per cent) of the more than 300,000 km of railway track were still owned or operated by private railway companies.[2] State railways were thus the exception in the nineteenth century and only the Prussian State Railways played an important role, operating around 9,400 km (75 per cent) of the total of 13,000 km of the German network in 1880, and more than 21,000 km (90 per cent) of the 24,000 km after 1890. Nevertheless, many European railway histories typically describe the national railway networks as if they were perfectly unified from the start, disregarding the dissimilarities that existed between the companies within one state.

The nationalization of the railways in Prussia and Italy, in 1879 and 1905 respectively, meant that these countries were the first in creating a fairly homogeneous national railway network and to have the largest part of their railway network directly operated by the state. In Italy, until 1905, the mixed railway system was an object of continuous debate in parliament and substantial criticism from the general public. Apparently, before nationalization large sectors of society thought that

---

[1] In this case, continental Europe includes Belgium, the Netherlands, United Germany, France, Switzerland, Austria-Hungary, Italy, Spain, Portugal and Greece.

[2] Leonida Leoni, *Testo-Atlante delle ferrovie e tramvie italiane e di quelle estere in contatto Francia, Svizzera ed Austria-Ungheria con un indice prontuario di tutte le linee, stazioni, fermate, scali, ecc. delle ferrovie tramvie e laghi italiani* (Novara, 1913), p. 89; a similar percentage is found for the years 1880 and 1889, see Great Britain, Statistical Office, *Statistical Abstract for the Principal and Other Foreign Countries in Each Year from 1879 to 1888–89* (London, 1891), pp. 209–10.

the railway companies were not providing an adequate service. After 1905, many of these problems were solved, but the financial benefits of the nationalized railways for the state were far from evident. By contrast, in Prussia the state railways were a financial success and generated substantial sums as revenue for the state.[3]

Generally speaking, trouble in the railway sector can be caused either by internal problems or by problems outside. During the nineteenth century in Italy, bad management, over-staffing, low labour productivity, the weak financial position of the railway companies, or conflicts between the companies and the state frequently caused severe difficulties. External economic factors, such as the low levels of economic development in the south, added to these problems. The argument that a railway infrastructure of the kind that was built in southern Italy in the nineteenth century could not be sustained by Italy's level of economic and social development will receive serious consideration in chapters 3 and 4.[4] In this chapter the set of problems directly related to the railway sector will be analysed with special attention to the relationship between the state and the Italian railway companies.

## II  RAILWAY REGIMES IN CONTINENTAL EUROPE, GREAT BRITAIN AND THE UNITED STATES

The great differences in the legal and political contexts in which railway companies operated in Great Britain and the United States of America on the one hand, and continental Europe on the other, warrant a distinct approach to their railway histories. First, in Great Britain and the United States, the state did not generally intervene directly in matters concerning the actual operation of the railway companies, whereas on the European continent state intervention and regulation were significant from the outset. In all concessions the state formulated its right to intervene in the widest sense in the management of the railway companies.[5] Continental railway companies, therefore, were not free to set their rates for all categories or all lines as were most companies in Great Britain and the United States. After the 1865 Railway Act, for example, Italian railway companies did not

---

[3] Rainier Fremdling, 'Freight Rates and the State Budget: The Role of the National Prussian Railways, 1880–1913', *JEEH* 9 (1990), pp. 21–2.

[4] Stefano Fenoaltea, 'Italy', in Patrick O'Brien (ed.), *Railways and the Economic Development of Europe* (Oxford, 1983), pp. 88–9.

[5] Upper Italy Railway Company, *Memoria difensiva della Società Alta Italia nella causa vertente coll'amministrazione generale dei lavori pubblici* (Turin, 1875), p. ix.

have the freedom to lower their rates without the government's approval.[6] Several lines which crossed international borders, to name another example, were operated with transport rates which were mutually agreed to by the states and could not be modified by the railway companies. Similarly, the governments established or at least approved most internal railway rates for goods traffic. In the nineteenth century the railway sector on the European continent was heavily regulated and sometimes the state intervened in the smallest details of the day-to-day operation of railways.

First, differences in political circumstance must be taken into account. The more unstable political systems and the frequent occurrence of wars in continental Europe restrained the growth of the European railway network. The risks of war and the consequent border changes had a great influence in the planning of the railway network and some lines were built for purely military and strategic reasons, or their construction was obstructed for these same motives. It is often argued that in those cases where military motives dominated, commercial interests were damaged.[7] These kinds of arguments are, of course, hard to prove since nobody knows what would have happened to commerce if these lines had been built differently or not at all.

Moreover, various European currencies, including the Italian lira and the Austrian gulden, were devalued during the second half of the nineteenth century, principally because of war debts, and this caused great problems for the railway sector.[8] For the Upper Italy Railway Company, for instance, the devaluation of the lira and the gulden in 1867 meant that it ran into trouble servicing its debt, since it had borrowed its capital in gold standard currencies on the Paris or London financial markets but obtained its revenue in devalued currencies. This company, one of the largest companies of its time, was a French–Austrian company which operated the northern Italian railway network until 1878. It also operated railways in Austria. This multi-national railway network had come into existence not so much as part of a deliberate strategy on the part of the company, but had been born out of necessity. When the company started building its

[6] Corbino, *Annali*, p. 196.

[7] Kostov, Alexandre. 'Les Balkans et le réseau ferroviaire européen avant 1914', in *European Networks, 19th and 20th Centuries. New Approaches to the Formation of a Transnational Transport and Communications System.* Eleventh International Economic History Congress, Session B8, Milan, September 1994 (ed. Paola Subacchi) (Milan, 1994), p. 96.

[8] Corbino, *Annali*, p. 196.

network in 1856 the Italian state had not yet come into being. To add to its financial difficulties after 1867 the Austro-Hungarian government began to exercise more and more pressure on the company to divide itself into two separate parts, an Austrian one and an Italian one. Eventually, the Italian part of the company went out of business mainly because of its bad financial situation and the continuous conflicts it had with the Italian government about unpaid subsidies and taxes.

Second, the state interfered considerably with the management of railway companies. Several semi-state companies came into being which had a hierarchical structure similar to bureaucratic or military organizations. In continental Europe it was therefore less likely that the railway companies would produce influential innovations in the field of management, as they had done in the United States of America.[9] The military and strategic interests of the European states also led to a variety of sometimes contradictory obligations and higher costs for railway companies operating international railway networks. Companies whose railway network happened to be lying in two different countries, for example, were pressured to divide their network, or compelled to set up two separate headquarters. Moreover, they had to fulfil different financial and technical requirements in each country.

Whereas the existence of joint-stock companies was firmly entrenched in England, in Italy company law was in a very crude state until the 1870s. This opened up many loopholes to foreign and national speculators in railway shares and the great number of unsuccessful companies in the 1840s and 1850s can partly be blamed on the speculation of European investors. When, in the 1870s, more stringent laws came into effect, most railway companies had already been formed and as a consequence several provisions of the new laws could not be enforced.

Third, most continental European railway companies regulated by national laws did not expand their networks into other countries, because of the technical, legal and political difficulties involved in crossing national boundaries. Although most European countries adopted the standard or Stephenson track gauge of 1,435 millimetres, other technical and administrative practices differed substantially between the various countries or even companies. Even in the same country it took considerable time before the problems with regard to

---

[9] Alfred Chandler, *The Railroads. The Nation's First Big Business. Sources and Readings* (New York, 1965).

different loading gauges (height and weight of rolling stock), types of coupling, braking systems and administrative practices such as ticketing, the division of revenue and scheduling, were solved.[10] Naturally, international agreement on these issues was even harder to attain.

To allow for the operation of cross-border lines in continental Europe, diplomatic conventions and more specific technical agreements between the railway companies were concluded. Apart from normal competition between railway companies, however, political and strategic interests made effective international cooperation in railway matters rather difficult. In the case of northern Italy, for instance, both France and Austria-Hungary offered special discounts for goods travelling from the ports of Marseilles and Trieste, respectively. Due to the geographical position of the Italian ports of Genoa and Venice, which were relatively close to the borders, rate cuts offered by the Italian railway companies were not as effective. Consequently, the Italian ports could not take full advantage of the European railway network. In sum, the existence in continental Europe of many competing states thus posed an obstacle to the expansion and the operation of the railway network across national boundaries. National boundaries thus formed a kind of railway frontier, which was virtually absent in the United States of America.

Next, the geographical differences in economic institutions between the European and the American continent must be considered. First, in contrast to America, in Europe the history of human occupation had to be taken into account, in the sense that the organization of the territory including the traditional infrastructure had been shaped over a period of many centuries. Generally, most major railway lines in Europe were created in an urban and sometimes industrialized setting. On the American continent, on the other hand, in many cases railways served to open up virgin territory and were mainly used to transport agricultural products. From the outset, therefore, in Europe the goods transported by railway were more diversified and travelled shorter distances.

Second, in Great Britain and the United States of America the transport market was practically free and the regulatory bodies for the railways fell far short of the kind of interference practised by the continental European states. Goods rates for the railways were set differently for each article according to its value on the local market. In Great Britain railway goods rates were determined according to the

[10] Douglas Puffert, 'The Technical Integration of the European Railway Network', in *European Networks, 19th and 20th Centuries. New Approaches*, pp. 137–9.

principle of 'what the traffic can bear'. This meant that British railway managers would increase a rate for an article on a specific route until the traffic flow began to decrease. This technique gave rise to great differences in rates even for very similar traffic flows, but it was a commercially sound strategy on the part of the railway companies for maximizing traffic and revenue. Nevertheless, the general public tended to resent these practices, feeling themselves to be victims of the railway companies' greed. On the European continent, conversely, the railways were considered more as a public service and a railway rate a kind of tax, which should be levied according to generally accepted principles of taxation.[11]

In the two Anglo-Saxon countries the railway companies generally bought the land on which they constructed the lines and exercised unlimited property rights over it. In North America a major share of the railway companies' assets was formed by the land on which the track was built. On the European continent the land was leased for a limited period, and after this lease period the railways would automatically become the property of the state.[12] The railway companies in continental Europe, therefore, continued to depend on the governments' good will to continue the lease, subsidize generously and tax moderately. The fact that the railway question remained on the political agenda in France and Italy, for example, can be explained directly by the large role played by the state in railway matters rather than by the cultural characteristics of the French and Italians.[13] The different legal framework explains why railways continued to be the subject of political debate in continental Europe. Moreover, in Great Britain, from the beginning of railway building, local or provincial bodies were involved in financing the construction of lines. On the European continent local authorities began to subsidize the construction of railway lines much later, particularly in Italy where this only started in the late 1870s.[14]

Lastly, in continental Europe the railway business was organized in a totally different manner. During the construction phase, the states usually gave subsidies to the company in the form of a guarantee on interest on capital invested or on net revenue. Once the railway

---

[11] Harold Hotelling, 'The General Welfare in Relation to Problems of Taxation and of Railway and Utility Rates', *Econometrica* 6 (1937), p. 242.

[12] Italy, Ministero di Lavori Pubblici, *Atti della commissione d'inchiesta sull'esercizio delle ferrovie italiane* (*Atti Commissione Baccarini*), 12 vols. (Rome, 1881), part 2, vol. 1, pp. 1–60.

[13] Jan Hole, *National Railways* (London, 1893), p. 265.

[14] Briano, *Storia delle ferrovie*, pp. 127–8.

company started collecting revenues, however, the states frequently claimed back some of these subsidies, either directly or by levying heavier and a greater variety of taxes. By contrast, in the Anglo-Saxon countries, subsidies were seldom given and taxes on railway transport were not so common. Because of this very different context, the continental European railway industry needs to be approached as a state-regulated sector rather than as an independent private sector. This implies that the railways were more strongly subject to political decision-making rather than to commercial logic. The arguments made in the literature for British and American railways as a breeding ground for modern company management, for example, can therefore scarcely be applied to continental Europe. Any examination of a continental European national railway system must therefore start with determining the influence of the state and include a detailed review of the Railway Acts.

### III  RAILWAYS AT WAR

Since on the European continent the states had great power over the management of railway companies from the outset, it was not difficult to use the railways during war. The first occasion on which railways were used to transport troops during an international armed conflict was in Italy in 1849.[15] In May of that year, during the war between Piedmont and the Austrian Empire,[16] the railways in Venetia were used by the Austrian army to transport troops on the 60 km stretch between Vicenza and Mestre, and in Piedmont the few lines that existed were also employed by the military.[17]

Ten years later, during the 1859 Italian campaigns, the railways were used by both sides for transporting troops to the war zone for the first time, as well as part of their tactical movements immediately before battle. The Austrian army used the railway network, which had grown considerably since 1849, to move its troops from Vienna to Lombardy and Venetia. The enormous demand for transport generated by military operations had, however, not been foreseen and general chaos characterized this operation. On certain sections great traffic congestion developed, and waiting times for the troops

---

[15] Italy is used here in the geographical sense, comprising also the Kingdom of Lombardy–Venetia which was part of the Austrian Empire until 1866.

[16] After 1867 it is called the Austro-Hungarian Empire.

[17] Andrew Wingate, *Railway Building in Italy before Unification* (Reading, UK, 1971), p. 38; instead of the Kingdom of Two Sardinias, its official name, I shall refer to it as the Kingdom of Piedmont.

increased even more for lack of rolling stock. On average, it took a military unit around two weeks to move from Vienna to Lombardy. Although this was considerably longer than necessary, it was about four or five times faster than could have been achieved with traditional means of transport. After the war, it took a long time before all coaches and wagons which had been kept in Italy by the military for their real or imagined needs were brought back to Austria.[18]

During the 1859 war the Austrian government did not tolerate foreign personnel operating the railways and all of the Upper Italy Railway Company's French employees based in Lombardy and Venetia had to leave Austrian territory. The Italian government was less strict and this attitude later proved to be to its advantage. The Austrian railway directors based on Italian territory in Bologna remained on duty and Italian troops were speedily transported on the recently opened line from Piacenza to Bologna, which greatly bene-fited the Italian army in Emilia and, as a consequence, undermined the Austrian army's objectives. Again the army's tremendous transport needs became evident and the company transported around 200,000 Italian troops in ten days, including all their war material.[19]

The use made of the railways by the Piedmontese and the French during the 1859 campaign was slightly more orderly. During the three months of the war the French Paris-Lyon-Méditerranée Railway Company transported around a quarter of a million men by rail to Italy.[20] The Piedmontese State Railways were also used to transport the allied French troops over the Savoyard and Piedmontese lines to the theatre of war in Lombardy. The Fréjus pass had not yet been opened, but this did not delay French troop movement unduly.[21] On arrival in Italy, however, it took some time before the troops were ready for action, since the military planners had not anticipated that the troops could move faster than their equipment. A second French army arrived by ship in Genoa and was subsequently transported by rail in the direction of Lombardy over the Genoa–Alessandria–Casale–Novara line.[22] The French–Italian side not only used the railways to move troops far behind the front lines, but also tactically to outflank the Austrians before the battle of Magenta in June 1859. It seems too much, however, to attribute a decisive role to the railways in this

[18] John Westwood, *Railways at War* (London, 1980), pp. 14–16.
[19] Atti Commissione Baccarini, part I, vol. I, p. 227.
[20] Westwood, *Railways at War*, p. 14.
[21] Peter Hertner, 'Il problema dei valichi e la politica ferroviaria internazionale', *Pa-dania* 4 (1990), p. 31.
[22] Briano, *Storia delle ferrovie*, pp. 103–4.

Italian–French victory.[23] Probably the Italian side, with French help, would have won in any case.[24]

Not only does the railways' contribution to increasing the scale and consequently the horrors of war during the Italian wars of independence deserve attention, but their humanitarian role was also important. After the battle of Magenta in June 1859, where railways played such an important tactical role before the battle, the wounded were transported by rail to the hospitals in Turin. Later, at the battle of Solferino at the end of June 1859, where Henry Dunant was inspired to create what was later to become the International Committee of the Red Cross, the railways could not at first play a similar tactical role since the Austrians had sabotaged the Milan–Peschiera line at various points. However, thanks to the efforts of Charles Brot, a Milanese banker and railway director, the damage to the lines on the newly conquered territory was quickly repaired. As a consequence, the thousands of wounded men from Solferino could be transported swiftly to the hospitals in Milan.[25]

In the 1867 war, the Upper Italy Railway Company transported 115,000 Italian troops with all their equipment to the front in two weeks at a greatly reduced rate. Curiously enough this company provided similar services to the Austro-Hungarian troops by transporting them across the Brenner pass, where the line had been partially opened, with the exception of the stretch between Innsbruck and Bolzano. Again, the Austrian government ordered all foreigners out and more than four thousand Italian workers who were employed in the construction of the Brenner line were evacuated.[26]

After this campaign we find the first mention of the financial consequences of war for a railway company. The Upper Italy Railway Company noted that damage to the track and works as a consequence of the war should be paid for by the governments of the armies which had caused it. Clearly, there was an increase in revenue from military transport, but the company complained that the cost of repair due to excessive wear and tear of the locomotives more than absorbed these benefits. Around fifty-four locomotives, 100 coaches and 1,800 wagons used during the war by both sides all needed to be repaired. Moreover, there was also a loss of revenue since regular transport had to be suspended for some time before and after the battles. Although these costs might be somewhat exag-

---

[23] Fenoaltea, 'Italy', p. 89.     [24] Westwood, *Railways at War*, p. 16.

[25] Henri Dunant, *Un souvenir de Solférino* (Geneva, 1990), pp. 104–7.

[26] *Economist*, 3 August 1867, p. 2; Josef Fontana, *Geschichte des Landes Tirol* (Bozen, 1987), pp. 39–43.

gerated it can be concluded that this war was far from lucrative for the company.[27]

The role of the Upper Italy Railway Company during the Italian wars of independence is particularly interesting since the company had both a French and an Austrian director (the French being Italy's allies and the Austrians being their enemies). In all Italy's wars of independence the company behaved in an exemplary fashion, and if anybody had to fear from its multi-national character it was not the Italians, a fact widely recognized in Italy. Maybe the company decided to remain neutral because both sides in the conflict were represented on the board of directors.[28]

Finally, in 1870, the railways played a less spectacular role during the war between Italy and the Papal States. The Papal army destroyed the three railway lines to Rome operated by the French Romane Railway Company at various points. This same company, however, put various groups of railway workers and engineers at the disposal of the Italian army to repair the damage. The Italian army were thus able to transport its troops by rail to Rome with a minimum of delay.[29]

It has been postulated that Italian governments were intolerant towards foreign railway companies primarily for military reasons. However, during all the military campaigns which took place in Italy from 1849 to 1870, the foreign companies operating the railways always cooperated with both parties to the conflict. Since no Italian government had reason to complain about the non-cooperation of railway companies during wartime, it could not have been military motives that lay at the root of their hostile policies, but rather the more nationalistic political atmosphere in Europe around the middle of the century. These hostile policies were primarily aimed at decreasing the power of foreign financiers over the management of railways in Italy and only after that were they directed towards eliminating the risk of the railway companies cooperating militarily with the enemy.

Although the first experiences of the military use of railways took place in Italy, there is no evidence that Italy continued to play an important or particularly innovative role in this field. In other theatres

---

[27] Upper Italy Railway Company, *Osservazioni generali relative alla statistica dell'anno 1867* (Milan, 1868), p. 7.

[28] The minutes of the directors' meeting are feared to have been destroyed together with most of the rest of the company's archives. This makes the task of writing a company history a difficult but interesting challenge for future historical research. For the names of the directors, see *Atti Commissione Baccarini*, part 1, vol. 1, pp. 228–9.

[29] Briano, *Storia delle ferrovie*, p. 127.

of war the railways were exploited to a greater extent. During the American Civil War, for example, the generals on both sides realized that correct use of the railways was a prerequisite for victory, and many observers remarked that this was a 'railway war'. The Confederates of the south, in particular, were heavily dependent on railways, although they were less successful in establishing control over the various railway managements.[30] In Europe, the railways played an important role in the 1870 Franco-Prussian War. In 1870, the French suffered a severe setback when its railways were used by the enemy which hastened the Prussian army's advance on Paris.[31]

Whereas in the United States the military role of the railways effectively ceased after the Civil War, the frequent occurrence of armed conflicts in Europe gave rise to continuous military involvement in various aspects of railway construction and operation. The 'strategic considerations' which held up various cross-border lines are frequently mentioned in the literature. Moreover, the military insisted that enough rolling stock should be available and that the stations should have sufficient loading capacity. By 1878, for example, in France and Prussia around 30 per cent of the railway network was double track whereas in Italy it was only 10 per cent.[32] After the experiences in the 1860s and 1870s many lessons were learned about the operation of railways during wartime. Most European countries began to draw up plans for the militarization of the railways in time of war. The First World War provides several examples of the implementation of these plans and the extensive use of railway transportation by the army. In Great Britain, for example, the government took control of the railways, forced the railway companies to transport military convoys free of charge, and limited civilian traffic by increasing passenger fares. In return, the railways companies were promised a net revenue equivalent to that of 1913.[33]

## IV  ITALY'S RAILWAY ACTS

Up until the present day, the degree to which the state should intervene in the railway sector has continued to be a heavily debated subject and in every country different solutions to the problem have been found. Historical experience provides no convincing arguments that the successful operation of railways, in either a state or a private railway system, can be exclusively achieved with either national or

---

[30] Westwood, *Railways at War*, chapter 2.        [31] *Ibid.*, chapter 3.
[32] *Atti Commissione Baccarini*, part 2, vol. III, pp. 1327–48.
[33] William Acworth, *The Elements of Railway Economics* (Oxford, 1924), pp. 170–83.

international capital. From the beginning the history of European rail-ways has shown that both systems and the various mixed versions have their own merits and pitfalls, but that the manner in which a particular arrangement is implemented in the given circumstances is decisive for success or failure. Given this mixed historical experience, the question of private versus state railways must be approached without ideological dogmas.

In the nineteenth century, the Belgian State Railways, the British private railway system, and the French mixed system were examples of the state owning the track or the rolling stock and the railway com-panies managing the railways under mutually agreed conditions. Important as the question of state versus private railways might be, the final criterion by which to judge the success of any railway regime is its ability to offer a good quality of transport services to the general public. For private railway companies acceptable net revenues must be generated and a stable rate of return on capital for the investors assured. In the case of a state system, the criterion is the capacity to create a sustainable railway system, guaranteeing transport services of both acceptable price and quality for the whole of the territory. Necessary conditions to achieve this are, among others, a management of sufficient quality and, in the case of a private system, a healthy capital structure and good relations with the state. Thus, the effects of railway regulation depended on the provisions which distributed the responsibilities between the state and the railway companies and deter-mined how the revenues and costs were to be shared between both parties.

After long debates the Italian parliament passed two major railway laws, the 1865 and the 1885 Railway Acts.[34] Both laws claimed to sti-mulate the construction of new lines and to create a viable railway system for the whole of Italy, and both failed to a large extent, although the first aim was achieved to a greater degree than the second. The question of whether a state or a private railway system was preferable was especially painful for the young Italian state. On the one hand, the dominant ideological influence of economic liber-alism and the belief in the beneficial effects of competition between different railway companies, made many of the Italian ruling class extremely reluctant to allow the state a major role in the construction and management of the railways. In particular, those Italian left-wing liberals who came to power after 1875, such as prime minister Agostino Depretis and his minister of public works, Francesco Genala,

[34] Act 2248 of 14 May 1865, Act 3048 of 27 April 1885.

tried to reduce state interference in railway matters.[35] On the other hand, only the state could counterbalance the power of the private railway companies which were dominated by foreign financiers. With the memories of the bitterly fought Risorgimento wars still fresh, Italian nationalism was easily aroused when foreigners threatened to influence Italian affairs. Thus for the Italian government the dilemma was that a state railway system would eliminate the competition thought necessary for the proper functioning of the railways, but that a private railway regime would give too much influence over the railways to foreign financiers.

The Italian governments experimented with various mixed forms and did not make an definitive choice between a state or a private railway system until full nationalization of the railways was decided by Act 137 of 22 April 1905 during the ministry of Alessandro Fortis.[36] Until nationalization, the compromises and frequent changes in the railway system caused great problems for the management of the railways. The continuous changes to the Italian railway regimes during the whole of the second half of the nineteenth century show the inability of government to handle the ideological divisions in parliament, and the local interests represented there. William Acworth, for example, author of several studies on railway economics and professor at the London School of Economics at the beginning of the twentieth century, notes, about Italy, that 'no country in the world experimented so much with different types of railway organization'.[37]

The troubled history of the Italian railways gave rise to various criticisms from foreign observers. Although the problems with the railway system cannot be denied, they can be seen in a different light when Italian achievements in other fields are taken into account. In the south, for example, very few roads had been built before 1860 and illiteracy and bad sanitation were common. The Italian state managed to create an education system, a medical service and even a railway network in most of its national territory, starting virtually from scratch.

As in other countries, there was an element of pork barrel politics regarding any piece of railway legislation and sometimes this led to downright corruption. As one English writer said at the end of the century: 'The country [Italy] is crushed with debt to provide an enor-

---

[35] Antonio Papa, *Classe politica e intervento pubblico nell'età giolittiana. La nazionalizzazione delle ferrovie* (Naples, 1973), p. 17.

[36] Carlo Ferraris occupied the post of minister of public works, see Papa, *Classe politica*, p. 121.

[37] William Acworth, *Railway Rates and the Traders* (London, 1891), p. 34.

mous army, an immense fleet, besides loans to municipalities for ornamental rather than useful purposes, and with swarms of needless civil servants. The railways seem to have had their share of the general corruption.'[38]

Another wry comment on Italy's railways from England at the end of the century ran thus:

> The mere financial aspect of this [railway] investment as loss is trivial as compared with the corruption it opened the way to in the management of affairs, and the demoralisation of the constituencies by the introduction of a system which readily lent itself to private ends. This system supplied the means of corrupting whole electoral colleges by the construction of roads for local purposes to the general loss, and degenerated into a plan, to use the expression of a Ministerial Journal, *Fanfula*, 'to place a station before every man's door' with the result of increasing enormously the mileage with little relation to the utility and in some cases only to the advantage of private estates English deputies formerly used their parliamentary influence to avoid railways approaching their mansions. The Italian Deputy reverses that example and wants it at his door.[39]

The quality of service too seems to have been below the English standards of the time: 'There is only one daily express along the plain of Lombardy from Milan to Venice and no fresh trains ever seem to be added. The connections are atrocious, i.e. a passenger from London to Venice has to wait six hours in Milan.'[40]

From the point of view of the railway regimes the history of Italian railways can be divided into four main phases.[41] From 1839, when the first line was built, to 1865, private and mostly foreign companies constructed the principal lines, for which they had obtained concessions from the pre-unification regimes. The one notable exception to this was Piedmont, where in the 1850s the state built and operated the greater part of the railway network. Accordingly, not only were the laws regulating the construction and operation of railways different between the Italian states, but within each state the individual concessions to the railway companies showed great disparities. After the achievement of political unity a first boom in railway construction occurred, and between 1861 and 1865 a record length of track was finished, mainly the important national trunk lines. Obviously, the

---

[38] Hole, *National Railways*, p. 274.          [39] *The Times*, 16 April 1892.

[40] E. Foxwell and T. C. Farrer, *Express Trains English and Foreign, Being a Statistical Account of All the Express Trains of the World* (London, 1889), p. 155.

[41] For a bibliography on Italian railways, see Andrea Giuntini, 'Le ferrovie nella storiografia italiana', *IC* (1990), pp. 327–32.

political unity of Italy facilitated the completion of these lines and had a positive effect on the willingness of foreigners to invest.

The 1865 Railway Act tried to bring some order into this situation by creating five large private companies for the whole territory. This marks the beginning of the second phase of Italian railway history. In order to achieve this the Piedmontese State Railways were sold and the Upper Italy Railway Company was formed. It was a case of privatization induced by the government's need for cash and this sale was a dramatic moment in the history of Italian railways – a tremendous humiliation that was never forgotten.[42] However, despite the disappearance of the state railways and of many other railway companies, most conditions formulated in the original concessions were kept in force. The 1865 Railway Act can be compared to the French Railway Act of 1858, by which six major companies were formed.[43] The declared purpose of the 1865 Act was to mobilize national investment in the railways, to expand the railway network and to guarantee acceptable rates of return on capital for the companies. After about ten years, however, the government proved incapable of compensating investors financially for the disappointing results and company after company got into trouble and was taken over by the state.

By 1878, the state had come into possession of most of the track and it also operated the railways. The government's unaccomplished aim was to rationalize the system and hand it over to private companies again. The period from 1878 to 1885 can be considered as a transitional phase, since the state did not change the organization of the railway companies and the majority of the personnel stayed in place.[44] From 1878 to 1885 the state was to run the railways in the worst possible circumstances and under continuous parliamentary investigation. It must be noted, however, that the basis for the rapid expansion of the network after 1885 was laid in 1879 with the adoption of an important law which decided on which secondary lines should be given priority over others. This law also instituted the Railway Enquiry Commission whose advice proved to be crucial during the reorganization proposed by the 1885 Railway Act.

From 1885, when the second Italian Railway Act came into effect,

---

[42] Rondo Cameron, 'Problems of French Investment in Italian Railways. A Document of 1868', BHR 33 (1959), p. 93.

[43] The Nord, Est, Ouest, Midi, Orléans and Paris-Lyon-Mediterranée Railway Companies.

[44] Michèle Merger, 'Origini e sviluppo del management ferroviario italiano, 1850–1905', ASI 8 (1992), p. 379; Atti Commissione Baccarini, part 2, vol. III, pp. 1088–90.

a mixed system existed until nationalization in 1905. This meant that the track was owned by the state but was operated by three private companies with largely national capital: the Mediterranean, the Adriatic, and the Sicilian Railway Companies. The Mediterranean Railway Company comprised the railways of the western half of the peninsula and the Adriatic Railway Company, the continuation of the former Meridionali Railway Company, those of the eastern half. The third company, the Sicilian Railway Company was created for the construction of the railways in the south and on the Italian islands.

Building on the aims of the 1865 Act, the 1885 Railway Act proposed to promote the economic integration of the north with the poorer south of Italy. The Mediterranean and Adriatic networks would thus form the 'inflexible axes' of Italian economic unification, eliminating the differences between north and south, as the prime minister, Agostino Depretis, put it during the presentation of the Bill to parliament.[45] A second wave of construction, with many new lines opened between 1885 and 1890, followed the 1885 Railway Act. Again it must be noted that these lines had been proposed in the Act of 1879.

The last phase of Italian railway history began with nationalization in 1905 and continues today. Because of the limited success of the Mediterranean and Adriatic Railway Companies in providing adequate transportation services, however, a consensus among historians has emerged that the takeover of these two companies by the state in 1905 was fully justified and almost inevitable. The mixed character of the two companies facilitated this operation.[46] From 1905 onwards the railways operated as a regular state company with the exception of the war periods during which they were militarized. Today, the viability of Italy's state railway system has once more been called into question after more than a decade of heavy losses and a series of corruption scandals which have put its director behind bars.

### Railways and the pre-unification states

Thanks to France's military and diplomatic support and a series of other favourable circumstances, Italian unification happened quite unexpectedly in 1859 and was practically completed within little more than a decade.[47] Railway construction had begun before 1859, and all

---

[45] Giustino Fortunato and Giovanni Zuccino, *Discorsi parlamentari di Agostino Depretis* (Rome, 1888); Papa, *Classe politica*, p. 18.

[46] Papa, *Classe politica*, pp. 32–3.  [47] Beales, *The Risorgimento*, p. 13.

Italian pre-unification states had granted building concessions to various railway companies.[48] After unification these states ceased to exist and some railway companies found that parts of their network lay within the territory of the new Italian state and parts either in France, the Papal States or the Austrian Empire. In particular, the secession of Savoy to France in 1860, and the belated incorporation of Venetia and Latium into Italy in 1866 and 1870 respectively, created an uncertain legal situation for the railway companies which found the new sovereign, Italy, either sometimes unwilling to recognize the agreements made with the former governments or else making additional demands. It was thus mainly during this first phase in Italian railway history that problems arose as a consequence of the formation of the Italian state.

In the 1830s, King Charles Albert and his ministers in Piedmont progressed significantly in their efforts to create a modern state by spending considerable amounts of money improving the army and building roads and canals. The Piedmontese state had been able to do this because, unlike the other Italian states, it had a relatively well-developed banking system. Before the outbreak in 1859 of the Second War of Independence between Piedmont and the Austrian Empire, only in Piedmont had a regional network been completed. At the time of unification Piedmont had experienced a decade during which construction and operation of the railways by the state had given many positive results. The railways in Piedmont were the only railways in Italy that were largely operated by the state, and had been conceived as such almost from the beginning. This did not mean, however, that they had no experience of foreign capital, engineers and technology, since several important lines were owned and operated by private companies, such as, for instance, the line from Savoy via Turin to Novara.

From 1837 onwards a governmental commission had been studying the requests for concessions and the first timid attempts to establish railway companies date from the early 1840s. Nevertheless, it was only around 1846 that the Piedmontese state itself embarked on a large-scale programme of construction of the main railway lines, leaving the secondary lines to private companies, following the French example of the period. The military campaigns of 1849 meant an interruption of these activities and only in the 1850s were the first lines opened. After

---

[48] For early European railway literature, see Appleton P. C. Griffin, *Selected List of Books on Railroads in Foreign Countries* (Washington, D.C., 1905); Daniel C. Haskell, *A Tentative Check-List of Early European Railway Literature, 1831–1848* (Cambridge, Mass., 1955).

this slow start, however, the network was quickly completed in the 1850s.[49] In 1846, Carlo Illarione Petitti, an advisor in railway matters to the Piedmontese government, analysed in great detail the contemporary railway legislation in Europe and the United States of America in the first Italian book on this theme.[50] He concluded that a state railway system following the Belgian experience would be most appropriate for Piedmont. Petitti argued that none of the Italian governments should leave the construction and exploitation of railways to private industry, since this would only lead to damaging speculation and bankruptcies. He insisted that it was always easier for governments than for private companies to obtain credit on European capital markets. Only when a government could not provide the funds, should it allow private companies to build railway lines and, again only if necessary, provide a guarantee of a minimum profitability of capital or a minimum net revenue. In any case, the buying and selling of railway shares should at all times be subject to various restrictive measures in order to prevent speculation. In particular, the trade in shares of railway companies which were not yet in operation should be restricted.

The waves of speculation in Italian railway shares in Tuscany and on the Paris and London financial markets in the 1840s proved Petitti's misgivings to be well founded.[51] Although most Italian governments shared his fear of speculation, his advice was not followed as regards direct state investment in railway construction and the institution of state railways. Some governments were simply unwilling to contract debt or spend state money for the construction of railways, and others did not have the means or were incapable of doing so because of their primitive banking systems and weak state finances. With the first construction of railway lines left to private and mostly foreign railway companies, speculation was almost unavoidable and was actually made easy by the crude state of legislation on joint-stock companies in all Italian states. Only with the adoption of the 1874 Italian code of commerce were more sophisticated rules for joint-stock companies adopted.[52]

Camillo Cavour, the Piedmontese statesman, was not so sensitive to the problems of the Italian pre-unification states and in a famous review of Petitti's book he argued that fear of speculation would cause

---

[49] G. Guderzo, 'Per una periodizzazione della politica ferroviaria sabauda, 1826–1859', *Studi Giuridici e Sociali in Memoria di Ezio Vanoni* (Pavia, 1961), p. 263.

[50] Carlo Illarione Petitti di Roreto, *Delle strade ferrate italiane e del migliore ordinamento di esse. Cinque discorsi* (Capolago, 1845).

[51] *Ibid.*, p. 496.

[52] E. Vidari, *Diritto commerciale*, 2 vols. (Milan, 1900), vol. II, p. 18.

the Italian governments to impede the growth of the 'spirit of association' or the creation of joint-stock companies, before this idea had even been born.[53] Of course, the validity of Cavour's argument depends on whether the railway companies concerned were solid enterprises or not. In any case, in 1846 the Piedmontese minister of public works, Desambrois, formalized the decision that the state would construct the main lines and only the secondary railways would be left to private industry, in line with Petitti's advice. These private companies, however, would enjoy a government subsidy.[54]

Piedmontese achievements during the 1850s in railway building were indeed remarkable. After a slow start in the 1840s, in 1853 and almost every year until 1858 around 100 km of new track were opened. The Genoa–Turin line was completed double track in 1853. Whereas other Italian states were hesitant to contract debt, Piedmont financed the modernization of the army and the road and canal infrastructure by borrowing on foreign capital markets.[55] Although this innovative policy was not exclusively to the credit of Cavour, who occupied ministerial posts during almost the whole decade, he does deserve credit for the decision to prefer the London over the Paris capital market, foreseeing the great dangers of depending on the Parisian Rothschild Bank.

The operation of the Piedmontese State Railways was quite successful. Its director, the Commendatore Bona, later director of the Meridionali Railway Company, could boast that the railways had always offered excellent service and provided a net return on capital of more than 5 per cent. On closer examination, however, this argument is not entirely convincing, in the first place because the Piedmontese State Railways' rates were relatively high and the rate system was rather inflexible: the railways did not, for example, provide return tickets. Second, in the accounts government transport was counted at full price which inflated gross revenues, contrary to later practice where the reduced rate was registered. The director of the railway had great personal authority and did not hesitate to take measures without waiting for ministerial authorization. He personally defended this course of action to Cavour to whom he remarked, time and again, that without some freedom for its director the railway could not func-

[53] Cavour, 'Des chemins de fer en Italie', in Francesco Cirugo (ed.), *Camillo Cavour. Scritti di Economia* (Milan, 1962), p. 236.

[54] Guderzo, 'Per una periodizzazione', p. 347, quoting a memorandum of 3 February 1845.

[55] Romano, 'L'industria italiana dalla restaurazione all'unità, 1815–1861', in *Storia della società italiana* (Milan, 1986), p. 121.

tion properly. It was thus the rather authoritarian character of the management of the Piedmontese State Railways, not its solid organizational structure, which determined its success.[56]

The loss of Savoy, which together with Nice went to France as compensation for its help in the 1859 war, caused various problems for the Victor Emmanuel Railway Company which had operated the lines in Savoy and was building the Savoy–Turin–Novara line. Now, the company needed to create two headquarters, one in Savoy and one in Turin. No satisfactory solution was found despite the French–Italian Convention on railways of 7 May 1862, and the company found itself in an uncertain juridical situation This was why in 1865 the company offered to exchange its concessions in Piedmont and Savoy for the ones in Calabria and Sicily.[57] This effort to find a better base to operate a railway network ended rather unhappily, however, with bankruptcy and the takeover by the Italian state in 1871.[58]

It is a commonplace to say that no one in Italy had envisaged a truly national railway network in contrast to, for example, Germany where Friedrich List had conceived the idea of a national railway system in the 1830s.[59] It must not be forgotten, however, that none of the German governments listened to List's dreams and that he finally committed suicide, depressed by this lack of interest.[60] Moreover, the competition between different German states with regard to their railway systems prevented effective unification until at least the First World War. The orderly nature of the growth of the Prussian railway network and its function as a national railway should therefore not be exaggerated.[61]

In the 1830s and 1840s the debates on the railway question were still rather theoretical, particularly in the lesser developed European states.[62] In Italy, one author even called Cavour and Petitti 'the

---

[56] *Atti Commissione Baccarini*, part 2, vol. II, pp. 1098–9.

[57] Upper Italy Railway Company, *Costituzione della Società del Sud dell'Austria e dell'Alta Italia nonche delle linee ad essa concesse od appaltate per l'esercizio e sull'organizzazione amministrativa della rete italiana. Dati raccolti e coordinati ad uso d'ufficio dal Segretario Generale del Consiglio d'Amministrazione di Milano* (Milan, 1867), pp. 131–3.

[58] B. Gille, *Les investissements français en Italie, 1815–1914* (Turin, 1968), p. 313.

[59] Friedrich List, *Uber ein Sächsisches Eisenbahn-System als Grundlage eines Allgemeinen Deutschen Esenbahn-Systems* (Leipzig, 1833).

[60] Wolfgang Heinze and Heinrich H. Kiel, 'The Development of the German Railroad System', in Renate Mayntz and Thomas P, Hughes (eds.), *The Development of Large Technical Systems* (Frankfurt am Main, 1988), pp, 106–34.

[61] Dieter Ziegler, 'Particularistic Competition and the Development of German Transport Networks, 1815–1866', in *European Networks, 19th and 20th Centuries. New Approaches*, p. 182.

[62] For a list of early railway literature, see Haskell, *A Tentative Checklist* and Giuntini, *Contributo alla formazione di una bibliografia storica*.

railway prophets' for their long digressions on Italian national character and dreams of Italian unity.[63] At that time, few people had practical experience in managing large construction projects or in the
technicalities of railway building, let alone in the running of railway
companies. There was still no agreement on certain rules of thumb for
the estimation of construction costs and the prediction of future traffic
flows, and in the requests for concessions rosy predictions abounded.
Cavour's personal experience in the 1830s as a railway director, for
example, had been disappointing. The railway company of which he
was one of the directors failed to complete the line between Lake
Bourget to Chambery in Savoy. The construction of what should
have been the first railway line in the Kingdom, was to connect Savoy
by rail to Turin rather than have a rail connection to Paris first. The
project miscarried because there was insufficient capital available; the
cost estimates in the construction plans had been much too low and
government aid was ineffective.[64] Eventually, in 1848 the first railway
line in Piedmont was a local line 13 km long between Turin, Monca-
lieri and Trofarello, which transported a great number of passengers.

Among the various writers on railway matters a consensus had been
reached on which were the major lines to be built in Piedmont, but
the layout of the rest of the Italian railway network remained hazy and
Italian authors expressed a great variety of ideas on the shape of a
national railway network. In Petitti's book, for example, the railway
network was planned on a limited northern Italian scale. He envisaged
that there would be two main 'arteries', from France to Turin and on
to Genoa through Alessandria, then from Alessandria through Piacenza, Parma, Modena, Bologna and Ancona. A second main line was
envisaged from Como to Milan and on to Venice and Trieste. The
railways in Tuscany would eventually be connected through the Florence–Bologna line but this network would fulfil a secondary role,
according to Petitti.[65] The rest of Italy was simply not taken into
account. This strictly northern Italian view follows from Petitti's political vision that Italian unification was still a long off. In his view, the
best manner to prepare for it was through a customs union on the
model of the German *Zollverein* of 1834. In this economic unification
of Italy, which was to precede political unification, the railways would
play an important role.[66]

Camillo Cavour looked at the Italian network from the perspective
of the great impact of steam shipping and railways on world trade

[63] Wingate, *Railway Building*, p. 5.
[64] *Ibid.*, p. 6.        [65] Petitti, *Delle strade ferrate*, p. 498.
[66] Wingate, *Railway Building*, p. 5.

flows, especially between northern Europe, southern Europe, India and China. The lines connecting Italy with its neighbours crossing the Alps and those connecting all the Italian ports from Taranto to Venice and Naples to Genoa were seen to be of the greatest importance. In his view, the city of Rome was ideally located to become the natural centre of the Italian railway network.[67] Although this view is certainly grandiose, it was certainly not realistic in 1847 to predict that the trade flows between East and West would again pass through Italy, as they did in the Middle Ages.

Carlo Cattaneo, another famous Risorgimento author, held an altogether different view on the development of the railway network, in line with his federalists views.[68] Each Italian state should concentrate on building a viable network within its borders. Cattaneo noted that interstate traffic was minimal and therefore the railways should first fulfil existing demand. At a later stage, the joining of the railway systems would not take long if this was to become necessary.[69] In the increasingly nationalistic atmosphere of the Risorgimento the idea of uniting the peninsula through a national railway network was more appealing than Cattaneo's federalist view, if only a plan could be agreed upon.

At one of the famous Italian Conferences of Scientists at Genoa in 1846 the ideas for a national railway system were discussed, together with topics such as the unification of the units of measurement, monetary unification, the formation of an Italian customs union, and the creation of a unified system of education. Cesare Cantú posed the rather theoretical question of whether it was better for Italy to have one central north–south railway line or two along both coasts. A year later at the Venice Conference similar questions were posed but were left unanswered, and no definitive project was drawn up.[70] After the First War of Independence in 1848 the time for these theoretical discussions had ended and Conferences of Scientists were no longer held.[71] In conclusion, the Italian debates with regard to the railways did not produce a concrete plan for a national railway system before political unification was a fact.[72]

Given the great political fragmentation in continental Europe at that time, it was soon realized that the necessary extension of the

[67] Cavour, 'Chemins de fer', p. 243.
[68] Carlo Cattaneo, 'Sui progetti di strade ferrate in Piemonte', *IP* 4 (1841), pp. 143–58.
[69] Wingate, *Railway Building*, p. 6.
[70] Carlo Carozzi and Alberto Mioni, *Italia in formazione* (Bari, 1972), pp. 271–2.
[71] Fiorella Bartoccini and Silvana Verdini, *Sui congressi degli scienziati* (Rome, 1952), pp. 40–2.
[72] Carozzi and Mioni, *Italia in formazione*, p. 276.

railway network would imply the crossing of international borders, and thus vital strategic and economic interests were involved. At first, the states used traditional means of diplomacy to make detailed arrangements with neighbouring states. In a later phase the technicalities with regard to the operation of the railways were left to the companies and high-level diplomats would no longer participate personally in the conferences. In all pre-unification states private capital from all over Europe was attracted to invest in railway construction and set up railway companies in the Italian peninsula. This same method was also used by many other continental European states: a concession or charter was granted to a private company which would build and operate a railway line for a relatively long period of ninety or a hundred years. A government subsidy was offered to the company in the form of a minimum revenue on operating lines or a minimum return on the building capital. A majority of concessions to private companies included a minimum revenue clause, which declared that the state would guarantee, for example, 5 per cent interest on the capital invested.[73] Since, after an initial period, the money lent to the companies had to be paid back to the state, these types of guarantees can be seen as a cheap loan. The government guarantees usually had a positive impact on the companies' prospects for finding credit, and on their general financial position.[74] Thus, from the beginning of railway building the creditworthiness of the Italian states was intimately linked to the fate of the railway companies.[75] Through this financial involvement in railway building they expanded their regulatory activities far beyond the limits of what was customary in Great Britain, for instance, where the state restricted its sphere of action to public safety and health.

In Lombardy and Venetia, part of the Austrian Empire until 1860 and 1866 respectively, the military and political interests of the Empire stimulated quick growth of the railway network. Although railway building did not proceed as quickly as in Piedmont, there is no reason to believe that the imperial government willingly hampered development of the railway network in its Italian provinces by provoking disunity among the different interest groups.[76] It was in this part of the Austrian Empire that the second line in Italy, the Milan–Monza line

[73] Leonardo Loria, *Le strade ferrate* (Milan, 1890), p. 64.
[74] *Atti Commissione Baccarini*, part 2, vol. 1, pp. 107–26.
[75] Gille, 'Les investissiments français', p. 293.
[76] Wingate, *Railway Building*, p. 20; Adolfo Bernardello, 'Imprese ferroviarie e speculazione di borsa nel Lombardo-Veneto e in Austria, 1836–1847', *Storia in Lombardia* 49 (1987), pp. 33–102.

(13 km), as well as the third line, Padua–Mestre (29 km), were opened in 1840 and 1842, respectively. In Italian historiography the fact is usually omitted that the Milan–Monza line was also the second line to be opened in the whole of the Austrian Empire.

It is also inaccurate to maintain that the Austrian administration was diffident towards any suggestion of a direct railway link to the other Italian states or that it obstructed the development of railways in Italy. From the beginning the Empire had connected its Italian territories with Austria and, as we have seen, it actively promoted the extension of its railway system towards central and southern Italy. It was thanks to Austrian involvement that Italy obtained its first direct railway connections across the Alps – the Semmering line, which opened in 1854 and connected Vienna with the port of Trieste. In 1860, Trieste was connected to Venice through Cormons, thereby linking Italy directly with Austria. The second transalpine line, the Brenner railway, opened to traffic in August 1867, was built principally to connect the Lombard-Venetian provinces of the Austrian Empire with Tyrol.

The Austrian policy of developing the railway network in its Italian provinces and the connection of this network to other Italian states, does not mean, however, that the government shared the same priorities as regards railway building as the Piedmontese government. It was Austria's principal aim to extend the railway network into Tuscany, in order to be able to project its power and transport its troops more efficiently in case of emergency and to connect the port of Trieste with Leghorn.[77] For this purpose in 1851 an international conference in Rome was organized in order to discuss the construction of this line with the participation of the Duchies of Modena and Parma, Tuscany and the Papal States.[78] The rulers of these states, except the Papal States, had dynastic connections with the Emperor, so could not mount real opposition to this plan. The Papal representative needed to be invited since the line was to pass Bologna, which was situated in the territory of the Papal States. Another result of this conference was a customs union between Lombardy-Venetia and Parma and Modena, which greatly stimulated Lombard exports to the Duchies.[79]

The view that no account of neighbouring states was taken in the planning of the Italian railway network is erroneous, since the Austrian government in particular was eager to sign treaties in this respect.[80] In the Austrian view a connection between the railway network in

[77] Andrea Giuntini, *I giganti della montagna. Storia della ferrovia direttissima Bologna–Firenze, 1845–1934* (Florence, 1984), pp. 48–53.

[78] *Atti Commissione Baccarini*, part 2, vol. 1, pp. 12–14.

[79] Luzzatto, *L'economia italiana*, p. 22.     [80] Corbino, *Annali*, p. 181.

Venetia with that of Emilia and Tuscany was more important than a line connecting Lombardy and Piedmont by rail. Nevertheless, in Vienna on 19 June 1856 an international convention was signed between Piedmont and the Austrian Empire in which both governments agreed to connect their railway networks at Buffalora on the river Ticin, which formed the border between Piedmont and Lombardy, and that the costs of the railway bridge would be divided equally between both governments. A border station would be established on Piedmontese territory and to study its location a bilateral commission was instituted at the end of 1858 which carried out an on-site inspection in February 1859. After the war in May 1859, however, this commission was rendered useless since the border between the Austrian Empire and Italy was established at Peschiera.[81]

The first international conference in Italy devoted exclusively to railways took place in Modena in 1856 with the participation of the ministers of foreign affairs of Tuscany, the Papal States, Parma, Modena and Austria-Hungary. During the conference the reactionary position of the Papal government soon became evident, since it vehemently opposed the clause concerning a minimum profit guarantee. It was only after great diplomatic pressure from the Tuscan and Austro-Hungarian government that the Papal States finally accepted this provision, although a clause stipulating the repayment of the sums was added.[82] Tuscany's indecision on whether the line should touch Prato or Pistoia also caused some problems during the negotiations.[83] Obviously, the completion of a railway line crossing several international borders took much more time than if Italy had already been a unified state. Moreover, traffic on the proposed line would have been hindered by the lengthy border control procedures customary at the period. Nevertheless, the results of the conference show that agreement on international railway lines could be reached and that it is incorrect to maintain that the planning of railways in the various pre-unification states did not take the activities of neighbouring states in this field into account. The line from Bologna to Piacenza, opened in 1859 and crossing the territories of the Papal States and the Duchies of Modena and Parma, was the first line linking two Italian states before unification, and was planned to connect Milan to Florence. However, before unification Emilia remained unconnected with Tuscany and Venetia. Clearly, the long border procedures hindered traffic, but

[81] Upper Italy Railway Company, *Costituzione*, pp. 127–8.
[82] Albert Schram, 'De Spoorwegkwestie in de Pauselijk Staten, 1844–1856', unpublished master's thesis, Rijksuniversiteit Utrecht, 1988.
[83] Giuntini, *I giganti della montagna*, pp. 44–50.

these examples show that the construction of international lines was not impossible. It may be added that the Turin–Milan line was almost finished in 1859, which means that planning had started some years earlier. Another constant strategic goal in Austrian policy was the development of the port of Trieste. Although the Austro-Hungarian government did not oppose the development of the port of Venice, as is shown by the early opening of the railway bridge connecting Venice to the mainland in 1846, this port could never be allowed to compete too fiercely with Trieste, which was the principal port of the Austro-Hungarian Empire. The Austrian government too had some trouble in determining its railway policy. It decided to nationalize the major line from Vienna to Trieste in 1844, but in 1856 sold the Southern Austrian State Railways, which had grown into an extensive railway network and was, moreover, the largest state railways in Europe.[84] If anything it can be blamed for failing to have a consistent Italian policy and the lack of a clear railway policy. Luckily, it found the Rothschild Bank willing to invest in these railways, which was an advantage that few of the other Italian states enjoyed.

Tuscan railway building in the 1850s shows less advance than in Piedmont or in the Lombardy-Venetian Kingdom. Probably, this state suffered from the isolation of its railway network from other states, since its population of barely two million could not by itself produce enough traffic. The connections with the other states to the north did not become operational until 1864 (Pracchia–Pistoia) and to the south in 1863.[85] In Tuscany, the state hardly played any role in railway building and did not provide a subsidy or a guarantee of interest, or else did so with great reluctance. This was the only state which participated fully in the European wave of railway building, or 'railway mania' in the years 1845–7. The state merely provided concessions to private companies without requirements as to their financial solidity. The ensuing speculation in railway shares in the 1840s was one of the main reasons for Petitti's fear of the unrestricted issuing of shares.

At the time of unification there were no railways in southern Italy except for Latium and Campania. Even more than in Tuscany, the Papal and Neapolitan governments were reluctant to provide state guarantees, and moreover were extremely hesitant and slow in granting concessions. A guarantee of a minimum revenue for railway lines once they were completed would not have led to significant

---

[84] H. Dietrich, 'Die Eisenbahnen in den Italienischen Besitzungen der Habsburger', *Eisenbahn* (1986), p. 6.

[85] Andrea Giuntini, *Leopoldo e il treno. Le ferrovie nel Granducato di Toscana, 1824– 1861* (Naples, 1991).

expenses and would therefore only slightly have increased state spending. Moreover, the first lines that needed to be constructed were also the most important ones economically and would generate sufficient revenue in any case. Despite the low risk for the state, in the Papal States and the Kingdom of Naples minimum profit guarantee clauses were seldom included in the concessions, which was probably one of the main reasons why railway building progressed at a much slower pace there. Paradoxically, it was in the least developed state in Italy – the Kingdom of Naples – where the first railway line in Italy was opened in 1839, the 13 km Naples–Portici line. This line mainly served the aristocracy by connecting the palace of King Federico II de Bourbon with the city, and commercial considerations thus took second place. After 1839 the construction of other lines stalled. The Naples–Rome line was completed only in 1864 when Naples was Italian and Rome was still a Papal dominion.[86]

The difficulties for the railway companies that political unification brought are seldom mentioned, although they were a direct consequence of the formation of the Italian state. A brief account of these cases reveals the vulnerability of the railway companies to political change. The problem of dual sovereignty over a railway company arose in 1860, when Umbria and the Marches were separated from the Papal States. In 1861, the French Romane Railway Company, which held the railway concessions in the Papal territory, was plagued by debts and chaotic financial administration and was taken over by the Société Générale de Crédit Industriel. The 1865 Railway Act required the Upper Italy Railway Company to absorb the small Tuscan railway companies and entrusted it with the Ligurian lines from Massa to Genoa. It became the basis for the later Mediterranean Railway Company.[87] Further problems arose after September 1870 when the Italian government refused to pay the 2 million lire subsidy guaranteed by the Papal government by the convention of 30 September 1868.[88] The reasons for this refusal are unclear but it certainly did not help the company.

After unification in 1860, the Italian state took over the debt and responsibilities of the pre-unification states and it recognized their railway concessions. It had to pay the expenses of the war of 1859: indemnities to France for ceding Savoy, and to Austria for taking over Lombardy's public debt. The Italian government's finances after unifi-

---

[86] Corbino, *Annali,* p. 185.
[87] Cameron, 'Problems of French Investment', p. 92; for a history of all the mergers, see Merger, 'Chemins de fers', p. 143.
[88] Gille, *Les investissements français,* pp. 294–7.

cation were very chaotic and it would take years of patient accounting to sort matters out. In any case, the pre-unification Italian states passed on a debt of more than 2,000 million lire to the new Italian state. With yearly revenues being barely 500 million lire and expenses more than that sum, it is quite clear why the interest on this debt could only be paid by contracting new debt during these first years. After 1866, however, new taxes were instituted and in 1875 the ministry of Minghetti finally announced that the deficit has been reduced to zero.[89]

The moving of the capital of Italy from Turin to Florence induced the directors of the Upper Italy Railway Company to consider moving its headquarters southwards. The company's directors deliberated so long, however, that the had capital moved again, from Florence to Rome, in 1870, and the company finally decided to move to the most central place on its network and transferred its headquarters from Turin to Milan in 1874.[90] Another Italian policy which hindered the railway companies was the effort to mobilize more national capital for the railways. In 1862, for example, the Italian parliament prevented the Rothschild Bank from buying the concessions in southern Italy. Subsequently, the Meridionali Railway Company was founded in which, on the face of it, Italian capital had a majority share. Before 1860, two foreign groups of bankers, the Rothschild and Talabot group and the Crédit Mobilier belonging to the Parisian Pereire brothers, had obtained the building concessions for the railways in the Papal States and the Neapolitan Kingdom. In 1862, the Italian government decided to renew these concessions, thus uniting the northern Italian network with that in the south. As no Italian candidates came forward, it looked as if these two foreign banks were about to take over the majority of Italian railway concessions. This, however, provoked fierce opposition in parliament and consequently the government had to revoke its decision.

The concessions in the south were consequently given to the banker and government minister Piero Bastogi of Leghorn, in order to ensure the participation of Italian capital.[91] Thus the concession went to the Meridionali Railway Company but it turned out that the Italian banker was not providing his own capital but was merely acting as a middleman for the French Crédit Mobilier bank. The first Italian political scandal erupted and it turned out that there had been several other irregularities in the constitution of this company. It is not sur-

---

[89] This historical moment is called in Italian *il pareggio*; Corbino, *Annali*, pp. 209–11.
[90] Upper Italy Railway Company, *Costituzione*, p. 172.
[91] Luzzatto, *L'economia italiana*, p. 73.

prising that Bastogi turned to the Paris financial market, since he had always been associated with foreign railway interests; in the 1850s he had been one of the commissioners of the Lombard Railway Company, which was later to become the Upper Italy Railway Company.[92]

If in 1862 the Rothschild Bank had succeeded in extending the network into southern Italy, there would have been little scope for any Italian railway company. The bank would have created the biggest international railway company that had ever been seen.[93] Without the interference of the Italian state possibly all Italian railways would have been taken over by this company. Since the bank was also one of the major creditors to the Italian state, this would have left little room for the state to exercise control over the railways or over its own financial situation. For the same reason, however, the government could not prevent the company from running its northern Italian network.

After 1860, it became evident that the Italian state, unlike the Piedmontese state, was not able to provide capital for the railways, and therefore had to opt for a railway system in which private companies would construct the railways. At that time the young state faced many urgent needs, including the setting up of a central bureaucracy, a national education system, and many other expenses, and it simply preferred not to provide the capital or credit to build a national railway network. The capital had therefore to be sought from the large European banks or private financiers. For Italy, according to the parliamentary enquiry, the foreign origin of capital did not have a negative influence:

> It was double luck for Italy to have foreign capital in the railways, first in order to have the railways at all, second to tie the interests of Italy to those of European capitalists and make war, for instance, undesirable. For this the influence of foreign capital must be considered excellent under all aspects.[94]

In the pre-unification states issues related to the construction of railways had become an important theme in their mutual diplomatic relations. Moreover, through guarantees given to the railway companies by these states, their finances had become intertwined with the

---

[92] Upper Italy Railway Company, *Costituzione*, p. 320; this first Italian political scandal will not be described further here. For an amusing account of the affair based on the newspapers of the period, read chapter 8 of 'La tangente di Garibaldi' in Vito Di Dario, *Oh mia patria! 1861 un inviato speciale nel primo anno d'Italia* (Milan, 1990). pp. 88–118.

[93] Kalla Bishop, *Italian Railroads*, p. 22.

[94] *Atti Commissione Baccarini*, part 2, vol. II, p. 129.

railway sector. These responsibilities were largely assumed by the Italian state, which, however, proved unable to provide a more solid financial basis or to stimulate the creation of a more homogeneous network. Moreover, the newly formed Italian state proved to be less supportive than its predecessors in the cases of the Upper Italy and Romane Railway Companies. Nevertheless, the tradition of state involvement in the railways started before unification, was continued by the Italian state, and was even further extended after the 1865 Railway Act.

### The 1865 Railway Act: five privately owned railway networks

Between 1861 and 1865, the first governments of right-wing liberals had tried to privatize all the railways, culminating in the sale of the Piedmontese State Railways to the Upper Italy Railway Company. The 1865 Railway Act marked a watershed, however, since from that moment onwards the law was changed and state involvement in railways increased. Whereas in 1865 there had been no state railways, in 1865 the state became closely involved in the building of railways for the Victor Emmanuel Railway Company. A year later the state became owner of the line from Florence to the French border, which represented around 7.5 per cent of the total operative Italian railway track.[95] In 1875 it became owner of 20 per cent, which in 1876 further increased to around 45 per cent with the purchase of the Upper Italy Railway Company.

The Railway Act approved by parliament on 14 May 1865 under the ministry of Alfonso Lamarmora, with Stefano Jacini as minister of public works and Quintino Sella as minister of finance, aimed at bringing some order into the relationship between the state and the railway companies. The situation had become chaotic for the great number of companies which operated railways in Italy. As specified by Quintino Sella in parliament, the building expenses were certainly considered, but the speed of construction was equally important. In Sella's words, the choice was between building the railways with some inconveniences or not building them at all.[96] Similarly, minister Silvio Spaventa declared that when something is urgently needed, it is far more important to do it quickly than to do it well.[97] His political adversary, the left-wing liberal Depretis, shared this opinion. The excessive haste led the state to grant an additional number of conces-

[95] 431 km out of a total length of 5,751 km.
[96] Quintino Sella, *Memorie*, 2 vols. (Rome, 1887), vol. II, p. 64.
[97] Silvio Spaventa, *Lo stato e le ferrovie* (Milan, 1876).

sions and at the end of 1864, there were twenty-two railway companies in Italy, all with different and mostly generous government subsidies and guarantees. Fourteen of these companies were running those lines in northern Italy which before 1865 the predecessor of the Upper Italy Railway Company had been unwilling to build.

The 1865 Railway Act was called the 'Law of the Great Groups', and it divided the Italian railway network into five segments: the Upper Italy Railway Company (almost the whole of Italy north of Florence: 2,422 km, of which 16 per cent was under construction), the Meridionali Railway Company (Tuscany and the Adriatic south: 2,362 km, of which 35 per cent was under construction), the Romane Railway Company (Central Italy: 2,840 km, of which 31 per cent was under construction), the Reale Sarda Railway Company (Sardinia: unspecified length, of which 100 per cent was under construction) and the Victor Emmanuel Railway Company (Sicily: 1,474 km, of which 89 per cent was under construction).[98]

The different levels of development between northern and southern Italy were a major cause of the problems of the southern Italian railway companies. In northern Italy (Piedmont, Liguria, Lombardy, Emilia and Venetia), with its high population density and numerous large cities, its rich agriculture and its industry, the Upper Italy Railway Company, which operated the whole network from 1865 onwards, was in an advantageous position to attract traffic. By contrast, in central and southern Italy smaller railway companies with a more limited and national capital basis had both to construct many new lines and create traffic flows. Soon it proved impossible for these smaller companies to sustain this double burden. Moreover, interests and amortization on loans made abroad in gold standard currency became substantially higher in local currency after the devaluation of the lira in 1867. Considering the great differences in the levels of development in Italy, the division of the railway network created by the 1865 Railway Act, whereby one company dominated the whole northern Italian network, appears economically unviable and politically unsustainable.

Subsequently, some existing lines passed from one of these companies to another and the conditions of the government guarantees were renegotiated several times. Under the law of 28 August 1870, for example, the operation of the small Tuscan railway companies was entrusted to the Upper Italy Railway Company.[99] With the Railway Act of 1885, however, the problems with railway building and opera-

---

[98] Briano, *Storia delle ferrovie*, pp. 124–5; for the situation in 1864, see Corbino, *Annali*, p. 186.

[99] Corbino, *Annali*, p. 188.

tion in the south seem to have been alleviated in some measure. The problems linked to changes of territory between different states also practically ceased to exist after 1870 when the Italian state took the shape it was to hold until 1918.

Almost at the same time as the Railway Act, a new law on public works had been approved by parliament on 20 March 1865, which regulated the construction of private but also of public railways. The railways of the private group were classified into a first and a second category. The terrain of the first-category lines was owned by the building company which was regulated by the government only in matters of hygiene and public safety. The land of the second-category lines was state property and therefore the building plans needed government approval. In practice this was the most common situation.[100]

The discussions about the 1865 Railway Act in pamphlets, articles and parliamentary papers show that the so-called 'railway question' was at the centre of political interest. The number of pages filled by the debates preceding the approval of the Act is staggering and the great number of details is mind-boggling. From every region of Italy local interest groups, railway companies, traders, industrialists, landlords and many others, made often vociferous attempts to influence the discussion in parliament on the Railway Act. The fact that during the ministry of Urbano Ratazzi and Luigi Federico Menabrea, between April 1867 and December 1869, four different ministers occupied the post of minister of public works shows how touchy a subject the railways remained.[101]

The controversial nature of the 1865 Railway Act was partly because of the ideological issues involved, but also because producing adequate legislation for such a relatively new and unknown enterprise as the railways was not an easy task for the new-born state. The dependency of railway companies on European financial markets, the swift expansion of the network all over the European continent and the continuous technological innovations in the railway sector were phenomena which all European states had difficulty in dealing with. The issues involved therefore transcended simple local or economic interests and should not be seen exclusively as a result of typical Italian bickering between rival cities and an unjustified resistance against efforts to build a national railway network.[102]

In 1865, the Italian state tried to create larger and more solid com-

[100] Briano, *Storia delle ferrovie*, pp. 123–4.
[101] F. Ippolito, 'Lo stato e le ferrovie dalla unità alla caduta della destra', *Clio* (1966), pp. 324–8.
[102] See for this last view, Jannattoni, *Il treno in Italia*, p. 49; Andrea Giuntini, 'La linea

panies in order to make the operation of the growing network feasible across the whole of its territory. Despite the 1865 amalgamation operation, however, for each line different legal conditions and guarantees continued to exist.[103] In view of this, the relations between the state and the new companies were necessarily complicated. The relationship between the state and the railway companies created by the 1865 Railway Act can be roughly divided into three phases: from 1865 to 1870, when there was a reasonably cooperative atmosphere; from 1872 to 18 March 1876, when the Minghetti ministry fell over the railway issue and the number of conflicts increased steadily;[104] and from 1876 to 1885, when the new Railway Act was adopted, most of the railway companies ceased to exist, and the state itself became responsible for the operation of the railways.

Despite the relatively cordial relations with the state, the years 1865 to 1872 were particularly difficult for the railway companies. In 1872, Paulo Amilhau, director of the Upper Italy Railway Company declared, for example: 'for the past seven years we have had only one normal year, all the other years there have been wars, cholera epidemics, floods, devaluations and the mobile wealth tax'.[105] The situation in Italy was far from peaceful and the reports suggesting that there were only minor disturbances were intended to hide from foreign eyes the fact that a large part of the Italian army had to be stationed permanently in the southern provinces, rendering the north more vulnerable to attack.[106]

In Italy in the 1870s, unlike other European countries, the issue of the relationship between railway companies and the state had not yet been resolved.[107] The changes in policy towards the railway companies were not casual, but part of a deliberate political strategy. During its wars of independence, the young state had first sought to attract foreign capital, thereby linking the interests of the European capitalists to the Italian cause. Afterwards, it had deliberately changed its policy and begun an effort to substitute these investments for national capital.[108] The lack of a solid capital basis and the hostility of the government to railway companies, and particularly foreign ones,

diretta Bologna–Verona e la formazione del sistema ferroviario italiano, 1866–1911', *Padania* 4 (1990), p. 102.
[103] *Atti Commissione Baccarini*, part 2, vol. 1, pp. 107–25.
[104] Aldo Berselli, 'La questione ferroviaria e la "rivoluzione parlamentare" del 18 marzo 1876', *RSI* 46 (1958), p. 188.
[105] *Ibid.*, p. 214.        [106] Corbino, *Annali*, p. 194.
[107] Gille, *Les investissements français*, p. 294.
[108] Papa, *Classe politica*, pp. 12–13; Berselli, 'La questione ferroviaria', pp. 187–91.

was the major cause of the problems in the railway sector, or in the words of the Railway Enquiry Commission:

> The present state of affairs cannot but have an adverse effect on the economic conditions of the country this railway regime [after the 1865 Railway Act] is the negation of a railway policy of whichever kind. In the beginning the government wanted private enterprise, when it was not able to build or operate the railway network. Actually, it sold the Piedmontese state railways (1865). When it saw that private enterprise did not produce the desired results, because it lacked true financial support, it changed it policy. How did it change it? The state went to war against the companies, and especially against the Upper Italy Railway Company as was admitted in Parliament by those who waged it.[109]

Even the payment of the promised subsidies and guarantees, which had been necessary to lure foreign investors, took place only partially and very slowly in the 1870s.

Up until 1876, the Minghetti government of right-wing liberals, with its public works ministers Quintino Sella and Silvio Spaventa, had worked resolutely to create the conditions for state-run railways as a means of eliminating foreign investment in Italian railways. Nevertheless, the Minghetti government fell over the railway question during the famous 'parliamentary revolution' of 18 March 1876. Proposal 19 dated 9 March 1876 for buying the Upper Italy Railway Company's network implied in effect the nationalization of the whole railway network, and this went too far for parliament.[110] As has already been mentioned, this constituted an extremely dramatic moment in Italian parliamentary history,[111] as well as in the history of railways, since it would take another thirty years before nationalization could again be discussed in parliament.[112] From the point of view of company history too this was an important moment, since the sale of the Upper Italian Railway Company was the biggest sale of a railway network in the world up to then. Instead of choosing between a state and a private railway system, the successive governments of Depretis and Cairoli appointed the Railway Enquiry Commission in 1878, which began touring the whole country, interviewing railway managers, merchants, the general public and anyone else it deemed neces-

---

[109] *Atti Commissione Baccarini*, part 2, vol. i, p. 1357.
[110] Corbino, *Annali*, p. 247.
[111] Berselli, 'La questione ferroviaria', pp. 413–20; Ippolito, 'Lo stato e le ferrovie', pp. 330–1; Corbino, *Annali*, pp. 247–51.
[112] Papa, *Classe politica*, p. 11.

sary. Obviously, this heated the national debate on the railway question even further.

The successful elimination of foreign railway companies by the governments of right-wing liberals before 1875 made it practically impossible to install a purely private railway system. The governments of left-wing liberals after 1875, although in principle in favour of private companies running the railways, paradoxically had to preside over the first experiments in the state operation of railways in a unified Italy.[113] Thus the 'parliamentary revolution' of 1876 did not lead to fundamental change in railway policy. The postponement of a decision on the state versus private railways issue was accompanied by an increasingly impassioned discussion on the railway question, which made it even harder to find an acceptable solution. Thus, this period marked the definitive end of a railway system where private companies played a major role and created the political conditions for the 1885 Railway Act.

At the origin of most of the problems between the state and the railway companies before the 1885 Railway Act lie the complicated arrangements with regard to taxes and subsidies. The Railway Act of 1865 provided for two main systems of guarantees on operating railway lines: one on the gross revenue and the other on the net revenue, that is, revenue minus expenses. For the state, the first system had the advantage that it was quite simple to obtain the necessary information for paying out the subsidies, as only the total amount of revenue from goods and passenger traffic needed to be known. However, this was offset by the disadvantage that in a case where operating expenses too were low subsidies would be given to companies that did not really need them. In the second case, however, the system was open to abuse, as a company could quite easily exaggerate its operating expenses and thus claim a higher subsidy.

In order to combine the advantages of both systems, the 1865 Railway Act introduced the so-called sliding-scale subsidies. This meant that when the company earned more than a certain sum per kilometre of line in operation the subsidy would diminish and finally the company would have to pay back the previously received subsidies. In practice this presented the company with the choice of trying to hold down traffic on certain lines or suffer losses. In 1873, for example, the average net revenue per kilometre of the Meridionali Railway Company exceeded 15,000 lire and, consequently, subsidies were withheld and no dividend could be paid to the shareholders. In this same

---

[113] *Ibid.*, p. 14.

year operating costs rose sharply, because of a rise in the price of coal and steel. Fortunately, a new convention with the Meridionali Railway Company was signed soon afterwards on 22 April 1874 to eliminate this absurd situation and the sliding-scale system was replaced with a fixed subsidy of around 25 million lire per year.[114]

The parliamentary commission made an estimate of the total benefits for the state and concluded that, during the whole period of 1859 to the first half of 1878, the state benefited to a total of more than 190 million lire. It received 122 million in taxes and 138 million in free travel, whereas it had paid only 50 million in subsidies and lost 19 million in unpaid taxes. The taxes received had thus largely reabsorbed the guarantees paid.[115] Conversely, there is hardly a reason to suppose that any Italian railway company was benefiting from its relations with the Italian state. Nevertheless, for the state too the subsidies proved cumbersome since they were financed from current accounts: 'the state, not wishing to augment the future of its inscribed debt, accredited to the companies a kilometric subsidy based on a calculation of probable expenses and revenues of each enterprise'.[116] This system of subsidies evidently did not help the companies to obtain an adequate return on the capital invested. The financial difficulties of the Meridionali Railway Company, the Victor Emmanuel Railway Company and the Romane Railway Company suggest that the 1865 Railway Act and the various conventions afterwards did not manage to support them adequately. The Upper Italy Railway Company did not depend on the subsidies in the way the other companies did.

The Meridionali Railway Company was the strongest of the three, but after 1865 it was crippled by the impossibility of obtaining an injection of new capital. In 1863–4, the average price per share had been between 233 and 211 lire, but in 1865 this went down to 183 lire, in 1866 to 142 lire and in 1867 to 127 lire. Faced with the impossibility of issuing new bonds the company asked for an advance on future subsidies, for which in 1866 a sum of 11 million lire was paid, in 1867 some 35 million lire, and again in 1868 a sum of 35 million lire. This extra aid saved the company from bankruptcy and made it possible to complete the lines it had promised to build in its concession in 1869. Less lucky were the Romane Railway Company and Victor Emmanuel Railway Company. The first prolonged its existence until 1873, but the second could not be saved from bankruptcy in 1868.[117]

---

[114] Berselli, 'La questione ferroviaria', pp. 201–2.
[115] *Atti Commissione Baccarini*, part 2, vol. i, p. 132.
[116] Cameron, 'Problems of French Investment', p. 96.
[117] Luzzatto, *L'economia italiana*, p. 77.

In 1868, the Romane Railway Company negotiated a fixed subsidy with the Papal government of 2.5 million lire per year for a period of five years for around 180 km of its track which was within Papal territory. The Italian government refused to ratify this agreement, however, and moreover wanted to impose on the Romane Railway Company the works made necessary by the relocation of the capital to Rome in 1870. In 1873 a meeting of the company's shareholders approved the selling of the network to the state, converting its shares into state bonds to a value of more than 800 million lire. However, the liquidation proved to be more complicated than expected, and it was only in 1879 that the Act was passed by parliament.[118]

The relationship between the Upper Italy Railway Company and the Italian and Austrian states merits special attention. From the beginning, both the Austrian and the Italian governments had difficulties with the multi-national Upper Italy Railway Company.[119] After 1860, the company realized it would be forced by the Austrian government to make its Italian network independent of its Austrian network. As the company felt that the network already in its possession in Venetia, Lombardy and central Italy was too small it was trying to take over other lines and concessions. It preferred an extension to the south, taking over the Meridionali Railway Company and its building concessions but, as we have seen, this move was blocked by the Italian parliament. To find new life for its Italian network in April 1863, the board of directors got full powers from the shareholders to negotiate buying the Piedmontese State Railways, which eventually happened in 1865.[120] The sale of the state railways has always been felt to have been a humiliation, made necessary by the immediate need for cash by the young state.[121] After 1865 the company had excellent prospects for growth, although it ran into a number of unforeseen circumstances: the war of 1867, floods, a cholera epidemic, etc. At the beginning of the 1870s it ran into trouble, because it needed to service its large debts and was the object of a number of hostile government policies, which meant that it had to pay high taxes and did not have the necessary freedom to develop traffic as it saw fit.

For the Upper Italy Railway Company the losses due to the devaluation of 1867 were grave because the Italian government, unlike the

---

[118] Gille, *Les investissements français*, pp. 294–6.

[119] No complete study of the history of the Upper Italy Railway Company has yet been written.

[120] *Atti Commissione Baccarini*, part 1, vol. i, p. 55; Upper Italy Railway Company, *Costituzione*, p. 260.

[121] Cameron, 'Problems of French Investment', p. 97.

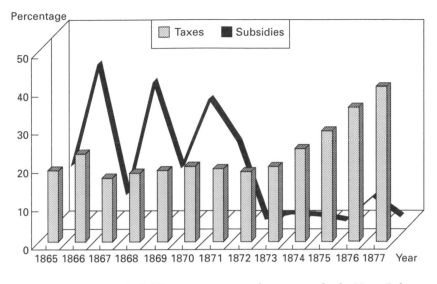

Figure 3 Taxes and subsidies as a percentage of net revenue for the Upper Italy
Railway Company

Austrian government, did not authorize a rate increase.[122] In Italy the
company had some lines falling under one and some under another
system of subsidies. On the whole the situation was questionable and
the unclear provisions in the arrangement were a source of continuous
conflict with the state. As can be seen from figure 3, there was a drop
in subsidies after 1871, accompanied by a progressive increase in the
tax burden on the company after 1874. It is reasonable to assume that
the rationale behind this policy was to bring the company into trouble
in order to take it over.

The collection of the taxes levied on the company was the main
cause of conflict with the state.[123] The ministry of the treasury wanted
to determine the tax on industrial profits (*richezza mobile* or movable
wealth tax) using the balance sheets of the whole company including
the Austrian network and not just the operation results of the Italian
sector. Year after year the taxes demanded by the state were not paid,
and in 1872 the ministry decided to postpone any subsidy payment.
The matter was referred to arbitration which resulted in a compromise
between the Ministry and the company signed in Rome on 16
October 1874, less than a year before the company was bought by the
state.[124]

---

[122] *Atti Commissione Baccarini*, part 2, vol. ii, p. 161.
[123] *Ibid.*  [124] Upper Italy Railway Company, *Memoria difensiva*, p. xix.

The delicacy of the relationship between the state and the railway company is exemplified by minister Quintino Sella's defence of his policy in parliament in 1876. Sella said that the commission in charge of verifying the accounts was unable to do anything because the company did not want to give any information. The situation was further complicated by the fact that the Rothschild Bank, which owed a majority share in the company, was also a major creditor of the Italian state. The government therefore had to manoeuvre carefully between regulating the company and maintaining its own prospects for further credit. These problems complicated the relations with the Rothschild Bank and the minister remarked during a parliamentary debate: 'Relations with the house of Rothschild were difficult because on the one hand there was no respect for the Italian law; on the other hand we had to be grateful for the help given to Piedmont and Italy.'[125] By 1875, however, not much of this gratitude was left.

The railway regime of 1865 very soon proved to be an impossible framework for Italian railway companies. All of them ran into financial trouble and were taken over by the state between 1872 and 1878. Moreover, through its complexity, the 1865 law had given rise to insoluble conflicts between the state and the companies. In conclusion, only the Meridionali Railway Company profited from the subsidies paid by the Italian state. For the other companies they were either too small or, as in the case of the Upper Italy Railway Company, they proved to be a continuous source of conflict.

### The sale of the Upper Italy Railway Company in 1875

The most dramatic moment in Italian railway history after the sale of the Piedmontese State Railways was probably the purchase of the Upper Italy Railway Company by the Italian state. It was the largest single takeover of a railway company by any European state up until that time, and it made the Italian state the owner of most of the national railway network. One critic of the purchase commented that it was absurd that Italy, which was among the poorest and weakest of the European states should try to do what the richest had not dared do up until then.[126] The purchase was widely publicized and caused commotion all over Europe. The story goes that the company's board in Turin first learned about it from the French newspaper *L'Opinion*, and

---

[125] Sella, *Memorie*, p. 255.
[126] Federico Gabelli, *Il riscatto delle ferrovie* (Padua, 1876), pp. 20–6.

when it asked the Paris Committee, the supreme financial organ of the company, for confirmation, it received the following telegram: 'C'est vrai. Rothschild.'[127] The fate of the company was thus decided by politicians and bankers in Paris and local interests were not heard.

A great upheaval followed in the Italian parliament, which was disastrously divided on the issue of state or private railways and increasingly worried about the consequences for the state's finances. Just after the Minghetti government had announced the *pareggio*, or elimination of the budget deficit, this move threatened the credibility of Italian finance once again by taking on a new financial obligation.[128] Moreover, the government's indecision on how to run the network meant problems ahead.

Prospects for the immediate future did not spell doom. The purchase of the roughly 2,000 km of the Upper Italy Railway Company's track made the Italian state the owner of the most profitable part of the Italian network with a revenue of around 28,000 lire per kilometre. The relatively low profitability and the modest revenue per kilometre of most of the rest of the Italian lines formed a more serious liability for the government. According to the calculations of the Railway Enquiry Commission in 1875, all Italian railways produced on average a gross revenue of 18,700 lire per kilometre of track, in contrast to the English 55,962 lire, the French 42,000 lire, the German 39,400 lire and the Austrian 37,000 lire per kilometre. All depended, however, on how the government would manage the railways, and at that moment they seemed to have no clue.

The negotiations leading up to this event had a long history. Both the 1860 Zürich Peace Agreement and the Vienna Peace Agreement of 1866 between the Austrian and Italian states stipulated that the Upper Italy Railway Company should be divided into an Italian part and an Austrian part. Neither government, however, could force the company to split itself up. The company would only accept a split on condition that the two halves could be profitable and viable enterprises. Article 12 of the Vienna Peace Agreement of 3 October 1866 stated that the moment it was possible, and in agreement with the Südbahn State Railways, a convention should be drawn up to put into effect Article 15 of the Convention of 27 February 1866, which called for separation.[129] It gave the company until 1 January 1872 to present new statutes dividing it into an Italian part and an Austrian part. Until

---

[127] *Ibid.*, p. 13.    [128] Papa, *Classe politica*, pp. 10–13.
[129] The convention between the Italian and Austrian governments with regard to the railways was ratified by the Italian parliament more than a year later on 13 April 1867.

1872, the company did not think it was in the interests of the share-holders to separate the company into two halves and that, if it did so, it would seriously damage its creditworthiness. The company there-fore did not hurry to separate the network, using the argument that it was in the interests of both states to wait for the moment when the two parts would be able to operate separately. In addition, there was the legal complication that no shareholder or bondholder could be forced to accept two companies instead of one.

Austria, however, insisted on separation, mainly for political reasons. Apparently, strategic considerations were at stake and the multi-national network was considered to be a threat to the Empire's security.[130] It was not financially motivated, although revenue from the Austrian network was probably used to cover Italian losses. Never-theless the company provided more a source of revenue than a liability. In fact, after 1860, the guaranteed minimum revenue for the Austrian lines never needed to be paid.[131] For the Italian state, on the other hand, the possible risk of not being able to count on the help of the foreign Upper Italy Railway Company in case of war did not balance the benefits of having the only financially healthy railway company in the country. The fact that revenue made on the Austrian network helped to cover the loss of the Italian operation irritated Italian national pride, but given the state of Italian finances, this argu-ment should not be taken too seriously.[132]

From 1872, the Italian government of right-wing liberals and the Austrian government began negotiations with the Upper Italy Railway Company for the separation of the Italian and Austrian net-works. On the extended deadline of 24 October 1873, the Turin and the Vienna headquarters presented an identical proposal to the Italian and Austro-Hungarian governments in which the necessary conditions for protecting the interests of the shareholders and the principle of solidarity between the two halves were clearly expressed. It was argued that for the moment it was best if the Paris Committee con-tinued to take care of common interests and funds. To convince the Austro-Hungarian government of this a member of the Paris Com-mittee, the banker Paul Talabot, travelled to Vienna and Pest to try to persuade the finance ministers not to press too much for separation, and a similar mission was undertaken to Rome. These arguments impressed the two governments and the international commission for separation of the two networks mentioned in the Convention of 1866

[130] Spaventa, *Sul riscatto ed esercizio delle ferrovie italiane* (Rome, 1876), p. 51.
[131] *Atti Commissione Baccarini*, part 2, vol. i, p. 107.
[132] Spaventa, *Sul riscatto*, p. 15.

was never convened. Nevertheless, the Austro-Hungarian government soon started to insist on total separation again, but now the company found a legal pretext for its refusal to cooperate, saying that first a new convention between the two governments was needed.[133]

After 1872, however, the company itself began to change its mind. Apart from the legal problems posed by these international treaties and the quarrels over the Italian accounts, the company experienced a series of problems concerning the operation of railways in Italy. The low traffic density of the Italian lines led to relatively modest revenues compared to the company's Austrian network.[134] Moreover, the increase in operating expenses, which was a European phenomenon during those years, was even steeper in Italy, first of all because of the need to import coal as fuel for the locomotives, as well as more of the other railway material, but most importantly because of the effects of the devaluation of the lira. The reason for this was that the company had to pay its bills for coal in gold, but received revenue in debased currency. The problem was exacerbated during the years 1873–5 by the fact that, unlike in Austria, in Italy the company was not allowed to increase its fares to compensate for the devaluation or the higher costs. Clearly, this was a further incentive for the company to sell its Italian network.[135]

Among all the writings by Italian supporters and opponents of the purchase of the Upper Italy Railway Company's network two documents stand out. For the supporters a very elaborate defence is given in the report by the minister of public works of the Minghetti government, Silvio Spaventa, *Sul riscatto ed esercizio delle ferrovie italiane* (Rome, 1876). The opponents are represented by the engineer Federico Gabelli in *Il riscatto delle ferrovie* (Padua, 1876). Gabelli, a former railway engineer, was a prolific author on railway questions and as a member of parliament for a Venetian district was ridiculed by some for his hypercritical attitude towards all railway legislation.[136] He was not without criticism of the Upper Italy Railway Company, but he considered other solutions to the problems feasible apart from state purchase. The opponents did not deny that the Upper Italy Railway Company had run the railway badly, but saw this as a consequence of

---

[133] Upper Italy Railway Company, *Costituzione*, pp. 258–64.

[134] Upper Italy Railway Company, *Geschäftbericht der K.K. Lombardisch Venetianischen und Zentral Italienischen Eisenbahn Gesellschaft* (Vienna, 1876).

[135] *Railway News*, 10 July 1875, p. 47; for a more extensive historical account see Corbino, *Annali*, pp. 240–51.

[136] Luigi Luzzatti, *L'esercizio di stato. Discorso pronunziato alla camera dei deputati nella tornata del 18/19 dicembre 1885* (Rome, 1886), p. 52; Gabelli, *Riscatto*, p. 65.

the particular arrangements made in 1865, and not as a hopeless situation. Moreover, they argued that these defects had been obvious for a long period of time and were not sufficient to justify nationalization at that moment. From 1870 onwards, the Upper Italy Railway Company had not carried out necessary maintenance in order to be able to pay its debts. Other major shortcomings were, first, the failure to construct the Coccaglio–Treviglio line, and the company's opposition to the building of the Pontebba line. Second, station maintenance was not regular, and third a second track on those lines where revenue per kilometre had reached 35,000 lire had not been built, as had been agreed in the concession.[137] The Upper Italy Railway Company was accused, therefore, of not carrying out the provisions spelled out in the concession.

The provinces in Venetia had special grievances against the company for failing to build several secondary lines that were urgently needed. The company's original concession in Venetia had only embraced the Peschiera–Venice, Mestre–Austrian border, Verona–Mantua, Verona–Tyrol border and Padua–Rovigo–river Po lines. For these lines a minimum revenue of 30,000 lire was guaranteed, the payment of which, however, after 1866 was never required.[138] With the conventions of 19 June 1875 and 3 August 1875 the Legnago–Rovigo–Adria line and the Verona (Dossobuono)–Legnago line were added to the network operated by the Upper Italy Railway Company, but without any form of guarantee.[139] The construction of other secondary lines in Venetia had not been undertaken by the company and led to numerous negotiations with the provinces and municipalities which desired new lines. It was decided that the Upper Italy Railway Company would pay for the rolling stock and stations and take care of operations. Not much was done, however, while the provinces squabbled over who would pay for which section.

Acting on the basis of the law of 29 June 1873, which opened up the possibility that secondary lines would be constructed and operated by private industry, provinces or municipalities, the provinces of Treviso, Vicenza and Padua proceeded on their own account without consultation with the Upper Italy Railway Company.[140] The company objected, however, considering that it had the exclusive right to build secondary lines. This affair was referred to arbitration which judged that these were in fact different lines and the company could not claim the right to build them. The provinces, however, did

[137] Gabelli, *Riscatto,* pp. 83–5.
[138] *Atti Commissione Baccarini,* part 2, vol. i, p. 109.
[139] *Ibid,* p. 116.          [140] Upper Italy Railway Company, *Costituzione,* pp. 246–56.

not make a serious effort and the company was also hesitant about undertaking the building of the lines. The whole matter of the construction of lines in Venetia was put to the shareholders' meeting, which, given the financial situation of the company, vetoed the plans.[141] In the end, these lines were opened at the end of the 1870s, but operated separately from the Upper Italy Railway Company network. The whole episode of the Venetian lines shows that accusations of negligence were justified since the strategy of the company had been to postpone any further investments and defer the maintenance of stations and tracks.

Another important point in a discussion of the purchase of the Upper Italy Railway Company was the way the value of the company had been determined at the moment of the sale. No independent inventory was made, but the declaration of the company was accepted on the basis of what was spent in the period from 1867 to 1875. The curious result was, according to Gabelli's calculations, that the Italian state paid more for the used rolling stock than the new value in 1875. Moreover, large reparations had been put on the capital account and not on maintenance, so the state now risked, for instance, paying twice for a bridge that had been destroyed. Furthermore, in the early years it had paid generous dividends in order to ensure future credit.[142] It is questionable, however, whether the state paid too much for the company since for a similar sum it would not have been able to construct a similar network.

The proponents of the purchase did not deny these facts but maintained that it was first and foremost justified by political necessity. According to Silvio Spaventa, sooner or later the state would have to buy all the railways. At that moment there was thus no other option left, because it seemed senseless to come to the aid of the companies again, knowing that in the end they would have to be bought in any case: 'There is no great company that can live without state aid thus there is no way railway operation can even have the appearance of being a free and independent industry.'[143] Strategic and military reasons too played an important role in favour of nationalization. Although the record of the companies during the 1859 and 1866 campaigns had been good, their future behaviour could not be predicted, argued the minister. In fact, the best and most secretive service was given by the Piedmontese State Railways during the 1859 campaign.[144]

[141] Ibid., pp. 249–53; Gabelli, Riscatto, p. 12.
[142] Gabelli, Riscatto, pp. 87–90, 133.
[143] Spaventa, Sul riscatto, p. 49.     [144] Ibid., p. 41.

The criticism that the Italian state paid too much for the Upper Italy Railway Company's network was not countered by the minister. Instead, considerable future savings in operating expenses were promised, the size of which was certainly somewhat overblown for the sake of the argument. Certainly, some economies could be made through the centralization of the Romane, Meridionali and Upper Italy Railway Company administrations, but it is doubtful whether the savings in the centralization of provisions, the reduction of subsidies and travel expenses for military and government personnel, would ever be substantial. The possibilities of attracting new international traffic flows were also somewhat overstated. It seems implausible that by regulating the rates, international trade flows would finally be attracted to the Italian network.[145]

It seems that it was the company who first suggested secretly that it would be willing to negotiate about the purchase of its network by the Italian state. Later, however, the company acted as if it were the Italians who had made the first move and accepted publicly the offer made by the Italian government to initiate negotiations.[146] At this time it had become the only practical solution left, as the company did not want to continue the costly conflict with the Italian government. The Italian government of right-wing liberals was willing to take over the Upper Italy Railway Company's network in line with its policy of gradually nationalizing all railways. It had already taken over the smaller companies, and it did not want to lose this big fish.[147] This led to the signing of the Basel Convention on 17 November 1875 and the Vienna Convention on 25 February 1876 between the Italian government and the company.

When the right-wing liberal government of Minghetti fell in March 1876, parliamentary support for the takeover evaporated. The left-wing liberal Depretis government did not want to ratify the Basel and Vienna conventions and negotiations had to be reopened. At this stage the Upper Italy Railway Company send a special representative to Rome where intense negotiations were carried out. The deed could not be undone, but a face-saving solution for the Depretis government had to be found. It was found in extending the operation of the network by the Upper Italy Railway Company for two more years until 1 July 1878.[148] Since neither the price nor the method of

---

[145] *Ibid.*, p. 51; see chapter 4.      [146] Berselli, 'La questione ferroviaria', p. 227.
[147] Gabelli, *Riscatto*, p. 47.
[148] These conditions were stipulated in additional conventions of 1876, on 11 June in Paris and 17 June in Rome. They were ratified by the Italian parliament

payment was affected by this additional agreement, this must be considered to be a mere political gesture.

The company was cautiously optimistic about the final result, as can be ascertained from the annual report to the shareholders in 1876: 'When we consider the circumstances which have led to the Paris and Rome conventions, as well as the spirit which is enclosed in these agreements and finally, the declarations made during the presentation in the Italian parliament, we can not imagine that these agreements will form a source of loss for the company.'[149] Act 3181 of 29 June 1876 approved the modified convention of Basel (17 November 1875) between the company and the Italian government, the possession by the Italian state starting from 1 July 1876. The Italian government promised to pay in gold a sum of almost 30 million lire until 1 January 1955, representing 5 per cent of a capital of more than 600 million.[150] About 120 million were paid at that time, financed through state bonds.[151] Great government uncertainty followed the purchase of the Upper Italy Railway Company network. In 1875 the Italian government had set itself a time limit to produce a law before 1877 for transferring the ownership and operation of the railways to private companies, but this goal was not achieved until the 1885 Railway Act.[152]

To answer the question whether, after the sale, the company's shareholders were better off, the history of the company's financial operations must be examined. The purchase of Piedmontese State Railways in 1865 had been financed by the issue of short-term shares. The risk that the interest payments of 5 per cent on bonds would weigh too heavily on the company's finances was justified at the time by the expectations of a fast-growing Italian traffic. This gamble of financing the purchase in this way did not work, since the positive predictions for an increase in net revenue did not come true. Unfortunately, the purchase contract did not take into account the possibility of a change in the value of the currency, and the *corso forzoso* – the lire being devalued – introduced a few months after the purchase involved great cost to the company. The Upper Italy Railway Company did not put the losses caused by the *corso forzoso* into its Italian balance sheets and kept the lire–gulden rate fixed at 2.5. The exchange losses have been esti-

on 9 August 1876, and later by a shareholders' meeting of the Upper Italy Railway Company.

[149] Upper Italy Railway Company, *Geschäftsbericht*, 1876, p. 10.

[150] *Atti Comissione Baccarini,* part 2, vol. i, p. 60.

[151] More details in Albert Schram, 'The Impact of Railways. Growth and Development in the Northern Italian Economy, 1856–1884', Ph.D. thesis, European University Institute, Florence, 1994.

[152] *Atti Commissione Baccarini,* part 2, vol. i, p. 61.

mated at between 4 and 8 million lire annually (or around 10 per cent of net operating profit in Italy) and net revenue decreased, especially in the years 1869–73, although traffic continued to grow in a healthy way. These disastrous effects of the floating of the lira were an important reason for the company to sell the Italian network.

In 1875, these problems had become quite evident. The following comment was made, for example, in a London stock-exchange year book: 'The great drawback of this important company is the loss incurred by the debased paper currency of Austria and Italy, more particularly as regards this latter country, the continued accession of new lines and the now expensive character of the huge bonded debt.'[153] The Upper Italy Railway Company had become specialized in operating railways rather than in building them and functioned as a kind of holding company. In 1875, around 25 per cent of the company's network of 3,301 km was not owned by the company. These were partly lines which had been built by other companies and partly newly built secondary lines. Local capital was used to build the secondary lines, which were then operated by the Upper Italy Railway Company. Since for each line separate conventions were drawn up, this led to an chaotic situation.

Comments after the deal were not unequivocally positive. The *Economist* of 29 July 1876 states that for the year 1875, net earnings minus debt charges left around 5,075 million lire. In that year, however, after deductions for the loss of exchange and general expenses plus the sums due from guarantees, for a total of 10,925 million lire, this left the company 5,850 million lire in the red. Although revenue in those years was on the increase, the company had to draw on its extraordinary reserves. The *Economist* wrote in the same article: 'The question of questions for the moment is whether the company gets a full equivalent for the net earning it surrenders.' On the face of it, the Upper Italy Railway Company received around 8 million lire more each year than the 1875 net earnings of 5 million lire. On the other hand, it may not have been able to reduce its general expenses and loss by exchange by so much as one half. Another drawback was that the shares were subject to the tax on moveable wealth. Moreover it is not clear by how much its debt was reduced in the end.[154]

---

[153] Thomas Skinner, *Stock Exchange Year Book For 1877 Containing a Careful Digest of Information Relating to the Origin, History and Present Position of Each of the Joint Stock Companies And Public Securities Known to the Markets of the United Kingdom* (London, 1878).

[154] To arrive at a more precise judgement on the financial consequences of the sale

In conclusion, it can be said that the deal was not unreasonable for the shareholders of the Upper Italy Railway Company, but that much depended on the future investment policies and debt management. The most important reason for the Upper Italy Railway Company to sell its Italian network was the difficulty of sustaining the Italian railway operation against a hostile Italian state, and the Austrian state's pressure to separate the two networks. Thus both financial problems and political pressures led to the sale of the Italian network to the Italian state. For the Italian state it was a good deal in the short run, although they could have driven a harder bargain by insisting on an independent inventory of the company. In view of its financial position, however, the decision could not have come at a less suitable moment, just after having announced the elimination of the budget deficit and the reduction of its principal debt problems.

### The 1885 Railway Act: the Mediterranean and Adriatic Railway Companies

In 1881, the Railway Enquiry Commission pronounced itself against nationalization and in favour of a mixed system, and proposed giving a concession to three private companies which was to be renewed after twenty years. The system was mixed in the sense that the state owned most of the lines and the companies the rolling stock. Territorially, the Italian peninsula was divided between two companies with an eastern half and a western half, with a third company running the lines in Sardinia and Sicily. The aim of this was to stimulate the integration of southern Italy by having each company compensate the low operating revenues in the south by the higher revenues from the north.[155] The companies would operate the railways, but the government would keep absolute control over the transport rates.[156] The Railway Enquiry had shown that the public wanted new investment in railway construction and rolling stock, higher productivity and lower rates, and thought the state should operate the railways. By pronouncing itself in favour of private railways and against public opinion, the Railway Enquiry Commission did not help the forming of consensus. Not surprisingly, the vote in parliament on the Railway Act was tight: 226 in favour and 203 against.[157]

When Act 3048, the Railway Act, was passed by parliament on 27

of the Upper Italy Railway Company, more specific information about the company's investment and debt strategy after 1875 is needed.

[155] Costantino Bresciani, *Die Eisenbahnfrage in Italien* (Berlin, 1905), p. 1045.

[156] *Atti Commissione Baccarini*, part 2, vol. iii, pp. 1397–8.

[157] Briano, *Storia delle ferrovie*, p. 134.

April 1885 hopes were still high. Francesco Genala, minister of public works in the Depretis government, boasted that this Act had ended the railway debate for the next fifty years.[158] After 1885, the Italian state began to regulate the railway industry even more intensively than it had done before. Previously transport rates could not be changed without government authorization but now the special and local rates had to be approved too. The timetable for the trains was decided by the ministry of public works and to control whether these provisions were carried out accurately the Royal Inspectorate of Railways was set up.[159] The 1885 Railway Act was certainly impressively detailed, spanning more than 2,000 pages in the parliamentary papers. The companies agreed to build all the lines mentioned in the 1879 Act. For the first time national industry supplying railway material was protected and only if its offers were more than 5 per cent more expensive could railway material be imported.[160]

The Railway Act of 1885 divided the Italian network between three large groups: the Mediterranean, the Adriatic and the Sicilian Railway Companies. Out of this network of about 8,900 km, 6,400 km were state property but were leased to the companies. The Adriatic Railway Company was really the Meridionali Railway Company which merely changed its name. It owned about 1,800 km of the 4,303 km it was operating and still had 1,560 km (27 per cent) under construction. The Mediterranean Railway Company had a network of 4,250 km and still had 1,824 km (30 per cent) under construction. Finally, the Sicilian Railway Company had 597 km and still had an unspecified length of track to construct. Concessions of 1,750 km were given to various other private companies. The Mediterranean and Adriatic Railway Companies had three Alpine passes each, with the stations of Chiasso and Milan used by both of them.[161]

The three conventions falling under this law were to have a duration of sixty years from 1 July 1885, divided into three periods of twenty years each, during which the companies would lease the lines. At the end of each sub-period both the state and the company would have the option to disengage with a notification period of two years. The companies became owners of the rolling stock and were responsible for its maintenance and that of the railway track. Four special reserve funds were created, the first for repair to the lines due to natural disasters or construction errors, the second for renewal of the

[158] Papa, *Classe politica*, p. 23.
[159] *Ibid.*        [160] Briano, *Storia delle ferrovie*, p. 133.        [161] *Ibid.*, p. 134.

rails, the third for renewal of rolling stock and the last for the improvement and expansion of the rolling stock and the track.[162]

The construction of new lines would be decided and paid for by the government, but the execution and the technical studies would be carried out by the companies. Of the 6,109 km of line which had been begun under the Act of 28 July 1879, about 3,276 km were in operation in 1885. On 24 July 1887 and again by the Act of 20 July 1888, fresh funds for railway construction and increased subsidies were allocated. This was the last large-scale government-sponsored plan for railway construction, which was supposed to bring about the railway unification of Italy. In 1891 state finances again were scarce and the companies began to have difficulties in dealing with the increase in traffic. Between 1894 and in 1899 subsidies again increased, but problems persisted.[163] The performances of the Mediterranean and Adriatic Railway Companies in 1898 were clearly below similar foreign companies such as the French Compagnie du Nord and the Paris-Lyon-Méditerranée Railway Company or the Prussian State Railways.[164]

The capital of the Meridionali Railway Company which ran the Adriatic network amounted in 1898 to 240 million lire, which had produced an average annual return to capital of 7 per cent and paid a dividend of 33 lire on its 500 lire shares in 1898. Its headquarters were in Florence and the Italian Bastogi and Balduino banks were behind it, together with the most famous names of the Italian financial aristocracy. It is no coincidence that it was this company which produced the best results, first, because it owned the network and second, because of its solid financial backing. Less florid were the results of the Mediterranean Railway Company. In 1898 it had a capital of 180 million lire which had given an average annual return of around 7 per cent over the period 1886–98 and paid a dividend of 25 lire in 1898. This company had its headquarters in Milan and was backed, among others, by the Banca Commerciale Italiana. German banks, too, backed the Mediterranean Railway Company and the 1885 Railway Act therefore marked the beginning of German investment.[165] The Sicilian Railway Company had given good results, and in the period

---

[162] Gaetano Eugenio Chelli, *Le nostre ferrovie. Origini e costituzione delle rete ferroviarie italiane* (Milan, 1889), pp. 41–51.

[163] Carlo Ferraris, 'Le ferrovie', in *Cinquant'anni di storia italiana* (Milan, 1911), pp. 7–10.

[164] Fenoaltea, 'Italy', pp. 83–4.

[165] Gille, *Les investissements français*, p. 317; Peter Hertner, *Il capitale tedesco in Italia dall'unità alla Prima Guerra Mondiale. Banche miste e sviluppo economico italiano* (Bologna, 1984).

1866–98 it had given a return to capital of 8 per cent and distributed a dividend of 32.5 lire on its 500 lire shares which formed a capital of 20 million. The company's headquarters were in Rome and its director was Ricardo Bianchi, who after 1905 was to become director of the Italian State Railways.[166]

Concerning the provisions for the operating revenues, the distribution of the gross revenue was as follows. The Adriatic and Mediterranean Railway Company would receive 62.5 per cent of the initial revenue of 112 million for the Mediterranean (110 for the Adriatic or Meridionali), 56 per cent of the 50 million lire between 112 and 162 million lire and 50 per cent of the sum collected over 162 million lire. For the Sicilian Railway Company these percentages were set more generously at 82 per cent of the initial revenue of 8 million, 72 per cent of the 6.5 million up to 14.5 million and 62 per cent of the sum earned over 14.5 million. Then a fixed sum would be paid to the reserve fund and the remainder would go to the state. Another limitation was set on net return on capital: half of everything earned over 7.5 per cent would go to the state. For various lines which were named as secondary railways it was decided that the state would provide the rolling stock and that the companies would receive a fixed sum of 3,000 lire/km plus 50 per cent (65 per cent on the Sicilian network) of the net revenue. If gross revenue exceeded 15,000 (12,000 for the Sicilian network) the branch lines would have to be included in the main network.[167]

On the operation of the railways, the 1885 Act failed completely, for quite simple reasons. The Railway Enquiry Commission had proposed a system of sharing revenues between the state and the company based on gross revenue but with a sliding scale, inspired by an earlier Dutch Railway Act. According to this principle, the more the company earned, the more it was to pay to the state. The two companies created after 1885 would receive 62.5 per cent of revenue from traffic and the rest would go to the state. If the company's total revenue was greater than 112 million lire, it would receive only 56 per cent of the extra and for over 162 million only 50 per cent. The main flaw of the Dutch system was the assumption of a fixed ratio between operating costs and revenue. The companies were thus encouraged to stay below the 112 million lire mark and to reduce operating costs to a bare minimum. The company was mainly interested in reducing operating costs, not in measures to increase traffic.

This system created a complicated and clumsy relationship between

[166] Papa, *Classe politica*, pp. 26–8.     [167] Ferraris, 'Le ferrovie', pp. 8–10.

the state – the owner of the lines – and the companies that ran the railways and owned the rolling stock. The contract between the companies and the state was based on the premise that only the operating and maintenance costs would be paid for by the company, but that all other construction costs would be paid for out of a reserve fund into which the company would pay a certain sum each year depending on its revenues. Contributions to this fund, however, were evaded and the money was used for other purposes. The arrangements also gave rise to continuous conflicts about what were construction and what were maintenance costs.

The complicated rules concerning the special funds proved inefficient and rolling stock and track deteriorated badly. The companies were tempted to take more than necessary from the special funds that had been created to cover for damage and renewal of rails and rolling stock. Government intervention, instead of guaranteeing the quality of the service, hindered the companies in the execution of their tasks. In the end, the 1885 railway system was neither a private nor a state system, and had the defects of both with none of the benefits.[168] According to Papa the system of self-financing through these funds for improvement of infrastructure was an important and positive innovation, but clearly only on the theoretical level, since in practice the total deficits amounted to around 100 million lire in 1899.[169]

The 1885 Railway Act failed to define exactly the spheres of action of the government and the companies and caused an inappropriate division of revenue between them. Problems in the operation of the railways and under-investment in rolling stock continued and in 1905, at the end of the first twenty years, the complete nationalization of Italian railways was decided upon by parliament. In 1905 Italy became, after Prussia which had nationalized the majority of its network in the 1880s, the second country to nationalize the railways. It had become evident that regulation had failed once more and that the two principal companies, the Mediterranean and Adriatic Railway Companies, had not been able to offer services of an adequate quality.

## V CONCLUSIONS

In every country it proved difficult to draw up a regulatory framework which struck a balance between enough economic freedom for

---

[168] For a somewhat dated but still very useful overview, see Ferraris, 'Le ferrovie', pp. 3–20.
[169] Ettore Jovinelli, *Il problema ferroviario. L'ordinamento delle strade ferrate e le convenzioni* (Florence, 1904), pp. 24–5.

railway companies to achieve efficiency and sufficient state intervention necessary to assure proper services. For the historian the wisest
approach to the issue of state or private railways is to remain agnostic,
since the historical record shows that both can be successful depending
on how particular arrangements are implemented. Attention should be
focused instead on the practical consequences of state intervention for
the construction and operation of railways. In general, the degree of
state intervention in continental Europe was greater than in the
United Kingdom or the United States of America. The railway companies had to subject the rates they charged to government approval,
leased the land on which they built the railways and received various
forms of subsidies which obliged them to present their accounts to the
government. In Italy, in particular, state intervention was considerable
from the start and increased gradually. After Prussia, which had nationalized its railways in the 1880s, Italy was the first country to nationalize the railways in 1905.

In the first book in Italian on railways, published in 1845, Carlo
Petitti advocated the creation of a state railway. For most Italian states
this advice could not be followed since only the Kingdom of Piedmont was in a position to choose a state railway system and to construct and operate the railways directly. For the other states this was
simply not an option, given their under-developed banking and financial systems. In practice, therefore, in the 1840s and 1850s many,
mostly foreign, railway companies obtained building concessions.
These requests for concessions were frequently accompanied by rosy
predictions of future traffic flows. Adequate technical studies were
seldom carried out and construction costs were greatly under-
estimated. The pre-unification governments were unprepared for
dealing with these requests and incapable of formulating coherent
railway policies. Most governments were extremely afraid of speculation in railway shares and suspicious of large companies. Therefore
they preferred to grant concessions to several smaller companies
instead of one larger one. As a consequence, within each Italian state
single railway lines were conceded to different companies under a
great variety of conditions. Although the states produced many different kinds of railway regulation, railway construction and operation
in those years proceeded chaotically. Since after unification these concessions were generally respected by the Italian state and seldom completely revoked, it was on this basis that the railway regime in Italy was
shaped.

In our view the principal problem with the railways in this period
was not the lack of desire on the part of the states to intervene or co-

ordinate the planning of the lines connecting the various regional networks, but rather the great ignorance of railway matters both on the
part of the governments and the railway companies. In the Papal
States, for instance, the government tried unsuccessfully to fix the
order in which the lines had to be built without bothering about the
technical difficulties involved in their construction. Moreover, it
entered negotiations with other governments on cross-border lines
but vehemently opposed any proposal for subsidies to railway companies. Between 1860 and 1870 the situation was further complicated
by the unification process, which gave rise to legal and financial difficulties for the railway companies. In some cases, the new sovereign
state proved to be less generous than the previous one. Moreover,
several companies found themselves in a delicate legal situation, as a
consequence of the border changes, in having to deal with two different sovereign states instead of one. Inevitably, the opaque legal
situation produced financial problems for the railway companies.

Railways were used in the 1849 War of Independence for the first
time when the great advantages of railways for the military were realized. Nineteenth-century armies, however, were notoriously slow in
absorbing the impact of technological innovations and applying them
on the battlefield: it would take several decades before the military
fully learned the lessons and developed contingency plans.[170] The
sheer size of military transport requirements, the necessity to repair
war damage to the installations quickly, and the need to coordinate
transport between different companies, were just some of the problems that had to be dealt with. The role of railways as a 'weapon'
during the Italian campaigns was therefore severely limited as a consequence of the infant stage of development of the railway network.
More significant than its role as a war machine, the railways played an
important humanitarian role transporting the wounded to the hospitals
in the cities after the bloody battles.

With the 1865 Railway Act and the sale of the Piedmontese State
Railways in the same year, Italy decided on a private railway system in
which the state subsidized the railway companies. Quickly, however,
the government changed its mind and decided that a state railway
system was preferable. It began to withhold subsidies, intervene in the
details of railway operation and institute new taxes. Railway companies could not defend themselves against this and company after
company ran into financial trouble and were taken over by the state.
Railway operation continued on the same footing as under the private

---

[170] John Ellis, *The Social History of the Machine Gun* (London, 1987), pp. 174–7.

companies with most of the management and personnel staying on. After the purchase in 1875 of the Upper Italy Railway Company the government hesitated to nationalize the railways, although the state had, *de facto*, come into possession of most of the track in Italy. In 1876, a political crisis with regard to the railways was reached, with the Minghetti government falling over the issue of the purchase of the Upper Italy Railway Company's network. This purchase meant the end of large-scale French investment in Italian railways and the beginning of the involvement of German bankers. It also produced a definite break in the trust of foreign investors in Italian railway policies. In order to break the political deadlock in the Italian parliament, a Railway Enquiry Commission was instituted in 1878. This Commission interviewed a wide cross-section of society and thus created even more debate than already existed. The following year a law was adopted proposing a plan to finish building the Italian railway network, but nothing came of this since the state did not provide the necessary funding. The issues of the organization of the railway companies, their ownership and management remained unresolved.

# CHAPTER 3

# RAILWAY BUILDING IN ITALY

## I INTRODUCTION

In 1861, Massimo d'Azeglio remarked that now political unity had been achieved and Italy had been created, the next step was to 'make Italians'. In other words, after the political unification, the social, cultural and economic integration of the country would have to follow. He also noted, however, that it would probably take more than a lifetime, and with the benefit of hindsight even this can be considered a conservative estimate. The great differences in development levels between north and south were hard to justify politically in the newly formed country and needed to be eliminated quickly. A prerequisite for 'making Italians' was to stimulate the use of a common language and develop official Italian cultural symbols. The establishment of a national education system, for example, would, it was hoped, both eliminate the relatively high levels of illiteracy and promote the use of Italian as a national language. Next, the necessity of creating a basic national healthcare system and the need to eradicate malaria by draining the many swamps and wetlands was also widely felt.[1] Finally, the construction of ports, roads and railways was considered to contribute greatly to the economic unification of Italy. In particular, the railways were seen as the most important bringers of economic progress. The great hope was that they would help both to eliminate regional differences and facilitate Italy's integration into Europe. A sustained rhythm of railway construction was a necessary condition for the railways to act as agents of Italy's economic unification.

In order to establish whether conditions existed in which the railway network could play this unifying role, Italian efforts in railway building are gauged against those of other countries. Next,

---

[1] Beales, *The Risorgimento*, p. 94.

the regional distribution of the Italian railway network is contrasted to that of Germany, in order to put the magnitude of the problem of the unequal spread of the railway network into perspective. Third, the level of economic and human development of the Italian regions before and after unification is assessed in order to evaluate if this can possibly be related to the effect of the construction of railways. Lastly, the process of construction of the network is described in relation to the measures taken in the 1865, 1879 and 1885 Railway Acts.[2]

It must be remembered that even if railway construction had proceeded in an optimal manner, it is most doubtful whether the railways alone could have fulfilled the double integrating task that was expected of them. Protectionist policies, the under-development of the financial and agricultural sector, the lack of competitiveness of export industries, and many other economic and social factors retarded Italy's economic integration.

## II RAILWAYS IN ITALY AND EUROPE

Data on a country's railway length and traffic have been used as indicators of national and regional economic development. This can be deceptive, however, since it overlooks the differences in the function of the railways in each country. In countries where, for instance, coastal shipping played a significant role, the impact of railways on the economy was necessarily smaller. Some studies even assume a direct relationship between the growth of railway construction and traffic on the one hand, and economic growth on the other. It would be hard, however, to construct a precise relationship between these variables, since railway construction and traffic seem to follow a dynamic of their own which is quite different from the rhythm of economic growth. Italy, Spain and the Austrian Empire were the countries where railway building started later and proceeded more slowly. In these countries the railways in the nineteenth century never followed the same dynamic growth path they followed in France, Germany or Great Britain (see tables 1–3).[3] In 1862 Italy caught up with the Austrian Empire, but lost its place again after some years. Not too much weight must be attached to this, since the networks in these

---

[2] For a detailed overview of the history of railway construction in Italy, see Antonio Crispo, *Le ferrovie italiane* (Milan, 1940). For a map of railway lines opened each year, see Briano, *Storia delle ferrovie*, pp. 260 *et seq.*

[3] If track density or kilometres of track per square kilometre is considered, this picture changes only slightly.

Table 1. *Population estimates for various European countries (in millions)*

| Year | Austria-Hungary | France | Germany | Great Britain | Italy | Spain |
|------|-----------------|--------|---------|---------------|-------|-------|
| 1840 | 16,650 | 34,080 | 32,620 | 15,730 | 21,975 | |
| 1850 | 17,490 | 35,630 | 35,310 | 17,770 | 23,617 | |
| 1860 | 18,740 | 36,510 | 37,610 | 19,900 | 25,017 | 15,640 |
| 1870 | 20,320 | 36,870 | 40,800 | 22,500 | 25,860 | 16,200 |
| 1880 | 21,900 | 37,450 | 45,090 | 25,710 | 28,210 | 16,860 |
| 1890 | 23,630 | 38,380 | 49,240 | 28,760 | 30,250 | 17,760 |
| 1900 | 25,790 | 38,900 | 56,050 | 32,250 | 32,350 | 18,530 |

*Sources:* Brian Mitchell, *International Historical Statistics. Europe, 1750–1988* (New York, 1992): Table A5, pp. 77–82.
*Notes:* For Italy, 1840, 1850 and 1860 data are for the census years 1838, 1850 and 1861, respectively. The other years refer to mid-year population estimates as given by Mitchell.

Table 2. *Length of railway track in various European countries (km)*

| Year | Austria-Hungary | France | Germany | Great Britain | Italy | Spain |
|------|-----------------|--------|---------|---------------|-------|-------|
| 1840 | 144 | 410 | 469 | 2,390 | 20 | |
| 1850 | 1,357 | 2,915 | 5,856 | 9,797 | 620 | 28 |
| 1860 | 2,928 | 9,167 | 11,089 | 14,603 | 2,404 | 1,649 |
| 1870 | 6,112 | 15,544 | 18,876 | 21,558 | 6,429 | 5,295 |
| 1880 | 11,429 | 23,089 | 33,838 | 25,060 | 9,290 | 7,490 |
| 1890 | 15,273 | 33,280 | 42,869 | 27,827 | 13,629 | 10,002 |
| 1900 | 19,229 | 38,109 | 51,678 | 30,079 | 16,429 | 13,214 |

*Sources:* Mitchell, *International Historical Statistics*, Table F.1, pp. 655–64.
*Notes:* The data given for 1870 for Great Britain are for 1871.

Table 3. *Length of railway track per 1,000 inhabitants in various European countries (km)*

| Year | Austria-Hungary | France | Germany | Great Britain | Italy | Spain |
|------|-----------------|--------|---------|---------------|-------|-------|
| 1840 | 0.009 | 0.012 | 0.014 | 0.152 | 0.001 | |
| 1850 | 0.078 | 0.082 | 0.166 | 0.551 | 0.026 | |
| 1860 | 0.156 | 0.251 | 0.295 | 0.734 | 0.096 | 0.105 |
| 1870 | 0.301 | 0.422 | 0.463 | 0.958 | 0.249 | 0.327 |
| 1880 | 0.522 | 0.617 | 0.750 | 0.975 | 0.329 | 0.444 |
| 1890 | 0.646 | 0.867 | 0.871 | 0.968 | 0.451 | 0.563 |
| 1900 | 0.746 | 0.980 | 0.922 | 0.933 | 0.508 | 0.713 |

*Sources:* See tables 1 and 2.

Table 4. *Length of railway track in Lombardy, Piedmont and Belgium (km)*

|          | Area (km²) | 1861  | 1870  | 1886  | 1912  |
|----------|-----------|-------|-------|-------|-------|
| Lombardy | 23,526    | 403   | 680   | 1,438 | 2,012 |
| Piedmont | 29,268    | 689   | 1,174 | 1,393 | 2,053 |
| Belgium  | 30,513    | 1,824 | 2,897 | 4,420 | 4,677 |

Source: Mitchell, *International Historical Statistics*, Table F.1, p. 655.
Associazione per lo Sviluppo dell'Industria nel Mezzogiorno, *Un secolo di statistiche italiane nord e sud, 1861–1961* (Rome, 1961): Table 252, p. 477.

countries remained substantially smaller than in other European countries.[4]

Some might think that it was the slow growth of the railway network in the south that put a drag on the national aggregate. Even if Piedmont or Lombardy, the regions with most railways, were considered as independent units and compared to Belgium, for example, which has a similar area, the differences remain marked as can be seen in table 4. Thus, even in its most dynamic regions the growth and size of Italy's railway network remained below the European average.

Similarly, when overall traffic levels are considered, it can be noted in tables 5 and 6 that, after Spain, the Italian railway network showed the lowest traffic density and little signs of catching up with other European countries.[5] By contrast, traffic density on the German network increased continuously. The low traffic density on the Spanish and Italian railway networks cannot wholly be blamed on an inefficient railway management or pernicious state interference, but was also determined to a large degree by the lower levels of economic development in these southern European countries which implied a lower demand for transport services, particularly with regard to goods traffic.

When railway building in Italy is considered separately, figure 4 shows how, after a modest beginning in the 1840s, in most pre-unification states railway building progressed slowly during the following decade, with the notable exception of Piedmont. In view of the relatively small amount of railway track completed before unification, only Piedmont can be said to have held an initial advantage over the rest of Italy. It is unlikely, therefore, that the initial layout of the railways at unification was a important factor in stimulating the growth of the economic divergences between the whole of northern Italy and

[4] Brian Mitchell, *European Historical Statistics, 1750–1975* (London, 1992), pp. 655 et seq.
[5] Antonio Gómez Mendoza, *Ferrocarril y mercado interior en España, 1874–1913* (Madrid, 1984).

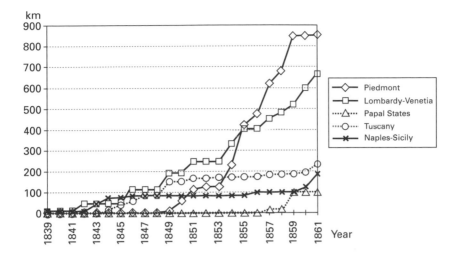

Figure 4    Railways buildings in Italy until 1861 (Source: Briano, *Storia delle ferrovie*, p. 108)

Table 5. *Traffic units (TU) in various European countries*

| Year | Austria-Hungary | France | Germany | Italy | Spain |
|------|-----------------|--------|---------|-------|-------|
| 1870 |                 | 9,329  | 9,700   | 1,632 | 732   |
| 1880 | 6,435           | 16,213 | 20,000  | 2,725 | 1,476 |
| 1890 | 11,003          | 19,703 | 33,800  | 4,251 | 2,006 |
| 1900 | 16,322          | 30,000 | 57,200  | 4,927 | 3,223 |

*Sources:* Albert Carreras, *Estadísticas históricas de España* (Madrid, 1989): Table 7.3, pp. 288 *et seq.*
Albert Schram, 'The Impact of Railways. Growth and Development in Northern Italy, 1856–1884', Ph.D. thesis, European University Institute, Florence 1994: pp. 68–9.
Mitchell, *International Historical Statistics*, Table F.2 and F.3, p. 665.
*Notes:* Traffic units (TU) are the sum of passenger kilometres (PK) and ton kilometres (TK).

Table 6. *Traffic density in various European countries (TU/km)*

| Year | Austria-Hungary | France | Germany | Italy | Spain |
|------|-----------------|--------|---------|-------|-------|
| 1870 |                 | 0.60   | 0.51    | 0.25  | 0.14  |
| 1880 | 0.56            | 0.70   | 0.59    | 0.29  | 0.20  |
| 1890 | 0.72            | 0.59   | 0.79    | 0.31  | 0.20  |
| 1900 | 0.85            | 0.79   | 1.11    | 0.30  | 0.24  |

*Sources:* See tables 2 and 5.

Table 7. *Railway construction in Italy in
five-year periods (km)*

| Years | Length railway track opened |
|-------|------------------------------|
| 1839–45 | 152 |
| 1846–50 | 468 |
| 1851–55 | 648 |
| 1856–60 | 1,167 |
| 1861–65 | 2,188 |
| 1866–70 | 1,838 |
| 1871–75 | 1,577 |
| 1876–80 | 1,172 |
| 1881–85 | 1,682 |
| 1886–90 | 2,716 |
| 1891–95 | 2,341 |
| 1896–1900 | 458 |
| 1901–5 | 650 |

*Source:* Ferrovie dello Stato, *Sviluppo delle ferrovie italiane dal 1839 al 31 dicembre 1926* (Rome,
1927).

the south. The initial length of railways completed was only around 15
per cent of the network which existed in 1900.

Between 1850 and 1859 the Piedmontese state managed to build an
extensive railway network according to a predetermined plan.
Although in 1859, in northern Italy and in Tuscany numerous lines
were already operating, only in Piedmont did they form a proper regional network. The discrepancy between Piedmont and the other
Italian states was large: in 1860 Piedmont had a network of 850 km or
38 per cent of the total Italian railway network at that time (2,237
km).[6] Nevertheless, in all other northern Italian regions the main cities
were connected by rail and plans to connect the regional networks
had been agreed upon.[7]

This said, it should be remembered that before unification more
railway concessions were given to private companies than were actually
completed and opened to traffic. Moreover, since these pre-unification
concessions were fully recognized by the Italian state, the 1840s and
1850s were a more significant period than these statistics on the
opening of lines would suggest at first sight.

After unification, data on the length of the regional networks
become scarcer. The geographic unit of measurement became the

[6] Ferrovie dello Stato, *Sviluppo delle ferrovie italiane dal 1839 al 31 dicembre 1926* (Rome,
1927).
[7] Luzzatto, *L'economia italiana*, p. 22.

Table 8. *Population in Italian regions (000s)*

| Region | Area | Population | | | | |
|---|---|---|---|---|---|---|
| | | 1861 | 1871 | 1881 | 1901 | 1911 |
| Piedmont | 29,268 | 3,041 | 2,900 | 3,070 | 3,317 | 3,424 |
| Liguria | 5,324 | 771 | 844 | 892 | 1,077 | 1,197 |
| Lombardy | 23,526 | 3,305 | 3,461 | 3,681 | 4,283 | 4,790 |
| Venetia | 23,463 | 2,239 | 2,643 | 2,814 | 3,134 | 3,527 |
| Emilia | 20,515 | 2,047 | 2,113 | 2,183 | 2,445 | 2,681 |
| North | 102,096 | 11,403 | 11,961 | 12,640 | 14,256 | 15,619 |
| Tuscany | 24,052 | 2,006 | 2,152 | 2,209 | 2,549 | 2,695 |
| Marches | 9,703 | 883 | 915 | 939 | 1,061 | 1,093 |
| Umbria | 9,663 | 513 | 550 | 572 | 667 | 687 |
| Latium | 11,917 | n.a. | 837 | 903 | 1,197 | 1,302 |
| Central | 55,335 | 3,402 | 4,454 | 4,623 | 5,474 | 5,777 |
| Abruzzi and Molise | 17,290 | 1,213 | 1,283 | 1,317 | 1,442 | 1,431 |
| Campania | 17,978 | 3,110 | 2,755 | 2,897 | 3,160 | 3,312 |
| Apulia | 22,115 | 1,755 | 1,421 | 1,589 | 1,960 | 2,130 |
| Basilicata | 10,675 | 493 | 502 | 525 | 491 | 474 |
| Calabria | 17,257 | 1,140 | 1,206 | 1,258 | 1,370 | 1,402 |
| Sicily | 29,241 | 2,392 | 2,584 | 2,928 | 3,530 | 3,672 |
| Sardinia | 24,342 | 588 | 637 | 682 | 792 | 852 |
| South | 138,898 | 10,691 | 10,388 | 11,196 | 12,745 | 13,273 |
| Total | 296,329 | 25,496 | 26,803 | 28,459 | 32,475 | 34,669 |

*Sources:* Mitchell, *International Historical Statistics*, Table A1, p. 1.
Italy, Ministero di Agricoltura, Industria e Commercio, *Censimento 1871* and *Censimento 1881* (Rome 1872, 1882).

state, and the pre-unification states which became regions were no longer of importance. It was inevitable that railways did not spread evenly over the whole national territory and that less densely populated, poorer or remoter provinces generally had to wait longer to be connected to the railway network, given the complicated mixture of business interests and the role of public policy which played a role during construction. As shown by tables 8 and 9 the population density in central and southern Italy was substantially lower than in the north, hence its prospects for producing substantial amounts of railway traffic were proportionally smaller.

The most appropriate measure for studying the spread of railways is the number of kilometres of track per 1,000 inhabitants in each region. This measure gives an indication of the provision for railways per region and can be interpreted as a crude approximation of transport

Table 9. *Population density in Italian regions (inhabitants per km²)*

|  | Population density | | | | |
|---|---|---|---|---|---|
|  | 1861 | 1871 | 1881 | 1901 | 1911 |
| Piedmont | 104 | 99 | 105 | 113 | 117 |
| Liguria | 145 | 159 | 168 | 202 | 225 |
| Lombardy | 140 | 147 | 156 | 182 | 204 |
| Venetia | 95 | 113 | 120 | 134 | 150 |
| Emilia | 100 | 103 | 106 | 119 | 131 |
| North | 112 | 117 | 124 | 140 | 153 |
| Tuscany | 83 | 89 | 92 | 106 | 112 |
| Marches | 91 | 94 | 97 | 109 | 113 |
| Umbria | 53 | 57 | 59 | 69 | 71 |
| Latium | 0 | 70 | 76 | 100 | 109 |
| Central | 61 | 80 | 84 | 99 | 104 |
| Abruzzi and Molise | 70 | 74 | 76 | 83 | 83 |
| Campania | 173 | 153 | 161 | 176 | 184 |
| Apulia | 79 | 64 | 72 | 89 | 96 |
| Basilicata | 46 | 47 | 49 | 46 | 44 |
| Calabria | 66 | 70 | 73 | 79 | 81 |
| Sicily | 82 | 88 | 100 | 121 | 126 |
| Sardinia | 24 | 26 | 28 | 33 | 35 |
| South | 77 | 75 | 81 | 92 | 96 |
| Total | 86 | 90 | 96 | 110 | 117 |

*Sources:* See table 8.

services offered by the railways. A better measure would be the number of railway stations per 1,000 inhabitants, but unfortunately data are not available for most of the period under study.[8] For 1880, map 1 shows that there were considerable differences in the number of stations between the various northern Italian provinces. Piedmont's initial advantage can be clearly seen, since the Piedmontese provinces have a substantially higher number of stations per inhabitant than the other northern Italian provinces.

In order to reach firm conclusions on the regional spread of the railway network a comparison with the German case is fruitful, since this country too was unified after railway construction had begun. The coefficient of variation of the kilometres of track per 1,000 inhabitants for each region shows whether the railways in Italy were spread

[8] More research is needed in order to estimate variables during different periods, concerning the shape of the network, whether single or double track, and the exploitation of the track, such as the frequency of trains and the number of stations.

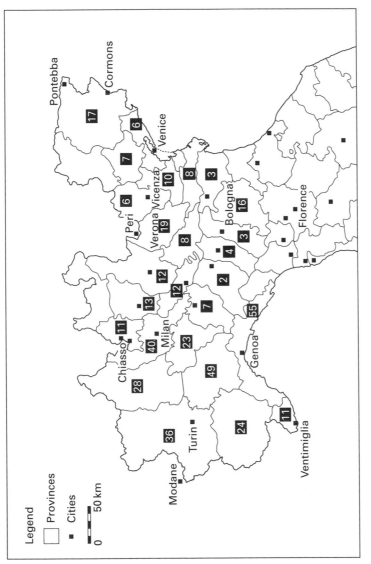

Map 1   The number of stations in Piedmont, Lombardy and Venetia, 1880

Table 10. *Railway length in Italian regions (km)*

| Region | Area (km²) | 1861 | 1886 | 1912 |
|---|---|---|---|---|
| Piedmont | 29,268 | 689 | 1,393 | 2,053 |
| Liguria | 5,324 | 54 | 366 | 451 |
| Lombardy | 23,526 | 403 | 1,438 | 2,012 |
| Venetia | 23,463 | 353 | 1,072 | 1,438 |
| Emilia | 20,515 | 302 | 735 | 1,271 |
| North | 102,096 | 1,801 | 5,004 | 7,225 |
| Tuscany | 24,052 | 361 | 954 | 1,299 |
| Marches | 9,703 | 74 | 327 | 503 |
| Umbria | 9,663 | | 460 | 460 |
| Latium | 11,917 | 100 | 435 | 787 |
| Central | 55,335 | 535 | 2,176 | 3,049 |
| Abruzzi and Molise | 17,290 | | 503 | 881 |
| Campania | 17,978 | 184 | 734 | 1,239 |
| Apulia | 22,115 | | 767 | 1,237 |
| Basilicata | 10,675 | | 187 | 352 |
| Calabria | 17,257 | | 507 | 796 |
| Sicily | 29,241 | | 893 | 1,033 |
| Sardinia | 24,342 | | 431 | 1,033 |
| South | 138,898 | 184 | 4,022 | 6,571 |
| Total | 296,329 | 2,520 | 11,202 | 16,845 |

*Sources:* Associazione per lo Sviluppo dell'Industria nel Mezzogiorno, *Un secolo di statistiche*, Table 252, p. 477.

more or less equally in relation to population over the national territory than in Germany. For Italy for 1861, 1886 and 1912 the length of track opened for each of its sixteen regions is known. For Germany, data on track length for twenty-four regions was analysed for 1860 to 1900.[9] The average size of the Italian region was almost 19,000 km² and the average population was between 1.7 (1860) and 2.2 million (1912). Germany's twenty-four regions were slightly more extensive, with an average size of almost 23,000 km², but with an average population similar to Italy's regions of 1.6 (1860) and 2.2 million (1900).

[9] The data were kindly provided by Dieter Ziegler, and can be found in his 'Eisenbahnen und Staat im Zeitalter der Industrialisierung. Die Eisenbahnpolitik der deutschen Staaten im Vergleich', unpublished Ph.D. thesis, University of Bielefeld, 1994, tab. A1, p. 522, tab. A2, pp. 523–30, tab. A3, pp. 531–3. Regrettably, Ziegler provides no data on railway length for the regions of Berlin, Hamburg and Bremen. For the sake of compatibility the regional division of Germany was taken from Mitchell, *European Historical Statistics*, Table B3, pp. 71–2.

Table 11. *Railway length per 1,000 inhabitants in Italian regions (km)*

| Region | 1861 | 1886 | 1912 |
|---|---|---|---|
| Piedmont | 0.23 | 0.45 | 0.60 |
| Liguria | 0.07 | 0.41 | 0.38 |
| Lombardy | 0.12 | 0.39 | 0.42 |
| Venetia | 0.16 | 0.38 | 0.41 |
| Emilia | 0.15 | 0.34 | 0.47 |
| North | 0.16 | 0.40 | 0.46 |
| Tuscany | 0.18 | 0.43 | 0.48 |
| Marches | 0.08 | 0.35 | 0.46 |
| Umbria | 0.00 | 0.80 | 0.67 |
| Latium | n.a. | 0.48 | 0.60 |
| Central | 0.16 | 0.47 | 0.53 |
| Abruzzi and Molise | 0.00 | 0.38 | 0.62 |
| Campania | 0.16 | 0.25 | 0.37 |
| Apulia | 0.00 | 0.48 | 0.58 |
| Basilicata | 0.00 | 0.36 | 0.74 |
| Calabria | 0.00 | 0.40 | 0.57 |
| Sicily | 0.00 | 0.30 | 0.28 |
| Sardinia | 0.00 | 0.63 | 1.21 |
| South | 0.02 | 0.36 | 0.50 |
| Total | 0.10 | 0.39 | 0.49 |

*Sources:* See tables 8 and 10.

Population density for the Italian regions was on average 90 inhabitants/km² (1860) up to 118 inhabitants/km² (1911), and for Germany the population density was between 76 inhabitants/km² (1860) and 106 inhabitants/km² (1900).[10]

As a measure of inequality, a weighted $V_w$ instead of a simple coefficient of variation is used in order to avoid giving the same importance in the calculations to less populated regions, and to compensate for the sometimes rather arbitrary division into regions of the two countries.[11] As can be seen from the values of $V_w$ in table 12, the initial distribution of railways in Italy in 1860 was much more uneven than in Germany, but by 1886 this difference had been greatly reduced. At the beginning of the twentieth century in both countries a trend towards a

[10] The coefficients of variation for Italy's total regional populations are between 0.52 (1861) and 0.45 (1911). For Germany, they are from 0.38 (1860) to 0.51 (1900). These data suggest that the regions in the two countries are roughly comparable in size and population.

[11] Different measures of inequality can be calculated, but the results are similar.

Table 12. *Weighted coefficient of variation (V_w) for railway length per 1,000 inhabitants*

|                       | 1860 |      | 1886 |      | 1912 |
|-----------------------|------|------|------|------|------|
| $V_w$ Italy           | 1.32 |      | 0.24 |      | 0.31 |
| $V_w$ Germany         | 0.35 | 0.27 | 0.17 | 0.18 | 0.25 |

*Sources:* See table 11 and Dieter Ziegler, 'Eisenbahnen und Staat im Zeitalter der Industrialisierung. Die Eisenbahnpolitik der Deutschen Staaten im Vergleich', Ph.D. thesis, Bielefeld, 1994: table A1, p. 522, table A2, pp. 523–30, table A3, pp. 531–3.

more unequal regional distribution can be detected. Nevertheless, according to the values calculated in table 12, the distribution of railways in the Italian regions remains more uneven than in Germany.

Of course, no comparison is ideal and two major differences between Italy and Germany must be taken into account. First, after unification Italy did not have powerful local government, so the obstacles in the way of inter-regional railway traffic were smaller and mainly related to such things as transport rates, the operation of the railways and the use of different technologies. Actually, the contemporary historical debate on the nineteenth-century railway network in Germany has mostly been focused on the failure to create an integrated system. The competition between the states, it is argued, created an excess number of lines, and this could have been avoided if proper planning had taken place.[12] Second, although Germany also had considerable differences in average income per region, it did not have Italy's north–south problem.[13] Third, in Italy there was a long tradition of coastal shipping which compensated for a possible lack of railways in certain regions in the south. In Germany, on the other hand, the use of rivers and canals was limited to certain regions. Both differences between Italy and Germany meant that a more uneven spread of the railway network in Italy would have less impact than in Germany.[14]

When the regional differences in track length per 1,000 inhabitants within Italy are considered, it can be seen from table 11 that by 1870 central Italy had attained the highest value and that by 1886 southern Italy too had reached a high score. The same is true when the length

[12] Ziegler, 'Particularistic Competition', pp. 182–3.

[13] Frank B. Tipton, *Regional Variations in the Economic Development of Germany during the Nineteenth Century* (Middletown, Conn., 1976), pp. 1–10.

[14] A more thorough comparative study of the Italian and German railway networks, which is not limited to the track length per region is called for.

of railway track opened in the north is contrasted with that opened in the south: the south scores well from 1886 onwards (see table 10). In view of this, the arguments that the south of Italy was particularly under-endowed with railways must be reconsidered. According to this measure, the construction policies in favour of the south after unification were a success. As a consequence, the supposed uneven spread of the railways cannot be considered an impediment to the development of the south. In fact, the spread of the railway network is one of the variables that shows the smallest difference between the northern and southern Italian regions.

### III ECONOMIC UNIFICATION

During the second half of the nineteenth century and up until the First World War Italy, unlike other southern European countries like Spain, Portugal and Greece, managed to join the ranks of European industrial nations.[15] The railways have repeatedly been mentioned among the reasons of Italy's miraculous ascent.[16] Despite this emphasis on railways, hardly any serious attention has been given to the relationship between railway construction and operation on the one hand, and regional differences in economic development, on the other.[17] Any serious questioning of this would overturn one of the axioms of railway history, since the railways were seen as the economic unifiers of the country.[18] Moreover, it would be contrary to many assumptions of mainstream neo-classical economics, which suggest a convergence of income levels when transaction costs decrease through cheaper transport.[19] Thus, paradoxically, the dominating belief that the railways in Italy contributed to regional integration has led to a neglect of research into the effects of the railways on the regional economies. Data on inter-regional railway traffic flows, for instance, have never

---

[15] Jeffrey Williamson, 'Globalization, Convergence and History', *JEH* 56 (1996), pp. 277–9.

[16] Douglas Fisher, *The Industrial Revolution. A Macro-Economic Interpretation* (New York, 1992), p. 232.

[17] The only exception is Zamagni, 'Ferrovie e Integrazione', pp. 1635–8; for an experimental method of arriving at provincial GDP estimates, see Schram, 'The Impact of Railways', pp. 206–36.

[18] James Vance, *Capturing the Horizon. The Historical Geography of Transportation since the Sixteenth Century* (Baltimore, 1990), p. 246; Kalla Bishop, *Italian Railroads*, p. 39; for a more critical view see Zamagni, 'Ferrovie e Integrazione', pp. 1635–6.

[19] Paul Krugman has suggested an alternative approach; Paul Krugman, *Geography and Trade* (Cambridge, Mass., 1992), pp. 97–8.

been carefully examined, and railway networks have been described on a national scale as if they were perfectly integrated.[20]

The national bias in railway history finds a parallel in economic history since most quantification of Italian economic development has produced national aggregates. Italy, however, is a country of regions whose industry towards the end of the nineteenth century developed in a relatively small area of Piedmont and Lombardy, in the so-called industrial triangle formed by the cities of Genoa, Turin and Milan.[21] National aggregates for both the economy and for the railways therefore obscure important regional differences and should be used with caution, particularly for the first decades after unification.[22]

Vera Zamagni's important study offers the first estimate of regional differences in GDP per capita levels for 1911.[23] As a consequence, not much can be said about a possible convergence of regional income levels during the second half of the nineteenth century. To make matters worse, even the aggregate estimates of Italian GDP for the nineteenth century are inaccurate and subject to constant revision.[24]

### The first decade after unification

In order to analyse the effects of unification on the economies of the Italian regions the situations before and after 1860 should be compared. Regrettably this is rather tricky since in the 1840s or 1850s the criteria for producing social and economic data varied widely between the pre-unification Italian states. There is certainly no absence of economic statistics for single Italian states before 1860 or, as was maintained by Cesare Correnti in 1857: 'in Italy there is no lack of statistical institutions or offices, but there is no constant method of gathering data, nor a coordinated and uniform way of publishing them'.[25] For this reason it is practically impossible to compare the statistics of different pre-unification states.

There is one exception, however. In theory, at least, the statistics for those regions which were part of the same political unit can be compared, since they were collected using the same criteria. This is

---

[20] In my Ph.D. thesis regional traffic for northern Italy is analysed from 1867 to 1884; see Schram, 'The Impact of Railways', pp. 206–36.
[21] Giuseppe Dematteis, Gino Lusso and Giovanna DiMeglio, 'La distribuzione territoriale dell'industria nell'Italia nord-occidentale', *SU* 40 (1979), pp. 117–21.
[22] Esposto, 'Italian Industrialization', pp. 353–4.
[23] Zamagni, *Industrializzazione e squilibri regionali*, Table 58, pp. 198–9.
[24] Paolo Ercolani, 'Il prodotto interno lordo dell'Italia nel lungo periodo: vecchie e nuove stime', working paper, University of Ancona, 1994.
[25] Cesare Correnti, *Annuario statistico italiano* (Turin, 1858), p. 397.

the case for the regions of Lombardy and Venetia which belonged to the Austrian Empire and all the southern regions which were part of the Kingdom of Naples. In the south, however, the collection of statistics was regarded by the government as a subversive activity and, consequently, there are few reliable data available.[26] To fill this gap, some authors have used data provided by foreign observers, such as the first statistics encompassing various regions of Italy which were collected in 1839 by an English consul for the British parliament. Nonetheless, these statistics are mainly commercial in nature and are of limited use.[27]

The socio-economic data collected by the Austrian state for Lombardy and Venetia are not sufficient to estimate precisely the relative levels of economic development in these regions.[28] Nevertheless, they provide enough information to make a preliminary assessment of the costs and benefits for these regions of being integrated into the new Italian state. All the same, the differences between these two regions should not be under-estimated for, as Vera Zamagni remarked, Lombardy and Venetia had and continued to have a separate economic development before and after their incorporation into Italy.[29] Although both regions were part of the Austrian Empire they were administered separately and even customs barriers between them continued to exist.

In the 1850s, Lombardy produced around a third of all Italian silk and accounted for more than 85 per cent of the value of all Italian exports.[30] Cotton and metal industries had already been established in the Milan and Como provinces of Lombardy.[31] Austrian protectionism supported the emerging industries in this region well, but at the same time it severely limited the export of Lombardy's products to other Italian markets. Therefore, in the long term, its incorporation into Italy in 1860 brought Lombardy more advantages than it had ever

---

[26] Domenico Demarco, 'L'economia e la finanza degli stati italiani dal 1848 al 1860', in *Nuove questioni del Risorgimento italiano* (Milan, 1962), p. 765.

[27] Sir John Bowring, *Report on the Statistics of the Italian States. Sessional Papers XVI* (London, 1839).

[28] Sergio Zaninelli, 'Una fonte per la storia dell'economia del Lombardo-Veneto nella prima metà del secolo XIX. Le "Tafeln zur Statistik der Oesterreichischen Monarchie"', in Carlo Cipolla (ed.) *Archivio Economico dell'Unificazione Italiana*, 12, series 1 (Rome, 1963), pp. 1–2.

[29] Zamagni, *Dalla periferia al centro*, p. 30.

[30] Pietro Maestri, *Dell'industria manifatturiera in Italia* (Turin, 1858); Cesare Correnti and Pietro Maestri, *Annuario statistico italiano* (Turin, 1864); Ira A. Glazier, *Il commercio del regno Lombardo-Veneto dal 1815 al 1865* (Rome, 1966).

[31] Bruno Caizzi, *La tessitura a Como dall'unità alla fine del secolo* (Bologna, 1981).

had as part of the Austrian Empire.[32] Assimilation into Italy in 1860 brought free access to the large Italian market, elimination of export duties and low imports which almost certainly greatly benefited this relatively rich region in the long run.

In the 1850s, Austria tried to stimulate the economies of Lombardy and Venetia by encouraging trade with the surrounding states. In 1851, free traffic on the river Po was agreed upon by the two small Duchies of Parma and Modena, the Papal States and the Austrian Empire.[33] Both Venetia and Lombardy took advantage of this customs union and expanded trade with Parma and Modena between 1854 and 1860. Nevertheless these measures went only half-way, since the far larger French and German markets for these regions' most important export product, silk, remained practically closed and subject to heavy export duties.[34]

The advantages to Venetia in joining Italy are less clear than they are for Lombardy, and it might even have been better off under Austrian rule, although this would be hard to prove. Venetia was less well developed than Lombardy and it counted only two major industrial establishments: Luigi Marzotto's and Alessandro Rossi's wool factories.[35] Data on per capita indirect tax collection indicate less economic activity in Venetia than in Lombardy.[36] The port of Venice played an important role in the region's economy, although Venice's port activity was considerably smaller than that of Genoa or Trieste.[37] Although the shipping statistics for Venice in the 1850s are not very detailed, they confirm the impression of a rather provincial economy. For 1857, for example, foreign trade accounted for only a minor part

---

[32] In the 1850s, however, at least one influential economist, Cesare Correnti, maintained the opposite, see Wingate, *Railway Building*, pp. 22–3.

[33] Massimo Costantini, 'Dal porto franco al porto industriale', in Albino Tenente and Ugo Tucci (eds.), *Storia di Venezia* (Rome, 1991), p. 889.

[34] Alberto Errera, *Documenti alla storia e statistica delle industrie venete e acenni al loro avvenire* (Venice, 1870), p. 127.

[35] Alessandro Rossi, *Dell'arte della lana in Italia e all'estero giudicata alla esposizione di Parigi. Note* (Florence, 1869); Alberto Errera, *Annuario statistico industriale del Veneto pel 1869* (Venice, 1870); Lucio Avagliano, *Un imprenditore e una fabbrica fuori del commune: Alessandro Rossi e il lanificio di Schio* (Bologna, 1981); Zamagni, *Dalla periferia al centro*, p. 33.

[36] Uggè, Albino. 'Le entrate del Regno Lombardo-Veneto dal 1840 al 1864', in Carlo Cipolla (ed.), *Archivio Economico dell'Unificazione Italiana* 1, series 1 (Rome, 1956), pp. 3–8; on the decline in agricultural production, see Bruno Caizzi, 'La crisi economica nel Lombardo-Veneto nel decennio, 1850–1859', NRS 42 (1958), pp. 204–8.

[37] Rolf Petri, 'Autarchia, guerra, zone industriali. Continuità e transizione dell'intervento straordinario nell'industria italiana', Ph.D. thesis, European University Institute, Florence (1987).

of total trade: 'Of the total of 577 ships (137,446 tonnes) coming into Venice, 501 ships (108,632 tonnes or almost 80 per cent) came from Trieste. The largest trading partner after Austria was Great Britain with 47 ships (19,939 tonnes)'.[38]

After unification in the 1860s the Italian statistical office, under the leadership of internationally recognized statisticians such as Pietro Maestri and Luigi Bodio, began to gather information about the development levels in the Italian regions. Nevertheless, it remains tricky to establish regional economic differences for the 1860s despite the availability of national statistics for Italy, which, however, do not include Venetia until 1866 and Latium until 1870. In the north, industrial activities had sprung up and modern agricultural practices had been introduced before unification. In Lombardy, for instance, landowners invested in the improvement of their estates and in research into better agricultural practices.[39] In the south, on the other hand, public administration had clung to its medieval concepts of government and impeded the construction of even the most basic infrastructure such as roads, canals and aqueducts. The elites in the south preferred court life in Naples to busying themselves with increasing the agricultural production on their *latifundia*, not to mention worrying about better living conditions for the peasants.[40]

According to Gino Luzzato, the enormous economic consequences of the extension of the Piedmontese tariff system to the whole of the Italian peninsula are not always fully realized. The essential characteristics of this system were that import tariffs were set as much as possible around 10 per cent, with the exception of colonial goods which attracted higher rates. No duties were levied on the imports of primary materials, including cereals, and almost no export duties existed. For most pre-unification states this meant a considerable reduction in import and export tariffs, with the exception of Tuscany which had exceptionally low import duties before unification.[41] Thus, in 1860–1 the various protective custom barriers which had existed between the

---

[38] Alberto Errera, *Saggio di statistica internazionale marittima comparata a cura del Prof. A. E. con particolare riguardo all'Adriatico superiore. Regno d'Italia e Impero Austro-Ungarico 1870* (Rome, 1873); Luzzatto, 'Introduzione', in Luigi Candida, *Il porto di Venezia* (Naples, 1950), p. 36; Costantini, 'Dal porto franco', p. 890.

[39] Greenfield, *Economics and Liberalism*, p. 51; Tom Barbiero, 'A Reassessment of the Agricultural Production of Italy. The Case of Lombardy', *JEEH* 17 (1988), pp. 103–5.

[40] Luigi Faccini, 'L'agricoltura italiana dal 1815 al 1859', *Storia della società italiana* (Milan, 1986), pp. 102–4.

[41] For Tuscany an exception was made so that customs duties remained at their pre-unification level. Luzzatto, *L'economia italiana*, pp. 26–8.

Italian states were replaced by the lower Piedmontese tariffs, except in Venetia and Latium.[42] Moreover, in these years commercial treaties were signed with France (1863), Great Britain (1863) and Austria-Hungary (1865 and 1867), which implied the elimination of most obstacles to free trade.[43] In contrast to Germany, where a process of elimination of internal custom barriers had started from 1834 with the *Zollverein*,[44] in Italy the elimination of internal trade barriers happened quite abruptly between 1859 and 1860. Moreover, the connection of the northern and central Italian railway network with the south opened up greater competition from the north for the industries of southern Italy. The previously protected industry of southern Italy suffered from this double shock and could not adapt quickly enough to the existence of a larger national market while having to compete with the cheaper products 'imported' from the north.[45]

During the 1860s many political changes took place which had a profound economic resonance both in the national and international sphere. First, towards the end of this decade the consequences of the 'transport revolution' – the introduction of steam technology for transport – were beginning to be felt on a worldwide scale. An integrated railway network became operational in the whole of northern Italy and steamshipping became more general in all Italian ports. Important international communications were opened in the second half of this decade, which influenced international trade flows and consequently activity in the ports. The Suez canal, for instance, was opened in 1869 and the Brenner railway in 1867, although the greatest effects of these two events probably only started to be felt during the 1870s.

Second, in 1860 the lira was introduced as the national currency, although tight control over financial policy was not possible since there was little coordination between the several issuing banks.[46] This increased the financial problems of the Italian state and its prospects for obtaining further credit on the European capital markets. The Italian

---

[42] On 10 October 1859, the customs union between Tuscany, Emilia, Romagna and Modena, Lombardy, Piacenza and Parma was declared. Almost a year later, on 9 September 1860 it was extended to Umbria, and on 10 October 1860 to the Marches. Finally, on 30 October 1860 the territory of the former Kingdom of the Two Sicilies was included in the Italian customs system; see Luzzatto, *L'economia italiana*, pp. 27–31.

[43] Corbino, *Annali*, p. 146.

[44] Rolf Dumke, 'Der Deutsche Zollverein als Modell Okonomischer Integration', in Helmut Berding (ed.), *Wirtschaftliche und Politische Integration in Europa im 19 un 20 Jahrhundert* (Göttingen, 1984), pp. 1–2.

[45] Luzzatto, *L'economia italiana*, pp. 26–7.    [46] *Ibid.*, pp. 60–3.

state became heavily in debt, since during its first five years of existence it ran an annual budget deficit of more than 25 per cent.[47] Soon after the introduction of the lira, however, after the Austro-Italian war of 1866, a financial crisis led to its devaluation, and it left the gold standard until 1881.[48]

Last, the interruption of cotton exports from North America and the subsequent price rise caused by the American Civil War (1861–5) affected the cotton industry both in Lombardy and Piedmont. The rise in cotton prices meant increasing the imports of Egyptian cotton, which started to enter the port of Venice in great quantities.[49] For all these reasons, the 1860s were a decade of great change in the world economy which had an important impact on the recently unified Italian economy.

Lombardy's and Venetia's economic prospects during the 1860s must be considered separately. For the years 1860–6 the dominating view is that Venetia's economy barely grew at all. The incorporation of Lombardy into Italy in 1860 meant for Venetia that an external customs barrier with Lombardy was erected, a situation which was to last until Venetia's own incorporation into the Italian state in 1866. Thus Venetia became separated from the rest of Italy, since the states of Parma and Modena, with which it previously had a customs union, ceased to exist. Venetia's adaptation to the new national reality in 1866 was probably more painful and slower than Lombardy's. Before 1866, the cotton industry in Pordenone, for instance, benefited from the protectionist policies of the Austrian Empire and from the export opportunities to the large Viennese market. The wool industry in the area around Vicenza received substantial orders from the Austrian army and it could 'export' to Vienna without paying custom duties.[50] When Venetia was integrated into Italy in 1866 this industry had to find new markets and switched toward the production of higher quality goods.[51] Indirect evidence suggests that, after its incorporation into Italy, Venetia continued to have severe adjustment problems. The emigration statistics demonstrate that during the 1870s many Venetians preferred to try their luck elsewhere. The first wave of Italian emigrants originated mainly from

[47] *Ibid.*, p. 85.
[48] Giulio Capodaglio, *Storia di un investimento di capitale. La Società Italiana per le Strade Ferrate Meridionali, 1862–1937* (Milan, 1939), p. 13; Ulrich Drumm, *Ferrovie italiane. Azioni e obbligazioni, 1840, 1861, 1941* (Frankfurt, 1986).
[49] Luzzatto, *L'economia italiana*, pp. 27–9.
[50] Rossi, *Dell'arte della lana*, pp. 210 et seq.
[51] Errera, *Documenti alla storia e statistica*, pp. 276–7.

this region, in contrast to the second wave in the 1890s when southerners predominated among emigrants.[52]

The causes of Venetia's economic problems were complex, but the failure of the Italian state to invest in the region contributed to the general disillusionment of the Venetians. Venetia missed the first round of government spending on public works, health and education in the early 1860s,[53] and was unable to take advantage of the 619 million lire invested in infrastructure during the first six years from 1860 to 1865, which amounted to an average of around 100 million lire per year out of a total budget of around 1,000 million lire. This delayed the development of transport infrastructure in the region. After the incorporation of Venetia into the Italian state, an effort was made by Venetian politicians to attract more public investment to compensate for this loss. Luigi Tatti, for instance, wrote: 'It is true that since this noble region has been embraced by the Italian fatherland, it has acquired its part of the national debt, but so far none of the benefits of pertaining to Italy. In particular, too little has been done to bring railway construction up to the levels of the rest of Italy.' In particular the lack of provincial railway lines was felt: 'This poverty was a natural consequence of prolonged foreign dominion, which abstained from investments in public works which it would have had to subsidize, or else for which the provinces would have had to pay money, which it could have earned itself. Another reason for this policy might have been that it was afraid that the revenues of the existing network . . . would decrease.'[54] This comment was not wholly fair to the Austrian government nor to the railway company, but it is clear evidence of the desire among Venetians for a more interventionist policy from the Italian state.

In conclusion, during the first decade after unification it were mainly the richer northern regions of Lombardy and Piedmont which benefited from access to the national Italian market. The south in particular had severe problems adapting to the new realities of free trade and more severe competition. Moreover, the southern territories were plagued by rebellious uprisings, the so-called *brigantaggio*, which hindered development. In the north too, however, Venetia remained, as it were, an under-developed island in northern Italy.

[52] A. Lazzarini, *Campagne venete ed emigrazione di massa* (Vicenza, 1981).

[53] Corbino, *Annali*, p. 177.

[54] Luigi Tatti, *Nota sulle ferrovie complementari del Veneto ai confini austriaci* (Milan, 1872).

## Regional difference in nineteenth-century Italy

The first national census in 1871 offers some ground for an preliminary appraisal of regional differences within Italy. The difference
in development levels between the Italian regions found in 1871 still
reflected the history of the separate Italian states. An analysis of the
regional spread of population and of the urbanization pattern reveals
striking differences between northern and central Italy on the one
hand, and southern Italy on the other.[55] A look at population data
shows substantially lower population density in the south, which in
turn influenced decisions to build railway lines there (see table 9).
Railway companies realized that population density substantially influenced the amount of traffic, since it was usual at the beginning of
the operation of a railway line for passenger traffic to predominate
over goods traffic. Another reason why railway lines were not constructed in the south is the relatively low number of cities of more
than 100,000 inhabitants (with the exception of Sicily). These large
cities played a leading role in the development of the regions.[56] As
has already been argued by Cattaneo, only in those areas where
medium to large cities are a reasonably short distance away from
each other will railway traffic grow rapidly. In southern Italy the
urbanization process had produced a different pattern from northern
Italy. A number of large cities had grown up in an otherwise sparsely
populated area unlike the network of cities which existed in the
north.[57]

In 1871, in Molise and Abruzzi there were no large cities and only
three medium-sized cities. In Campania there were no less than eight
medium-sized cities but only one very large one, Naples. Moreover,
the medium-sized cities were all concentrated in the vicinity of
Naples. In Apulia, there were twelve medium-sized cities along the
coast of which only one, Bari, had reached the 100,000 mark by 1911.
Sicily shows a more advanced pattern of urbanization with a greater
number of medium-sized cities and two large cities, but despite its
higher urbanization it was among Italy's poorer regions. In Basilicata
there were no medium or large-sized cities and on Sardinia only two
medium-sized ones. As shown in table 13, this pattern remained stable

---

[55] The analysis of population data starts in 1871, when the first national census was
held which included Venetia and Latium. The 1881 census is of substantially better
quality, in particular with regard to the more precise classification of occupational
groups. The 1890 census is not particularly rich for occupational groups and a
complete economic census was held in 1911.

[56] Carozzi and Mioni, *Italia in formazione*, p. 41.          [57] *Ibid.*, pp. 49, 275.

Table 13. *Large cities in 1871 and 1911*

|  | 1871 | | 1911 | |
| --- | --- | --- | --- | --- |
|  | Medium | Large | Medium | Large |
| Piedmont | 6 | 1 | 10 | 1 |
| Liguria | 3 | 1 | 4 | 1 |
| Lombardy | 8 | 1 | 16 | 1 |
| Venetia | 6 | 2 | 8 | 3 |
| Emilia | 12 | 1 | 16 | 1 |
| North | 35 | 6 | 54 | 7 |
| Tuscany | 10 | 1 | 17 | 2 |
| Marches | 4 | 0 | 9 | 0 |
| Umbria | 6 | 0 | 6 | 0 |
| Latium | 1 | 1 | 3 | 1 |
| Central | 21 | 2 | 35 | 3 |
| Abruzzi and Molise | 3 | 0 | 6 | 0 |
| Campania | 8 | 1 | 17 | 1 |
| Apulia | 12 | 0 | 19 | 1 |
| Basilicata | 0 | 0 | 0 | 0 |
| Calabria | 2 | 0 | 3 | 0 |
| Sicily | 15 | 2 | 14 | 3 |
| Sardinia | 2 | 0 | 3 | 0 |
| South | 42 | 3 | 62 | 5 |
| Total | 79 | 11 | 151 | 15 |

*Source:* Carlo Carozzi and Alberto Mioni, *Italia in formazione* (Bari, 1972): pp. 34, 40.
*Notes:* Large: more than 100,000 inhabitants.
Medium: between 20,000 and 100,000 inhabitants.

and did not show substantial regional shifts until 1911. The location of cities was also different in northern and southern Italy. In southern regions most cities were very near the sea, so coastal shipping was a formidable competitor to rail transport. Without considering other factors, therefore, it is quite clear that the geography and the spread of population made the south a less attractive region for building railways.

The disadvantaged position of the south with regard of the possibility of constructing a railway network becomes even clearer when other socio-economic data are examined. The concept of development as envisaged by the United Nations Development Programme, as a combination of education, health and income indicators, is particularly suitable for analysis of the often incomplete historical record.[58] By considering these three factors in conjunction, the gaps

[58] For another methodology, see Federico and Toniolo, 'Italy', p. 201.

in information can sometimes be filled, since in most cases there is a high correlation between levels of health, education and income.[59]

Unfortunately, the data from the 1871 and 1881 censuses concerning occupational groups are not very reliable, particularly for the south, where the percentage of persons working in agriculture has certainly been under-estimated. Reliable data for the percentage of the active population working in industry can be found only after 1911.[60] The percentage of the economically active population working in agriculture for the whole of Italy was comparatively high and was higher still in southern Italy (see table 14).

A quantitative analysis of the health and sanitary conditions of nineteenth-century Italians has not yet been carried out.[61] A little-quoted publication by Giuseppe Sormanni, a doctor in the Italian army, however, shows that certain diseases related to bad sanitary conditions were more common in the recruits from the southern provinces.[62] Sormanni analyses the occurrence of seventeen health problems among 2,333,288, twenty- to twenty-five-year-old recruits examined between 1863 and 1876. The health of this large male sample of the population partially reflects the sanitary conditions before unification. Diseases related to poor nutrition, inadequate water supply and low standards of hygiene were more common in the south, although high levels were also reached in the poorer provinces in the north. In particular, the existence of many wetlands and the lack of provision for drinking water played an important role. Intestinal diseases and ringworm, a fungus which attacks the skin, particularly the scalp, and leads to a loss of hair, for instance, were more common amongst southern Italian recruits (see table 15).

With regard to literacy, Italian data should be analysed in a similar way to valuable research which has been undertaken for the regions of Spain, in which a time-lagged model, relating income growth rates and literacy rates for the population over ten years of age, revealed that

---

[59] Up until recently, European economic historians have failed to use methodologies which measure economic and human development, although separate research on income, health and educational data has flourished recently; Joerg Baten, 'Der Einfluß von Regionalen Wirtschaftsstrukturen auf den Biologischen Lebensstandard. Eine Anthropometrische Studie zur Bayerischen Wirtschaftsgeschichte im frühen 19. Jahrhundert', *VSW* 83 (1996), pp. 1–3.

[60] Vera Zamagni, 'Istruzione e sviluppo economico. Il caso italiano, 1861–1913', in Gianni Toniolo (ed.), *L'economia italiana* (Bari, 1973), pp. 158–62.

[61] Franco Della Peruta, 'Malattia e società nell'Italia dell'ottocento', *Storia della società italiana* (Milan, 1986).

[62] Giuseppe Sormanni, *Geografia nosologica dell'Italia* (Rome, 1880).

Table 14. *Percentage of active population working in agriculture*

|  | 1871 | 1911 |
|---|---|---|
| Piedmont | 67 | 56 |
| Liguria | 55 | 35 |
| Lombardy | 56 | 43 |
| Venetia | 63 | 61 |
| Emilia | 58 | 58 |
| North | 60 | 51 |
| Tuscany | 57 | 51 |
| Marches | 67 | 68 |
| Umbria | 70 | 70 |
| Latium | 55 | 45 |
| Central | 62 | 58 |
| Abruzzi and Molise | 71 | 77 |
| Campania | 51 | 54 |
| Apulia | 58 | 63 |
| Basilicata | 65 | 77 |
| Calabria | 46 | 67 |
| Sicily | 45 | 53 |
| Sardinia | 66 | 59 |
| South | 57 | 64 |
| Total | 58 | 56 |

*Source:* Associazione per lo Sviluppo dell'Industria nel Mezzogiorno, *Un secolo di statistiche*, Table 10, pp. 18–22.

*Notes:* The data from 1871 for the proportion of the active population working in agriculture in the south are almost certainly too low. For slightly different but equally improbable percentages, see, Vera Zamagni, 'Istruzione e Sviluppo Economico', Table 11, p. 158, Table 12, pp. 160–1.

the literacy rate is a good predictor of future growth.[63] In particular, a large gender gap in literacy rates proved to be an impediment for future economic growth. This is hardly surprising when one realizes that women comprised between 70 per cent and 95 per cent of the workforce in the textile industry, which was the leading industry in many countries at the time. Regrettably, for Italy no comprehensive study for the second half of the nineteenth century has been undertaken and the literacy data from the different censuses still have to be reworked.

[63] Carla Eugenia Nuñez, 'Literacy and Economic Growth in Spain, 1860–1877', in Gabriel Tortella (ed.), *Education and Economic Development since the Industrial Revolution* (Valencia, 1990).

Table 15. *Percentage of rejected Italian recruits, 1862–76, with reasons for rejection*

| | Height | Sickliness | Weight | Intestinal Diseases | Ringworm |
|---|---|---|---|---|---|
| Piedmont | 11 | 30 | 4 | 0.0 | 0.4 |
| Liguria | 9 | 24 | 5 | 0.1 | 0.3 |
| Lombardy | 9 | 40 | 10 | 0.1 | 1.1 |
| Venetia | 4 | 32 | 8 | 0.3 | 0.4 |
| Emilia | 7 | 25 | 5 | 0.1 | 0.4 |
| North | 8 | 30 | 6 | 0.1 | 0.4 |
| Tuscany | 6 | 32 | 8 | 0.2 | 0.4 |
| Marches | 10 | 28 | 6 | 0.3 | 0.4 |
| Umbria | 9 | 28 | 7 | 0.1 | 0.6 |
| Latium | | | | | |
| Central | 11 | 39 | 9 | 0.2 | 0.6 |
| Abruzzi and Molise | 16 | 21 | 3 | 0.3 | 1.6 |
| Campania | 14 | 26 | 5 | 0.3 | 1.5 |
| Apulia | 18 | 25 | 4 | 0.8 | 2.2 |
| Basilicata | 25 | 25 | 4 | 0.9 | 1.4 |
| Calabria | 24 | 34 | 8 | 1.4 | 1.7 |
| Sicily | 17 | 33 | 6 | 1.3 | 1.0 |
| Sardinia | 27 | 35 | 8 | 1.3 | 0.9 |
| South | 20 | 29 | 6 | 0.9 | 1.5 |
| Total | 12 | 31 | 6 | 0.4 | 0.9 |

*Sources:* Giuseppe Sormanni, *Geografia nosologica* (Rome, 1880), pp. 22–61.
*Notes:* The recruits were born between 1843 and 1856 and medically tested at 20 years of age.
The data for Rome are included in Campania.

In Italy in the 1870s the overall literacy rate was considerably lower than in the rest of Europe, and this gap was closed only very slowly (see tables 16 and 17).[64] Of Italian conscripts in 1881, for instance, which form a sample of the young male population between twenty and twenty-five, almost 48 per cent were illiterate, whereas in the German Empire the average was only 1.32 per cent, in Bavaria it was 0.18 per cent and in Württemberg it was nil. The number of teachers in Italy was also below the European average and elementary

---

[64] Italy, Ministerio di Agricoltura, Industria e Commercio, *Censimento della popolazione del regno d'Italia al 31 dicembre 1881* (Rome, 1882), p. 61. Of the European states only Austria-Hungary, Spain, Portugal, Belgium, Ireland, Finland and Italy have kept data on literacy.

Table 16. *Illiteracy rates in Europe (percentage of population over 6 years old)*

| Date | Belgium | France | Great Britain | Italy | Spain |
|------|---------|--------|---------------|-------|-------|
| 1850 | 47 | 42 | 38 | 75 | 75 |
| 1860 | 42 | 37 | 31 | 72 | 73 |
| 1870 | 36 | 32 | 24 | 69 | 71 |
| 1880 | 31 | 27 | 17 | 62 | 69 |
| 1890 | 26 | 22 | 8 | 55 | 61 |
| 1900 | 19 | 17 | 3 | 48 | 56 |
| 1910 | 15 | 13 | 9 | 39 | 50 |

*Sources:* Gabriel Tortella, 'La historia económica de Espana en el siglo XIX: un ensayo comparativo con los casos de Italia y Portugal', in: *El desarrollo económico en la Europa del sur. España e Italia en perspectiva histórica* (Madrid, 1992): Table 2.3, p. 72.

Table 17. *State spending on education in Europe (percentage of GDP)*

| | France | Germany | Great Britain | Italy |
|------|--------|---------|---------------|-------|
| 1860 | 0.4 | 1.0 | | |
| 1870 | | | | |
| 1880 | 0.9 | 1.6 | 0.9 | 1.0 |
| 1890 | | | | |
| 1900 | 1.3 | 1.9 | 1.3 | 1.2 |
| 1910 | | | | 2.0 |

*Source:* Zamagni, 'Istruzione e Sviluppo Economico'.

schooling for children between six and ten years old only became compulsory in 1877.[65]

By 1881, it had become clear that illiteracy was a deeply rooted problem and that compulsory elementary education would not immediately be effective. In fact, most progress in this area was made in those provinces which already had the lowest level of illiteracy in 1866. [66] Thus the slow rise of literacy among Italy's population cast a shadow on the prospects of attaining higher levels of development (see table 18). As regards health, the census data are not sufficiently precise to reach unequivocal conclusions. The number of sanitary personnel is not comparable between the different census years, since the definition of what was a doctor became more stringent. In other words, the 1871 census counts a great number of quacks as doctors. Other data concerning health standards, such as the height of recruits and illness in the army, have not yet been sufficiently explored. Today's development economists tell us that a literate population is

[65] *Ibid.*, p. 90.     [66] *Ibid.*, p. 59.

Table 18. *Illiteracy rates in Italian regions (percentage of population over 6 years)*

|  | 1871 | 1911 |
|---|---|---|
| Piedmont | 42 | 11 |
| Liguria | 56 | 17 |
| Lombardy | 45 | 13 |
| Venetia | 65 | 25 |
| Emilia | 72 | 33 |
| North | 54 | 19 |
| Tuscany | 68 | 37 |
| Marches | 79 | 51 |
| Umbria | 80 | 49 |
| Latium | 68 | 33 |
| Central | 72 | 40 |
| Abruzzi and Molise | 84 | 57 |
| Campania | 84 | 54 |
| Apulia | 84 | 59 |
| Basilicata | 84 | 65 |
| Calabria | 84 | 69 |
| Sicily | 85 | 70 |
| Sardinia | 86 | 58 |
| South | 84 | 62 |
| Total | 69 | 39 |

*Source:* Vera Zamagni, 'Istruzione e sviluppo economico', Table 13, p. 164, Table 14, p. 165.

more easily assimilated in industry and is more likely to attain better sanitary conditions. Female literacy is especially crucial for attaining better health and nutrition standards and lower infant mortality. Better health also has a considerable influence on economic development.

The debate about overall growth rates from 1860 onwards for Italian national income, or gross domestic product, has reached a considerable degree of sophistication, which is not matched by an improvement in the quality of the underlying data.[67] Economic historians generally agree that growth rates during the first decades after unification have been significantly under-estimated.[68] This is probably due to the inherent limitations of national accounting methods which failed to take account of much of the growth in a pre-industrial

[67] Giorgio Fuà and Mauro Gallegati, 'An Annual Chain Index of Italy's Real Product', working paper, University of Ancona, 1994.

[68] Ercolani, 'Il prodotto interno lordo', pp. 1–3.

economy undergoing significant structural change.[69] Some data indicate a more dynamic growth process than is suggested by these
national income estimates. Coal imports, for example, more than
quadrupled between 1870 and 1890 and raw cotton imports increased
more than five times in the same period, a feat not equalled by any
other country: Spain, for instance, roughly doubled its coal imports
and trebled its raw cotton imports in the same period.[70] These data are
hardly compatible with the static view of the economy that the
national accountants provide, which means that nineteenth-century
estimates of Italian GDP should be used with some caution.

   The theoretical issue of whether during the process of development
regional per capita income levels increased, decreased or remained
roughly equal, has not yet been solved in a satisfactory manner. The
role of improvements in transport and wage levels in this process has
been perceived as crucial, but so far no definite conclusions have been
reached and more research on transport costs, wage levels and regional
trade is needed. Nineteenth-century Italian economists were not
worried that the railways might damage some regional economies.
They all agreed that railways would stimulate the growth of industry
and agriculture everywhere and facilitate the formation of a unified
national market. This belief was not exclusively Italian, however, since
most nineteenth- and early twentieth-century economists thought
that the application of steam power to transportation industries made a
significant contribution to the economic growth of the whole nation.
One of the founders of neo-classical economics, for example, Alfred
Marshall, stated that: 'the dominant economic fact of our own age is
the development not of the manufacturing but of the transport
industries'.[71] Although Marshall had a fine feeling for the location of
industrial activity, later economists largely ignored the geographical
aspects of economic growth.[72]

   Nineteenth-century regional income levels in Italy cannot adequately be determined, but as we saw in the previous section it seems
improbable that the south could keep pace with the north, or even
reduce its backwardness. In the twentieth century, on the other hand,
a more definite pattern emerges. In a classic article in 1965 Jeffrey

---

[69] Julian Hoppit, 'Counting the Industrial Revolution', *EHR* 43 (1990), pp. 174–6.

[70] Great Britian, Statistical Office, *Statistical Abstract 1880*, pp. 72, 76; and *Statistical
  Abstract 1891*, pp. 88–9, 92–3; C. Bardini, 'Ma il vapore era davvero importante?
  Consumo energetico e sviluppo industriale di un paese privo di carbone. Italia,
  1885–1914', Ph.D. thesis, European University Institute, Florence, 1994.

[71] Alfred Marshall, *Principles of Economics* (London, 1920), p. 674.

[72] For a critique and an attempt to reintroduce locational elements into international
  trade theory, Krugman, *Geography and Trade*, pp. 1–5.

Table 19. *Gross domestic product per capita in Italian regions, 1911 (lire)*

|  | VA per capita | Index |
|---|---|---|
| Piedmont | 615 | 126 |
| Liguria | 700 | 143 |
| Lombardy | 673 | 138 |
| Venetia | 436 | 89 |
| Emilia | 557 | 114 |
| North | 589 | 121 |
| Tuscany | 490 | 100 |
| Marches | 428 | 88 |
| Umbria | 443 | 91 |
| Latium | 615 | 126 |
| Central | 501 | 103 |
| Abruzzi and Molise | 342 | 70 |
| Campania | 397 | 81 |
| Apulia | 407 | 83 |
| Basilicata | 338 | 69 |
| Calabria | 296 | 61 |
| Sicily | 341 | 70 |
| Sardinia | 387 | 79 |
| South | 364 | 75 |
| Total | 488 | 100 |

*Source:* Zamagni, *Industrializzazione e squilibri regionali in Italia. Bilancio della età giolittiana* (Bologna, 1978), Table 58, pp. 198–9.
*Note:* VA = value added; Index = index number on a scale of 0 to 100.

Williamson developed an ingenious methodology for measuring these regional differences.[73] Calculating the coefficient of variation of regional per capita income weighted by each region's population, Williamson found a value of 0.31 for 1928, 0.35 for 1938 and around 0.34 for most of the 1950s, which led him to conclude that the speed of divergence was diminished in the 1950s.[74] For 1911, I computed a value for the Williamson coefficient of 0.25, based on Vera Zamagni's estimates for regional income (see table 19).[75] This shows, first, that

[73] Jeffery G. Williamson, 'Regional Inequality and the Process of National Development. A Description of Patterns', *Economic Development and Cultural Change* 13 (1965), pp. 4–84.
[74] A simple coefficient of variation would show even greater differences.
[75] Zamagni, *Industrializzazione e squilibri regionali*, pp. 71–2.

in 1911 the regional differences in income levels were smaller than at any other time in the twentieth century. Second, from 1911 disparities in regional income levels was increasing, so that if convergence had taken place in the previous period this was probably largely compensated for during the latter period. On this regional scale the evidence for convergence between Italian regions seems rather thin, although within the more similar northern Italian regions income levels in the provinces might have converged from the 1860s onwards.[76]

A comparison with Germany is again instructive. The value of the Williamson coefficient for Italy in 1911 of 0.25 is similar to the value found in the German Empire in 1913 of 0.23. Whereas for Germany the values of this coefficient slowly decrease to around 0.20 in the 1950s, in Italy divergence takes place. For 1911, however, regional income data clearly demonstrate the divide which existed at that time between the north, the centre and the south of Italy.

The fact that income levels between Italian regions diverged should not be read, however, as if the north developed at the expense of south. Economic growth is no zero-sum game. The view that a kind of colonial relationship based on exploitation existed between northern and southern Italy has been discredited, principally because the mechanisms through which this supposed exploitation took place cannot be detected or do not make sense economically.[77] It can be concluded, therefore, that the north developed using its own resources, taking advantage of its proximity to the northern European markets, but it is equally clear that the south could not keep pace and needed more time to adapt to the national market. The overall result is that the gap between north and south probably grew continuously from unification until at least the 1950s.

An interesting comparison between the provisions for road and railway infrastructure can be made for the years 1885 (roads) and 1886 (railways) (see table 20). Again the lengths of roads and railways per 1,000 inhabitants are taken as a measure. It must noted that the data for the length of roads per 1,000 inhabitants follows broadly the north–south gradient that can be found in the income data. Notable exceptions are Liguria, which due to its geographical position and mountainous character had few roads. Other exceptions are Umbria and Sardinia which due to their small populations show high values for road and railway provision. For the railways, on the other hand, a very different pattern is found: the differences between northern and

---

[76] See Schram, 'The Impact of Railways', pp. 237–42.
[77] Zamagni, *Dalla periferia al centro*, p. 219.

Table 20. *Rail and road length per 1,000 inhabitants in Italian regions,*
*1885–6*

| | Population 1881 (000) | RW 1886 (km) | R 1885 (km) | RW(km/ 1,000 inh.) | R(km/ 1,000 inh.) | RW Index | R Index | Average |
|---|---|---|---|---|---|---|---|---|
| Piedmont | 3,070 | 1,393 | 14,989 | 0.45 | 4.88 | 115 | 106 | 111 |
| Liguria | 892 | 366 | 2,694 | 0.41 | 3.02 | 104 | 66 | 85 |
| Lombardy | 3,681 | 1,438 | 17,130 | 0.39 | 4.65 | 99 | 101 | 100 |
| Venetia | 2,814 | 1,072 | 13,722 | 0.38 | 4.88 | 97 | 106 | 101 |
| Emilia | 2,183 | 735 | 12,706 | 0.34 | 5.82 | 86 | 127 | 106 |
| North | 12,640 | 5,004 | 61,241 | 0.40 | 4.85 | 101 | 105 | 103 |
| Tuscany | 2,209 | 954 | 10,997 | 0.43 | 4.98 | 110 | 108 | 109 |
| Marches | 939 | 327 | 4,836 | 0.35 | 5.15 | 88 | 112 | 100 |
| Umbria | 572 | 460 | 4,079 | 0.80 | 7.13 | 204 | 155 | 180 |
| Latium | 903 | 435 | 3,700 | 0.48 | 4.10 | 122 | 89 | 106 |
| Central | 4,623 | 2,176 | 23,612 | 0.47 | 5.11 | 120 | 111 | 115 |
| Abruzzi and Molise | 1,317 | 503 | 7,792 | 0.38 | 5.92 | 97 | 129 | 113 |
| Campania | 2,897 | 734 | 7,798 | 0.25 | 2.69 | 64 | 59 | 61 |
| Apulia | 1,589 | 767 | 5,297 | 0.48 | 3.33 | 123 | 73 | 98 |
| Basilicata | 525 | 187 | 3,798 | 0.36 | 7.23 | 90 | 157 | 124 |
| Calabria | 1,258 | 507 | 7,280 | 0.40 | 5.79 | 102 | 126 | 114 |
| Sicily | 2,928 | 893 | 7,988 | 0.30 | 2.73 | 77 | 59 | 68 |
| Sardinia | 682 | 431 | 5,961 | 0.63 | 8.74 | 161 | 190 | 175 |
| South | 11,196 | 4,022 | 45,914 | 0.36 | 4.10 | 91 | 89 | 90 |
| Total | 28,459 | 11,202 | 130,767 | 0.39 | 4.59 | 100 | 100 | 100 |

*Source: Annuario Statistico,* 1886.
*Notes:* RW = railways
R = roads

southern Italy are less marked and some southern provinces have
values above average. Clearly, railway construction at this point had
greatly reduced the gap in railway density between northern and
southern Italy.

Regrettably, no significant correlation between these railway and
road provision series was found and even a rank correlation coefficient
proved to be insignificant. The Williamson coefficient of variation for
the railways has a value of 0.24, whereas for the roads a higher value of
0.35 is found. In northern Italy, Liguria, which ranks seventh for the
railways, ranks only sixteenth for roads. In southern Italy, Apulia pre-
sents a similar case, ranking third in railways but only twelfth in roads.
Emilia and Venetia are at the other extreme, having well-developed
road networks in relation to the size of their populations and being

relatively under-endowed with regard to railways: Emilia and Venetia rank third and fourth for roads but eleventh and fourteenth for railways, respectively. Sicily is under-endowed both with railways, ranking fifteenth, and roads, ranking fourteenth.

In conclusion, the reasons for the lower education, health and income levels in the south are complex and multiple: the distinct role of the states before unification, the different urbanization and population patterns, the historically low standards for literacy and health are just a few elements among a wider set of causes. Most social and economic data show lower levels in the south during the nineteenth century – a gap which probably grew more slowly during the twentieth century. Income data, however, show a growing gap after 1911. For some reason convergence in regional income levels did not occur, as predicted by neo-classical economic models. The data on the provision of railway infrastructure provide a development indicator by themselves, but are probably the only ones showing a relatively small divide between north and south by 1886. Obviously, the abundant provision of railway infrastructure did not, and probably could not, by itself have the desired income and development effects.[78]

## IV  RAILWAY BUILDING BEFORE THE 1865 RAILWAY ACT

During the first five years after political unification in 1860 more than 2,000 km of track were opened by private companies, a feat that was improved upon only during the second wave of construction in the period 1885–90. Although the major construction wave occurred just after political unification in 1860, it must be noted that the planning of these lines had taken place much earlier. Thus, political unification led to the realization of the plans formulated in the 1840s to build the great Italian trunk lines. The debates in these decades about the construction of railways created a great amount of political heat, which is understandable since the decision on the routing of a line, once taken, can hardly be undone later. Another explanation which has been advanced is that the pre-unification states regarded the railway debate as one of the few political themes not censored by the Austrian governments.[79]

The significance of the original decision on standardization and the phenomenon of path-dependency for the development of large technical systems has been well studied and documented. Path-dependency means that all other decisions concerning the growth of the system are

[78] Zamagni, 'Ferrovie e integrazione', p. 1635.
[79] Wingate, *Railway Building*, p. 31.

limited by the initial decision.[80] The decisions on the routing of railway lines, which were usually taken before a concession was requested, is such a decision and creates, quite literally, a path-dependency. Decisions on the railway gauge to be adopted in Italy were not critical, however, since English engineers had introduced the standard Stephenson gauge in almost every Italian state, and this consequently dominated the Italian peninsula.

Given the importance of the initial decision on the routing of railway lines, it is appropriate to take account of the early debates on the railways in the 1840s and 1850s and assess their consequences. The slower growth of cities in the central Po valley, for example, has been attributed to the development of the communication lines at the foot of the Alps and the Apennines at the expense of the central axis, a decision which can be traced back to the planning phase of the railway network in the Po valley.[81] Commonly, the slow progress in railway construction before unification – in the five states only 2,405 km of track had been built before December 1860 – is interpreted as a sign of Italy's general backwardness. In addition, the persistence of political divisions of Italy before 1860, the lack of interest on the part of private companies to build minor regional lines, or the particularly difficult terrain are mentioned. During the European 'railway mania' in the mid 1840s, a considerable number of concessions were granted to private companies in most Italian states, and railway building proceeded in a disorderly fashion, although not completely uncoordinated. As we saw in chapter 1, Italy's political divisions did not stand in the way of opening lines linking the different regions, although it certainly slowed down their construction. In fact, before 1859, the Piacenza–Bologna line was the only one that connected different pre-unification states. The Austrian government was especially successful in finding workable solutions, because railways served the empire's military and economic interests. If Italy had not become one country, its railway network would probably have been unified more slowly and with a more unequal geographical spread.

### The Po valley

Piedmont's successes in railway building in the 1850s clearly show the importance of effective government policies. The Piedmontese government did not allow the inevitable controversies between

---

[80] Paul David, 'Clio and the Economics of QWERTY' *AEAPP* 75 (1985), pp. 332–7; Paul David, *The Economics of Gateway Technologies* (Stanford, 1987).
[81] Carozzi and Mioni, *Italia in formazione,* p. 276.

railway companies and local and national authorities to hold up the completion of lines for too long. In the Po valley, on the other hand, the Austrian government was less successful in balancing the various interest groups and completing the railway lines rapidly, possibly because it could not count on much goodwill from its Lombard and Venetian subjects. Austria's Italian subjects also deeply distrusted the foreign bankers who held majority shares in many railway companies, and not without reason. Certain Viennese bankers, for instance, had speculated that a line would go through Bergamo and had already issued shares, although this line was not built until several decades later. Nonetheless, as Wingate and more recently Bernardello have convincingly demonstrated, there is no reason why the Austrians would hamper the construction of railway lines which benefited them both economically and militarily.[82] It is rather for the lack of direction of its railway policy and for bureaucratic meddling that Austrian governments should be blamed. Moreover, the company constructing the main line from Milan to Venice, for example, had to wait for the Austrian government to produce a law on joint-stock companies. When this law finally appeared, however, it proved enormously complicated to apply, even for the most courageous and persistent entrepreneur.[83] The unprecedented length of the Milan–Venice line and the inexperience of the Italian engineers were other factors complicating this enterprise.

In a technical sense, the building of railway lines in the Po valley was relatively straightforward, since this is one of the least hilly areas of Italy. Although it is crossed by many rivers and canals and many bridges had to be built, this is usually less expensive and less technically complex than tunnelling through mountains. Nonetheless, for various reasons the political difficulties of railway building in the Po valley were much greater. It was a relatively wealthy area and powerful local elites tried at all costs to include their city or locality on the railway map.

The debate about the Milan–Verona line is a good example of what could occur before unification. The controversy was at its height from 1837 to 1845 when the Ferdinandea Railway Company tried in vain to advance the construction of the Milan–Venice line.

[82] Wingate, *Railway Building*, p. 20; Adolfo Bernardello, *La prima ferrovia fra Venezia e Milano. Storia della imperiale regia privilegiata strada ferrata Ferdinandea Lombarda-Veneta* (Venice, 1996), p. 520. For a detailed review of Wingate's *Railway Building* and many bibliographic references on the railways in Lombardy-Venetia, see Bernardello, 'Imprese ferroviarie', pp. 17 *et seq.*

[83] Bernardello, *La prima ferrovia*, pp. 515–20.

The most contentious point was whether to include the city of Bergamo on the route. The leading newspapers of the period devoted many pages to the Bergamo question and famous economists like Carlo Cattaneo devoted several studies to it.[84] In the years from 1837 to 1841 at least seven different plans were made for this line. The complicated mixture of local and business interests these plans represent will be left aside here but are amply described in the literature.[85] The Austrian government's initial concession had left out Bergamo, but after years of pressure the city was finally included on condition that the rate would be calculated as if the line was direct and did not pass Bergamo. In the 1856 charter of the Upper Italy Railway Company, which took over the line, it was stated that if the direct line from Treviglio to Rovato was built an additional rate would be charged on this section, making travel just as expensive as the route through Bergamo. The decision to include Bergamo lengthened the line by about 50 km, and considering the average speed of the passenger trains of the period (about 25 km/hour) this increased travelling time by some two hours. The direct line Treviglio–Rovato was not opened until 1877.

The Ferdinandea Railway Company succeeded only in operating the Venice–Vicenza and the Milan–Treviglio sections. When, after several years of discussion, it was finally decided in 1841 to route the line through Bergamo, the government in Vienna refused to give it additional financial aid. The company's capital was only about 25 per cent Italian, so nationalist motives for Vienna's refusal can be excluded.[86] In the end, in July 1852, the company gave the concession back to the state and it was liquidated. Insufficient financial support from the Vienna government and a lack of direction in railway policy were the main reasons of the failure of this enterprise.[87] In 1856, Austria's railway policy suddenly changed and the lines previously owned and operated by the state were privatized. After 1856, the predecessor of the Upper Italy Railway Company achieved considerable progress in railway building, after having obtained all concessions for railways in Lombardy, Venetia and Emilia.[88]

---

[84] Wingate, *Railway Building*, pp. 23–8.
[85] Bernardello, *La prima ferrovia*, p. 186; Carrozzi and Mioni, *Italia in formazione*, pp. 304–29.
[86] Wingate, *Railway Building*, pp. 28–41.
[87] Carrozzi and Mioni, *Italia in formazione*, pp. 304–28.
[88] H. Strach, *Geschichte der Eisenbahen Osterreich-Ungarns von den ersten Anfängen bis zum Jahre 1867* (Vienna, 1898), pp. 213–30.

## Railway building in the Papal States

It is telling that the first request for a concession in the Papal States came from Bologna, the richest part of the Papal territory. On 4 July 1846, the Cini Railway Company requested permission to build a railway line between Bologna over the Apennines to Pistoia. The company had secured the concession for the Tuscan part of the line on 5 April 1845, and attempted to obtain the concession for the connecting line on Papal territory from the new, and more liberally minded Pope Pius IX. Unfortunately this request was completely ignored by the Papal government and even diplomatic pressure by the Tuscan government did not help.[89] On 7 November 1846 the Papal government issued a declaration explaining its railway policy and fixing the order of construction of the various railway lines. The first line mentioned was from Rome to Ceprano in the Neapolitan Kingdom, the second and third lines from Rome to the ports of Anzio and Civitavecchia, the fourth from Rome over Foligno to Ancona. No mention was made of subsidies to the companies and the line to Tuscany was not excluded but was clearly not considered a priority.

The announcement made by Pope Pius IX in 1846 inviting companies to present proposals for building railway lines in the Papal States had a tremendous political impact. The previous pope, Pope Gregory XVI had been known for his corrupt government and reactionary policies until his death in 1839. The 'declaration' on the railways, made public in 1846, seemed to predict that 'railway mania' would soon engulf the whole of the Italian peninsula. Moreover, the event was interpreted as a sign that a modern Pope would place himself at the head of the movement for Italian unification or, as the *Economist* wrote: 'For the first time for many ages a chord has been struck at Rome, which now vibrates from Calabria to Piedmont and through the whole of Catholic Europe.'[90]

From this date many building proposals were presented to the Papal government by French and British, but also several Italian companies. Few of these proposals, however, were based on reliable exploratory studies. The Papal government was overwhelmed by this rather wild response, and the Pope soon retracted and started to postpone the granting of concessions. The Papal government let it be known that it made no difference whether requests for concessions were presented in crystal frames if the technical and financial arguments were not

---

[89] Archivio di Stato di Roma, Prefettura Generale di Acque e Strade, vol. LXXIII, f. 238, Società Cini al Secretario di Stato, 4 July 1846 and 5 April 1845.

[90] *Economist*, 18 September 1847, p. 1074.

based on thorough studies.[91] The Pope's distrust became even greater after the failed revolution of 1848, when both Giuseppe Mazzini and Giuseppe Garibaldi took power in Rome for sixteen months from February 1848 to June 1849, and the Pope was forced to spend a year in exile in Gaeta.

But even before revolution broke out, an English visitor on semi-official business, Thomas Waghorn, acting as a consultant to the Papal government, wrote that:

> both government and companies congratulated themselves with the result thus far . . . I found the plans to consist of exceedingly neat and elaborate drawings, executed with extreme care and trouble, covered with a profusion of detail and figured dimensions and with precisely that appearance which would entirely deceive the unprofessional and induce the belief, which I found prevalent, that they were works of talent and subject for congratulations . . . The plans were prepared by men without practical experience, but with the most complete ignorance of the subject. It was my duty of dispelling this fair dream [sic].[92]

Waghorn's stay at the court of the king in Naples had a similarly sobering effect on the idealistic railway plans formulated there. The English interest in a railway line to the port of Brindisi is explained by the British Empire's desire for speedy communications between England and its Indian colonies. Since the Austrian government could obstruct British passengers and mail passing over its territories in Lombardy or Venice, the railway line to the port of Brindisi would need to pass through Papal and Neapolitan territory. Unfortunately, as Waghorn found out, the lack of technical competence and entrepreneurial experience in the Papal States and the Kingdom of Naples made progress in railway construction exceedingly slow.[93] Italian unification brought an end to English worries and in the 1860s contracts were signed allowing English mail to go to Brindisi.

It is unfair to depict the Papal government as completely unwilling to concede the construction of railways lines. It cooperated with other governments for the construction of international lines, albeit with extreme caution. In Modena on 1 May 1851, diplomats from Austria, Parma, Modena, Tuscany and the Papal States instituted a commission to decide who would obtain the concession for the Piacenza–Parma–Modena–Bologna line, with secondary lines to Tuscany and Mantua.

[91] Schram, 'De Spoorwegkwestie', p. 111.

[92] Archivo di Stato di Roma, Prefettura Generale delle Acque e Strade, vol. LXXIV, f. 249, Report 1, Waghorn to Palmerston, 19 May 1847.

[93] Nicola Ostuni, *Iniziative private e ferrovie nel Regno delle Due Sicilie* (Naples, 1980), pp. 129–34.

On 26 June 1852, the commission issued a booklet listing ninety conditions for obtaining a concession. The Papal government had refused to include a clause on minimum return to capital, but finally it accepted a modified version of Article 14 which stated that all the subsidies had to be repaid afterwards. These conditions effectively hampered the completion of the line and until the building was taken over by the predecessor of the Upper Italy Railway Company very little progress was made.

In the 1850s and 1860s, Austrian and French political intervention in the Papal States was significant since the Papal government had lost all credibility for its inability to control political events. The only thing that kept it in power was the presence of a French garrison, which was to stay in Rome from 1848 until 1870. In the 1850s railway building in the Papal States progressed very slowly. Eventually in 1857 the first line was opened between Rome and Frascati, where the Pope has his summer residence, and in 1859 a second one between Rome and the port of Civitavecchia became operational. Given the presence of the French garrison, it comes as no surprise that both railway concessions went to French companies so that provisions for the French garrison could be conveniently brought by rail from the port of Civitavecchia.[94]

The examples of the Austrian and the Papal governments show clearly that much of the delay in railway building in the pre-unification states (with the exception of Piedmont), was not due to obstructionist, 'anti-Italian' policies or Austrian imperial interests, as was maintained by many nineteenth-century writers, and echoed by later Risorgimento historiography.[95] In order to reach its goals with regard to railway building in Italy the Austrian government had to cooperate with other governments and this proved to be both time-consuming and complicated. Various other factors explain the delays. The governments did not know how to deal with large joint-stock companies and were afraid of speculation and financial crises. In the Papal States and Tuscany the under-developed banking system did not help either. Their hesitation in deciding between a state, mixed or private system also implied unclear policies with regard to the subsidies, which were a *conditio sine qua non* for railway building in Italy at this time.

---

[94] Pietro Negri, 'Le ferrovie Stato Ponteficio, 1844–1870'. In *Archivio Economico dell'Unificazione Italiana* (Rome, 1967); Allesandro Chiarvalotti, *Le strade ferrate nello Stato Ponteficio, 1829–1870* (Rome, 1969).

[95] For a thorough analysis of the railway debate in Tuscany, see Giuntini, 'La linea diretta Bologna–Verona', pp. 101–9, and Giuntini, *I giganti della montagna*, pp. 21–88.

## V RAILWAY BUILDING AFTER THE 1865 RAILWAY ACT

Although political unification in 1859 made diplomatic problems with regard to the construction of railway lines largely disappear, another type of difficulty arose. As we have seen, the 1865 Railway Act did not invalidate the previous concessions, so there was continuity rather than change with respect to the preceding period. The opaque legal situation concerning the obligations of the railway companies which arose from this, gave rise to many conflicts between the railway companies and the government.

Length of track opened to traffic is only a rough indicator of progress, but it is the only indicator available for the whole period. It can be seen from table 7 that the greatest advance in railway construction was during the five years after political unification and not after the Railway Act of 1865. During the twenty-one years from 1839 to 1860 a total of 2,435 km of line had been opened, most of it in northern and some in central Italy. In the five years from 1861 to 1865 the total amount was almost doubled and 2,188 km of new line was opened, a feat only improved upon in the five years after the 1885 Railway Act when 2,716 km of line was opened.

### Railways across the Alps

The period from 1867 to 1884 was significant in the sense that most of the lines to neighbouring countries were opened, and this necessarily meant crossing the Alps. The rapid progress of rail technology in those years is impressive and it is surprising that in such an early phase of railway history the Alps were crossed using tunnels. Italian engineers acquired much experience in tunnelling, since railway building in Italy, with the exception of the Po valley, required the construction of a great many tunnels. Currently, 5.5 per cent of Italian railway lines consists of some 1,850 tunnels.[96] In general, the international lines which presented the fewest technological problems were opened first, but information about the amount of traffic and about the physical characteristics of the line must also be taken into account. The Brenner railway, for instance, was operated on a single track until 1889–91, which obviously limited its traffic capacity. The connections with France on the other hand were operated double-track from the beginning.[97] Moreover, international agreements on trans-

[96] Vance, *Capturing the Horizon*, p. 250.
[97] Upper Italy Railway Company, *Costituzione*, p. 11.

port rates and the detailed operation of the lines influenced the transport capacity.

The Semmering line, connecting Vienna and Trieste, was the first line across the Alps; it was opened in 1857 and reached Udine in 1860. Asked for advice in the 1840s, English engineers had considered it impossible to operate a similar line, with gradients larger than 2.5 per cent, with the locomotives existing at the time. Despite this, the Austrian engineer, Karl von Ghega working for the Südbahn State Railways continued with the project. Studying American locomotives and railway construction he foresaw technological progress in locomotive power. Compared with the other Alpine passes the line was an easy one, its highest point being around 1,000 m and its longest tunnel only 900 m long. Since Trieste was the Austrian Empire's only major port, this line was economically and strategically of vital importance.[98]

The next line to be opened across the Alps was the Brenner line in 1867. This line reached an altitude of around 1,400 m, but required no major tunnelling and by making use of a side valley the maximum gradient was also kept to around 2.5 per cent. The Austrian Empire had a great concentration of troops in the western part of Venetia and the fortified cities of Verona, Peschiera, Mantua and Padua were the basis of its defence system in Italy. The Brenner line was thus militarily of great importance for supplying these fortresses in case of war. Until 1856 the Südbahn State Railways and afterwards the Upper Italy Railway Company which took over the concession, made great haste in completing it. The Kufstein–Innsbruck section was opened in 1858 and was also designed by Karl von Ghega. The Verona–Bolzano section was opened in 1859 and engineered by Luigi Negrelli. This last section had no less than 280 bridges and the 1,200 metre long bridge over the river Etsch was hailed as a technological wonder of the time. In 1867, the missing part between Bolzano and Innsbruck, designed by Karl von Etzel was finally opened.[99] It should be remembered that Trieste and the Brenner pass only became Italian in 1919, and were on Austrian territory until that date.[100] The Brenner line from Innsbruck to Peri was operated by the Südbahn, the sister company of the Upper Italy Railway Company which operated the Verona–Peri section until 1878.

Next, the lines between Italy and France were opened. In 1871 the

---

[98] For more information on the Alpine lines Vance, *Capturing the Horizon*, pp. 254–9, or Victor Röll, *Encyclopädie des gesamten Eisenbahnwesens in Alphabetische Anordnung*, 7 vols. (Vienna, 1890–5).

[99] Fontana, *Geschichte*, pp. 39–40.

[100] Hertner, 'Il problema dei valichi', p. 32.

Fréjus pass linking the French and the Piedmontese networks was completed and in 1872 the line between Marseilles and Genoa. At the Col de Fréjus[101] a 12 km tunnel was drilled at an altitude of around 1,300 m, using a new system invented by the Swiss physicist Collandon. His idea was that compressed air would both drive the drill and furnish ventilation for the workers at the same time. At first, the tunnel advanced at only 14 m a month, but after the engineer, Sommeiller, adopted the air drill in 1857 the tunnel advanced at almost 75 m a month. In 1860, when Savoy passed to France, a French team began drilling at the other side. This was the first time that a railway tunnel was drilled through a true mountain and across an international border as well.[102]

The Gothard line between Italy and Switzerland was opened in 1883. Although the tunnel lies entirely within Switzerland the construction of the 15 km tunnel at an altitude of 1,100 m was a cooperative project with Germany, Italy and Switzerland, with Italy paying 53 per cent of the cost and Switzerland and Germany the rest in equal parts. The Upper Italy Railway Company was obliged to contribute around 10 million lire of the 60 million lire Italian contribution to the construction of the Gothard pass, whereas in the construction of the Fréjus tunnel it had not contributed anything.[103] Technologically interesting was a circular tunnel in the approach to the main tunnel which kept the maximum gradient at 2.6 per cent. A third international route between Italy and Austria in the east was the Tarvis pass, opened in 1879, which, however, developed only a limited amount of traffic. Between Italy and Switzerland one of the longest tunnels in the world is the Simplon tunnel, 20 km long and reaching an altitude of 640 m, which opened to traffic in 1905. It must be mentioned, however, that it is only a single-track tunnel, in contrast to the other tunnels mentioned. Building began in 1898, but progressed very slowly due to the unfavourable condition of the terrain.

Although it did not cross the Alps, the Pustertal line, connecting Trieste with Tyrol and southern Germany, was a formidable competitor for the Italian lines. Austria was able to transport goods to southern Germany on this line without passing through Italian territory. Primarily strategic considerations lay behind the Austrian government's pressure to construct the line. The Südbahn Railway Company was obliged to build it as a condition of its concessions. After the Austrian–Prussian war and the demise of the Deutscher

---

[101] This line is sometimes wrongly called the Mt Cenis line.
[102] Vance, *Capturing the Horizon*, pp. 249–51.
[103] *Atti Commissione Baccarini*, part 2, vol. 1, pp. 1–6.

Bund in 1866, the railway link between Vienna and North Tyrol presented a security risk since it had to pass through Bavaria, which was no longer an ally. The company contended that it did not have the money to build the line so soon after the completion of the Brenner line.[104] After offering 13 million gulden (32.5 million lire), the government and the company agreed to build it and it was opened in November 1871.

In general, solutions to the technical and financial problems of building lines across the Alps were found promptly and by 1883 Italy's main railway connections with neighbouring countries were completed. Only the Simplon tunnel was opened in the twentieth century. Probably the fact that all affected parties saw the great advantages of rail transport over traditional transport over the Alps greatly helped to facilitate successful cooperation in the construction. As we shall see in the following chapter, however, cooperation with regard to transport rates between the railway companies which operated these lines proved much harder to achieve.

## The Apennine lines

The Apennines, being an internal mountain range, did not present the problems of international cooperation and competition of the Alpine lines, but similar technological and operational challenges had to be confronted.[105] The Genoa–Turin line over the Giovi pass was opened in 1853 and reached a height of 360 m with a gradient of 3 per cent. Before the railways, transport from the region surrounding Genoa and Liguria to Piedmont was very time-consuming and costly. The lines connecting Genoa with Alessandria have always been the busiest lines in Italy, since Genoa is one of the largest Italian ports and with much Italian industry being located in Turin or Milan. In fact, these lines were among the first lines to be electrified.[106] Electrical traction has great advantages over steam traction which loses power at higher altitudes due to lower atmospheric pressure. Another reason for introducing electrical traction on mountain sections was to avoid accidents caused by smoke in tunnels, such as happened in the Giovi tunnel in 1898 when ten people died of suffocation.[107] The limited capability of

[104] Fontana, *Geschichte*, p. 15.
[105] Laurent Tissot, 'Les traversées ferroviaires alpines suisses et leur rôle sur l'economie européenne, 1880–1939', *HES* 11 (1992), pp. 91–108.
[106] Camillo Laché, 'Il valico dei Giovi', *IF* (1978) p. 1; Renato Giannetti, 'L'électrification des chemins de fer italiens, 1899–1940', *HES* 11 (1992), pp. 131–3.
[107] Laché, 'Il valico', p. 1.

the railways for facilitating traffic between the port of Genoa and its hinterland put an important constraint on the development of the port.

At first, however, it was Genoa's port infrastructure which limited its development and this was in urgent need of modernization. When the Upper Italy Railway Company bought the Piedmontese State Railways in 1865 its willingness to improve the port was eroded by the endless discussions which took place between the proponents of a great variety of projects. At its own expense it undertook the construction of the tunnel between Sampierdarena and the maritime railway station. Nonetheless, it left the initiative to begin the work to the government, which was to approve the construction plans. The company's position was that these improvements should be undertaken at the same time as it was improving the tracks and that its contribution of 3 million lire would be paid gradually while the work progressed. The government objected to this position and the problem went to arbitration, but in 1876 a generous gift from the Duke of Galliera enabled the work to go ahead.[108]

In the 1860s other lines across mountain ranges or difficult terrain were completed. In 1866 the Upper Italy Railway Company opened the bridge over the river Po at Pontelagoscuro, completing the Padua–Rovigo–Ferrara line, and in 1874 another bridge was opened at Borgoforte, which completed the Verona–Mantua line. In 1864 the line from Bologna to Florence across the Apennines was completed, which opened the way for the direct line to Rome which was completed in 1866. Earlier, the Roman and Neapolitan systems had been linked in 1863. Many short tunnels were needed to reach Pracchia at 600 m, but conventional drilling methods could be used.

The first lines across the Apennines were completed in the 1860s, and in the twentieth century, mostly during the fascist period, the *direttissime*, or direct lines were constructed to improve the capacity and speed of rail transport within Italy. The Genoa–Turin line through the lower Giovi tunnel was opened in 1923, the direct Bologna–Florence line opened in 1933, and the direct line between Rome and Naples opened in 1927. The last *direttissima* between Genoa and La Spezia was opened in 1970 with 60 per cent of the track being subterranean. The direct Bologna–Florence line in particular improved transport dramatically, compared to the much older Porrettana line. The line boasts the world's third longest tunnel, 'la Galleria del Appennino', an 18 km double-track tunnel at an altitude of only 320 m. The Bologna–

---

[108] Elisabetta Bianchi Tonizzi, *I Ducchi di Galiera* (Genoa, 1991), p. 740.

Florence *direttissima* is also famous for the large number of workers that died during the building of the line.[109]

The railway line to the south on the Adriatic coast did not present major natural obstacles and was completed quickly: in 1861 the section of the Milan–Ancona line to the port of Ancona was opened by the Romane Railway Company and in 1865 Brindisi was reached by the Meridionali Railway Company. On the Tyrrhenian coast the construction of the line connecting Rome with Genoa was entrusted to the Romane Railway Company, which however, was unable to complete it. Eventually, it was built by the state in 1874 and its operation was entrusted to the Upper Italy Railway Company. The railway from Rome down to Naples was opened in 1863. This line was constructed inland to avoid the large area of coastal marshes where malaria was endemic. From Naples to Calabria there was no direct line, but in 1880 the line to Taranto was completed, through which a connection to Reggio Calabria was established.[110]

When Giuseppe Garibaldi proclaimed himself dictator in Naples, he created a 'Technical Office for the Railways' and in 1860 granted a concession for the major southern Italian lines to a foreign company. This concession was, however, revoked by parliament since the conditions were judged too burdensome for the state. A new concession was given to the Rothschild–Talabot group, but this was also revoked in favour of a national banker, Bastogi. The completion of the railway was further complicated by the civil war in the south which was to last well into the 1870s and which absorbed a substantial amount of state spending.[111]

On the islands of Sicily and Sardinia, building proceeded very slowly. The first line was opened in Sicily in 1863 and in 1866 two more lines were completed, but thereafter building practically halted until the 1870s. In Sardinia the first line was only opened in 1871. In the years 1860–6, while Venetia was still under Austrian rule, few railway lines were opened due to the insecure political situation.

This short resumé of the first decades of Italian railway building shows how, despite the problems caused by the process of political unification, the main railway lines were finished, most natural obstacles were overcome and international lines were completed. This technological success story contrasts markedly with the huge financial problems of the Italian railway companies, and the disappointing development of traffic which will be treated in the next chapter.

---

[109] Giuntini, *I giganti della montagna*, pp. 250–61.
[110] Briano, *Storia delle ferrovie*, pp. 63–107.    [111] *Ibid.*, p. 106.

## VI RAILWAY BUILDING AFTER THE 1879 AND 1885 RAILWAY ACTS

The period from 1878 to 1885, when the state temporarily ran the railways, is significant for the passing of Act 5002 of 29 July 1879, which provided for the construction of more than 4,000 km of secondary lines. This project can be compared to the French Freycinet plan which also provided for the construction of many local lines. The parliamentary debates preceding the approval of this Act consist of more than 1,500 pages in the parliamentary papers and more than 600 amendments were proposed and defended in many speeches, one of which lasted for two days. Clearly, given the parliamentary system of the first republic, the members of parliament could not resist the temptation to advance their electoral interests by promoting the construction of a railway line in their own constituencies.[112]

After four major changes to the 1879 Act, it was finally decided that the state would spend around 1,200 million lire over a period of twenty years and that private capital from the provinces would participate with a share of between 10 per cent and 40 per cent. The more important the line was economically, the higher the category and the participation of the state in the construction costs. In 1880, however, it was realized that the participation of private capital was practically non-existent and with Act 240 of 5 June 1881, it was decided instead to issue state bonds to finance the secondary lines.

These lines, often on difficult terrain, were of great utility since on many of the routes no alternative forms of transport existed. Moreover, they stimulated regional development and produced traffic for the main lines.[113] All of the existing problems with regard to the operation of railways, however, were left unsolved by this Act since it avoided the politically sensitive issue of delimiting the spheres of action between the state and the companies. Consequently, the management and personnel of the previous railway companies remained in place.

The 1885 Railway Act brought some order in the management of railways and instituted three large companies. The Sicilian Railway Company operated the railways on the Italian islands. The Mediterranean Railway Company operated the lines on the western side of the peninsula and the Adriatic Railway Company those on the eastern side. The aim of this territorial division was to facilitate north–south traffic and thereby the economic unification of Italy. Although the

---

[112] Merger, 'Chemins de fers et croissance économique', p. 125; Camillo Laché, 'La politica ferroviaria in Italia tra il 1876 e 1900', IF (1975), p. 5.

[113] Fenoaltea, 'Italy', p. 93.

Table 21. *Percentage of double-track line
in European countries, 1910*

| Country | Percentage |
| --- | --- |
| Great Britain | 56 |
| Belgium | 46 |
| France | 43 |
| Germany | 38 |
| Italy | 18 |
| Switzerland | 15 |
| Austria-Hungary | 11 |

*Source:* Leonida Leoni, *Testo atlante* (Novara
1913), p. 89.

building plans were not affected directly by this Act, in some cases the
reorganization of the companies forced a decision on the exact routing
of, for example, the Bologna–Verona line.[114] Moreover, through
special financial laws adopted between 1887 and 1889, extra funds
were made available for the construction of railway lines.[115]

With regard to the goal of stimulating the national railway industry
the 1885 Railway Act was successful and in the decade from 1885 to
1895, 5,057 km of new line were opened, more than in any other ten-
year period. Nonetheless, the quality of the railway stations and other
railway equipment remained below the European standards of the
time.[116] By 1910, Italy still lagged behind other European countries as
regards the number of double-track lines, with only 18 per cent of
lines being double track (see table 21).

In Article 21 of the 1885 Railway Act it said that the companies had
to give preference to national industry in procuring railway material,
on condition that prices were not more than 5 per cent higher than
the imported material. This provision stimulated industries such as
Breda, Officine Meccaniche di Milano and Costruzioni Meccaniche
di Saronno in the Milan area, which produced railway wagons and
coaches, and later locomotives. Although less important than the
Milanese industries, in the Genoa area the Ansaldo Company continued to play an important role. Many of these companies still exist
today.

After 1885, the density of regional networks increased in those areas
which had been relatively under-endowed with railways. This was

[114] Giuntini, 'La linea diretta', p. 112.
[115] Merger, 'L'industrie italienne de locomotives', p. 344.
[116] Foxwell and Farrer, *Express Trains*, p. 95.

part of the policy of the left-wing liberal governments, which favoured the extension of the railway network into the provinces.[117] Before 1875, right-wing liberal governments had placed importance on the construction of the great trunk lines. The aim of stimulating local traffic, however, was only partially achieved since the companies were not so successful in operating their networks and net revenue diminished. It is doubtful whether the typical Italian gusto for municipal battles was the main cause of the delay in constructing the lines.[118] More likely is the lack of a financially sound basis for railway policy and an inability to attract private capital.

## VII CONCLUSIONS

An evenly spread railway network and a well-developed railway industry are two conditions which determine the effects of railways on the economy. A comparison of Italian data with that of other European countries with regard to railway traffic and construction clearly shows the backward state of Italy's railway sector during the nineteenth century. Construction lagged behind other European countries and Italy was superior only to Spain. Railway traffic density was also below the European average. These facts should be kept firmly in mind when the Italian railways are analysed.

The extent to which the railways contributed to the formation of a national Italian economy is better understood when the spread of the railway network is contrasted to the different levels of human and economic development in the regions. Any assessment of regional differences in Italy in the nineteenth century, however, is tentative since the first reliable estimate of regional income is for 1911. When data on the provision of railways – the kilometres of track per 1,000 inhabitants – and railway traffic are disaggregated for the Italian regions, regional inequality is smaller compared with other regional socioeconomic data. Nevertheless, compared with the German railway network, Italian railways were less evenly spread over the territory in relation to the population.

By the 1850s railway construction had not progressed far, with the exception of Piedmont, and the socio-economic data for the pre-unification states are hard to harmonize. Only for Lombardy and Venetia, which both figure in the statistics collected by the Austrian Empire, can some educated guesses as to their general level of development be made. Lombardy probably benefited more than Venetia

---

[117] Feneoltea, 'Italy', p. 93.      [118] Giuntini, 'La linea diretta', p. 102.

from its railway links and its incorporation with the rest of Italy in 1860. Venetia, which became part of Italy in 1867, missed out on the first round of public spending on infrastructure and continued to be plagued by relative backwardness.

Next, the available regional statistics on health, education, income and the provision of roads and railways were examined for the period 1870–1911. They show that regional disparities in socio-economic development between the northern and southern regions remained large. Nevertheless, after 1885, the railways were spread relatively evenly in relation to the population of the regions and therefore did not follow this pattern. It might be said, therefore, that the only field in which the Italian state was effective in bridging the gap between north and south was the railways, certainly after around 1885.

With regard to all three railway construction waves, in the 1840s, the 1860s and after the Railway Act of 1885, it must be said that the opening of a railway line is the end of a process of planning and discussion which takes several years. In the Po valley, for example, a long and intense debate in the 1840s among powerful local elites delayed completion of the lines. The quality of railway construction projects was generally below standard and the government grew more and more diffident. The Austrian government was unable to play the role of mediator, for it had great difficulty in proposing compromise solutions and having the lines built. It would be unfair, however, to blame the government for the delay, since it was genuinely interested in linking its Italian possessions with the Austrian network and with the Italian states to the south. In the Papal States, the situation with regard to railway building was even worse. The government had fixed the exact order in which the railways had to be built, but opposed any kind of subsidy or guarantee to the railway companies. Nevertheless it cooperated with Austria and other Italian states in the planning of the line from Milan and Bologna to Florence, as a result of which the Piacenza–Bologna line was opened before unification in 1859. The completion of many lines between 1860 and 1865 was therefore not possible without the planning of the 1840s and 1850s.

The relatively early completion of the principal cross-border lines showed that the technical and financial obstacles to international cooperation could be overcome. The opening of the Gothard line in 1883 was probably the culmination of the effort to integrate the Italian railway network into the European one. As will be shown in the next chapter, the opportunities offered by these early rail connections to northern Europe could not be fully exploited, due to the competition from foreign railway companies which were given preferential treatment by the French and the Austrians. The crossing of the other natural obstacle, the Apennines, also progressed reasonably quickly, although the line from Genoa to Turin continued to present many technical and capacity problems. The most important trunk lines and connections to foreign railway networks were thus mostly completed by the 1870s or early 1880s. After 1885 secondary lines, particularly in Venetia and the southern provinces, were completed.

The sums spent by the Italian state during the nineteenth century on education and health were insufficient to narrow the gap in literacy and health levels between north and south. On the whole the state's actions in these fields were ineffective. Considering the urgent needs for building schools, hospitals and roads, the large sums spend on subsidizing the railways seem rather frivolous, particularly in the south where other needs were more urgent and coastal shipping played an important role.

# CHAPTER 4

# RAILWAY TRAFFIC

## I INTRODUCTION

As we have seen, the plans to build railway lines in the various pre-unification states were not completely uncoordinated and envisaged the opening of border crossing lines within the Italian peninsula, although particular policies slowed down the construction of these lines. When the Italian regions became connected by rail in the 1860s, however, several factors continued to impede the smooth flow of railway traffic between the regions. The lack of cooperation between the six main railway companies proved to be one of the principal obstacles to the development of free inter-regional railway traffic. In 1881, the Railway Enquiry Commission, for example, wrote that while the political barriers between provinces had fallen, a commercial barrier remained in place through the different rates levied by the various railway companies, who continued to act like strangers to each other.[1] Even after 1885, when only two main companies existed and railway rates were unified, problems arose with regard to the traffic between them. The 'railway unification' of Italy was therefore a long drawn-out process which was only solved satisfactorily after nationalization in 1905, when the operational difficulties of connecting different railway networks were practically eliminated.

The only truly comprehensive way of analysing railway traffic in Italy would be to construct a complete matrix of all traffic flows, whether by rail, river, canal, land or sea. Only in this way could it be verified how changes in one part of the transportation system affected the other parts. Unfortunately, so far this has proved impossible to do. Even for railways a complete traffic matrix cannot be reconstructed. Nevertheless, with regard to railway traffic, several topics can be

[1] *Atti Commissione Baccarini,* part 2, vol. 1, p. 823.

examined such as, for example, the share of northern Italian traffic out of total traffic, the influence of the opening of cross-border railway lines in changing the 'openness' of the railway network, traffic on the railway lines to the major ports, the contribution of railways to inter-regional integration, and the role of traditional transport.

## II RAILWAY RATES

Before traffic patterns can be analysed in more detail, some reflection is required on the economics of railway transport and particularly on the way transport rates are determined. On the demand side, the ratios between income levels and transport rates are crucial. Moreover, the location of industries and agricultural markets should be considered. On the supply side, the quality of service, the optimal frequency of trains, load factors, and a series of other factors need to be taken into account. The assumption that the railway companies acted like normal firms, trying to maximize their profits, cannot be taken for granted in the Italian case since the railway industry was heavily regulated and labour productivity was particularly low.[2]

In the nineteenth century two ways of establishing railway rates were practised: either rates were fixed by the government or they were established by the companies and left to market forces. Some regarded a railway rate as a kind of tax which should be levied in accordance with a principle of equity like other taxes, and in this view the state was the only appropriate institution to establish them.[3] Others thought it was better to leave it to the market to determine railway rates. In this case, traffic coordination between the different companies became a problem and regulatory bodies had to be set up like, for instance, the Interstate Commerce Commission in the United States.[4] Moreover, there was no guarantee that similar rates would be charged for similar services, since everything depended on the principle of 'what the traffic will bear'. It must be noted that in the twentieth century even the most fervent proponent of free enterprise in railway matters or privatization of state railway companies does not favour similar free rates.

A brief example taken from a study by William Acworth shows the

[2] Gianni Toniolo, 'Railways and Economic Growth in Mediterranean Countries. Some Methodological Remarks', in Patrick O'Brien (ed.), *Railways and the Economic Development of Europe* (Oxford, 1983), pp. 227–31.

[3] H. Hotelling, 'The General Welfare in Relation to Problems of Taxation and of Railway and Utility Rates', *Econometrica*, 6 (1937), p. 242.

[4] Thomas McCraw, 'Regulation in America. A Review Article', *BHR* 49 (1975), p. 166.

consequences of the application of the principle of 'what the traffic will bear'.[5] There were two ports where oysters were produced, connected to each other by rail and both connected by a railway line of roughly equal length to the market Z, which lay further inland. The traffic for oysters could be charged at a maximum of $1 for a full car-load, given the prices for oysters at the market Z. The problem was that the supply at X was only enough for half a car-load. To attract traffic from Y to fill the car in X the railway company would charge clients in Y 25 cents for Y to X and 75 cents from Y to the market Z. At first, the people in X were outraged, because for the same goods and on the same route from X to Z, they had to pay more than the people in Y. The company presented its case for charging the oyster producers in X more, stating that:

> 1 – a whole car-load at 75 cents would not pay the expenses of handling and moving; 2 – at higher rates than 75 cents they could not get a whole car-load but only half a car-load and half a car-load at $1 rate (the highest charge the article would bear) would not pay expenses. Therefore 3 – on any uniform rate for everybody the road must lose money, and 4 – they would either be compelled to take the oyster-car away altogether (between X and Z) or else get what they could at a dollar and fill up at 75 cents. There was no escape from this reasoning, and the oyster-men of X chose to pay the higher rate rather than lose the service altogether.

Clearly, the case was not always as straightforward and the end not always so happy. The public continued to suspect that the railway companies were manipulating the information about markets and transport demand in their own favour, and using their monopoly power to give customers a raw deal.

Charging free-market railway rates meant that in Great Britain and the United States an enormous variety of transport rates for each route existed, and railway rates became very complicated. It also implied that there was no uniformity of rates between companies or even between different railway lines belonging to the same company. The problem with the free-market way of rate setting was that, since competition between railway companies was imperfect, very few market forces would incite the railway companies to lower their rates, to cooperate with other companies or to improve the quality of service. All the same, an advantage of commercial transport rates was that in Great Britain, for example, the railway companies were able to respond swiftly to the particular needs of a region or create traffic on newly opened lines, providing fierce competition for traditional

[5] Acworth, *Railway Rates*, pp. 98–91.

transport. For this purpose, on newly opened railway lines rates were kept relatively low in the start-up phase in order to attract new traffic flows. Similarly, where competing services from canal boats were offered, for example, the railway companies could always undercut their rates quickly. In continental Europe, on the other hand, where rates were at least partially fixed by governments, the railways were less responsive to the particular traffic demands of certain regions and competition with traditional transport was therefore milder in character and in many cases complementarity between railways and traditional transport rather than competition can be observed.

The history of Italian railway rates is therefore less complicated than that of British railway rates and it is an exaggeration to say that the study of railway rates is like the study of the Chinese language in the sense that it takes a lifetime to learn.[6] In 1881, the Italian Railway Enquiry Commission asserted that the basis of all the rates on the Italian network was that established by the royal decree of September 1860.[7] In 1866, cumulative rates between the different companies and more special rates were introduced, predominately for primary materials over long distances. In 1870, for example, the Upper Italy Railway Company transported around 65 per cent of the goods *piccola velocità* under special free rates, the remaining 35 per cent being transported at fixed rates approved by the government.[8]

The introduction of cumulative rates meant that with one ticket goods could travel over networks operated by different companies. Six years later, in 1872, the Upper Italy Railway Company introduced differential rates for goods to encourage long-distance traffic, which meant that for each additional zone of 100 km the rate would be reduced. After 1885, the Mediterranean and Adriatic Railway Companies used the same basis to calculate their rates and the unification of transport rates was achieved to a large degree. However, the rate system and the division of revenue between the state and the companies was a continuous source of conflict. In fact the failure to improve services during the closing years of the nineteenth century was a major reason for public resentment towards the railway companies and facilitated the nationalization of the railways in 1905.

Due to the complicated nature of the rate system in the various

---

[6] *Atti Commissione Baccarini*, part 2, vol. II, p. 822.  [7] *Ibid.*, p. 813.

[8] *Piccola velocità* means slow traffic and it is the rate category for most goods traffic. By contrast, goods that needed quick delivery are in the *grande velocità* rate category; Upper Italy Railway Company, *Servizio della contabilità e del controllo della statistica*, 1868–1885; Ministero di Lavori Pubblici, *Riposte al questionario della commissione parlamentare d'inchiesta sull'esercizio delle strade ferrate italiane* (Rome, 1880), p. 148.

Table 22. *Railway goods revenue of various European railway companies,*
*(lire per TK)*

| Country | Railway company | Rate obtained | Difference from | |
|---------|-----------------|---------------|-----------------|--|
| | | | Upper Italy | Meridionali |
| France | PLM | 0.057 | −20% | 4% |
| | Nord | 0.055 | −23% | 0% |
| Belgium | Belgian State Railway | 0.046 | −35% | −16% |
| Germany | Baden State Railways | 0.076 | 7% | 38% |
| | Bavarian State Railways | 0.073 | 2% | 33% |
| | Prussian State Railways | 0.070 | −2% | 27% |
| Austria | Austrian State Railways | 0.082 | 15% | 49% |
| | Südbahn Railway Company | 0.076 | 7% | 38% |

*Sources: Atti Commissione Baccarini*, Rome, 1881: part 2, vol. II, p. 813.

European countries it is practically impossible to compare the rates charged for similar transport. Nonetheless, the Railway Enquiry Commission made a comparison of the average revenue obtained for 1 tonnekilometre (TK) between various European companies. This figure, of course, does not depend exclusively on the rates charged, but also on the quality of the supply of goods offered for transport. If a railway company, for instance, had lots of cheap-category transport, the average revenue per TK would be low too. In table 22 it can be concluded that no easy generalizations can be made. The Upper Italy Railway Company obtained a relatively high revenue per TK, since only the German Baden and Bavarian State Railways and the Austrian Südbahn Railway Company produced higher revenues. The Meridionali Railway Company, on the other hand, obtained very low revenue per TK, with only the Belgian State Railways obtaining a lower value. It would be more interesting to know, however, what the average rates were in relation to prices and income levels for those countries. Clearly, this would require a more detailed study and would have to take into account, for example, local transport rates and income levels. The difference in average per capita income between Italy and France or Germany, for example, could be compared to the difference in the cost of rail transport. This exercise is hardly meaningful, however, since as we saw, the levels of income and development between northern and southern Italy were too great.[9]

[9] According to the estimates made by Angus Maddison, the difference between Italian GDP per capita in 1985 dollars ($1210) at purchasing price parity and France's ($1571) in 1870 is around 30 per cent and between Italy's and Germany's ($1300) only 7 per cent; Angus Maddison, *Dynamic Forces in Capitalist Development. A Long-Run Comparative View* (New York, 1991), pp. 6–7.

In addition, a transport rate comparison is not very meaningful since it is questionable whether the Italian railway companies in the 1870s were able to offer the same quality of transport services as in Germany, for example, in terms of frequency of trains, speed, insurance against damage, loading, unloading and storing of merchandise. The remark of the English parliamentary Board of Trade that 'it was not in tariffs but in service that the chief drawback of the Italian railways system was to be found' was valid for the whole of the second half of the nineteenth century, although it was referring to the Italian State Railways after 1905.[10]

With the Railway Act of 1885 the railway rates were changed markedly, and little of the freedom in rate setting was left. The south in particular was harmed by the unification of railway rates, since the low rates previously charged by the Meridionali Railway Company came to an end. Although the rates of the previously existing five railways were unified and rates for inter-regional traffic were simplified, the responsiveness to changes in local transport demand was reduced. So what was won on one side – a clearer rate system and better procedures for inter-regional traffic – was lost on the other side by a lack of responsiveness to local traffic needs. What was even worse, these changes were hardly beneficial for the railway companies, since operating ratios increased and net revenue diminished.[11]

In addition, after 1885 it became virtually impossible for the railway companies to reduce rates on their own initiative.[12] If it was assumed, for example, that goods traffic would double, with a rate decrease from 6 lire per TK to 4 lire per TK, according to the 1885 Railway Act two cases needed to be distinguished. If the government decided to lower the rate, the company would earn an extra 15 lire and the government 5 lire per TK. If the company on the other hand took the initiative to lower the rate, it would receive only 12.5 lire per TK extra and the government 7.5 lire. It comes as no surprise, therefore, that effective Italian railway rates for both goods and passengers were hardly ever reduced as they were in other European countries.[13] In fact, only with nationalization in 1905 did an improvement in service and a rate reduction produce a marked increase in traffic.

[10] Great Britain, Parliamentary Board of Trade, *Continental Railway Investigation* (London, 1910), p. 259. For 1911, Fenoaltea finds that the rates of the state railways are on average higher than elsewhere in Europe; see Fenoaltea, 'Italy', p. 82.

[11] The operating ratio of expenses to revenue. Net revenue is gross revenue minus operating expenses.

[12] Laché, 'La politica ferroviaria', pp. 1–2.

[13] The example comes from T. Van den Wall Bake, *De Italiaansche Spoorwegen* (Utrecht, 1910).

The following example shows why other details of the arrangements in the 1885 Railway Act encouraged the construction of new lines, but not their use The companies were stimulated to attract traffic to their trunk lines, but discouraged traffic on the new secondary lines due to the particular characteristics of a state subsidy concerning the exploitation of these lines. For a new line a company would receive a subsidy of 3,000 lire per kilometre plus half of the revenue up to a sum of 15,000 lire, instead of the normal 62.5 per cent of revenue like the other lines. At a level of net revenue of 14,900 lire per kilometre the company would receive 14,900/2 + 3,000 = 10,450 lire instead of 62.5 per cent of 14,900 = 9,313 lire, but once revenue reached 15,000 lire/kilometre it would again receive the 62.5 per cent or 9,375 lire. Consequently, as this simple calculation shows, the company's interest was to maintain the level of revenue roughly between 12,700 lire and 15,000 lire or else above 16,800 lire, this last value being difficult to achieve on secondary lines.

In sum, in Great Britain and the United States railway rates were subject to market forces rather than government regulation to a much greater degree than in Italy and many other continental European countries. Until political unification in 1860, in most Italian states, with the exception of Piedmont, railway companies were free to set their own transport rates. After 1865, regulation became more restrictive, but the private railway companies commonly charged local, or special rates which implied significant reductions. Freer rates were to the advantage of the lesser developed regions, since, as opposed to a nationally unified rate, the principle of 'what the traffic can bear' allowed for lower prices in local markets. Nevertheless, in the 1885 Railway Act railway rates were fixed and unified completely by the state, thereby prohibiting the cut-price policies which had been experimented with by, for instance, the British railway companies. Consequently, no more reductions could be given to poorer customers in the south and the competition with traditional transport became less effective.

## III  THE DEVELOPMENT OF RAILWAY TRAFFIC IN ITALY

In 1983, Stefano Fenoaltea stated that any comprehensive assessment of the overall impact of railways should measure the effects of both railway construction and transportation, but so far very few have taken up the challenge.[14] Potential researchers have probably been repelled

---

[14] Fenoaltea, 'Italy', p. 89; Maurizio Zani, 'Gli incassi delle stazioni ferroviarie per la ricostruzione delle gerachie urbane, 1880–1990', *Padania* 4 (1990); Schram, 'The Impact of Railways', pp. 4–8.

by the great amount of numerical data on railway traffic that needs to be processed. For Italy, excellent data exist for the period 1867–84, but for the period 1885–1905 only a more limited traffic analysis can be carried out, since many changes were made in goods categories.[15] Recently, the availability of spreadsheet programs and geographical information systems for personal computers have greatly facilitated the analysis of railway traffic.

A second reason for the failure to investigate railway traffic might be the absence of paradigmatic studies for Great Britain and the United States of America due to the deficient manner in which railway statistics were kept in those countries. In the British and North American literature, this aspect of the operation of railways has not been given much weight, since the data are unavailable. The statistics in Britain, for example, do not even allow for an accurate estimate of overall traffic output.[16] In contrast, the French tradition of keeping traffic statistics for every station and every line which was followed by many railway companies in Italy and other continental European countries, allows a much more specific analysis.[17] It is no coincidence, therefore, that French historians are among the pioneers of railway traffic analysis.[18]

Three preliminary remarks concerning Italian railway traffic must be made. First, in Italy coastal shipping continued to be relatively important because of the country's long coastline and because of the location along the coast of many population centres, particularly in the south. Second, railway traffic density for Italy was substantially lower compared to that of other European countries for which such data are available (see table 4). As a consequence, in order to run the railways profitably, operating costs had to be proportionally lower too. Italy's hilly terrain and its dependence on imported coal, however, put a severe constraint on the reduction of operating costs. Operating results were therefore very meagre, and return on capital for the investors hardly ever reached 4 per cent. For 1877, return on capital for the various Italian railway companies was reported to be 3.26 per cent for

---

[15] Maurizio Zani, 'Il reticolo urbano dell'Italia settentrionale. Mutamenti nel ventennio post-unitario', *SU* 39 (1978), p. 167; Schram, 'The Impact of Railways', 1994, pp. 1–4; So far, these traffic data have not been thoroughly analysed.

[16] Derek H. Aldcroft, *British Transport. An Economic Survey from the Seventeenth Century to the Twentieth* (Leicester, 1969); Gary R. Hawke, *Railways and Economic Growth in England and Wales, 1840–1870* (Oxford, 1970), pp. 48–50; Terry Gourvish, *Railways and the British Economy, 1830–1914* (London, 1980), p. 60; Phillip S. Bagwell, *The Transport Revolution* (London, 1974), pp. 95 *et seq.*

[17] Acworth, *The Elements of Railway Economics*, p. 60.

[18] François Caron, *Histoire de l'exploitation d'un grand réseau. La Compagnie du Chemin de Fer du Nord, 1846–1937* (Paris, 1973), pp. 143 *et seq.*

the Upper Italy Railway Company, 1.41 per cent for the Romane Railway Company and 1.62 per cent for the Meridionali Railway Company. The Sicilian Railway Company and the Reale Sarda Railway Company showed a negative return on capital.[19]

The lines across natural obstacles such as mountain ranges and rivers continued to present a number of problems which hindered traffic. Due to climatic factors such as snow or floods, for example, traffic on these lines was frequently interrupted. In other regions, cholera epidemics broke out or the risk of contracting malaria was high.[20] Moreover, the imperfection of railway traction technology at the time meant that steam locomotives were very slow in crossing mountain ranges. Steam technology could not solve the problem of the bad performance of steam engines at higher altitudes caused by lower atmospheric pressure. The lines across Italy's national borders fall mostly within this last category, and on these lines customs procedures were also bound to slow down through traffic even further.

Third, traffic imbalances within the network were great and had not been foreseen when construction was taking place. Around the middle of the nineteenth century in particular the primitive state of railway technology created great capacity problems for the busiest lines. The technology to enhance the capacity of a railway line such as the Porettana line or the Giovi pass, for instance, was not available or was too expensive. The lines connecting the large ports with their hinterlands, such as the Genoa–Turin line, had difficulty in handling the enormous quantities of passengers and goods traffic.

Stefano Fenoaltea maintains that the secondary lines with less traffic had a higher 'social return' because they opened up areas where no other traditional transport was available.[21] Despite their usefulness, however, these lines produced heavy losses for the companies and a more thorough cost-benefit analysis would be needed to support Fenoaltea's thesis. At the same time, some foreign observers realized that Italy's concentration on extension of its railway network after 1885 was ill-advised.[22] The operating ratio on the main network, taking all the railway companies together, was around 87 per cent, but for the secondary networks it was over 100 per cent, implying that these made severe losses.[23]

---

[19] Corbino, *Annali*, pp. 270–1.

[20] Upper Italy Railway Company, *Osservazioni*, pp. 8–9.

[21] Fenoaltea, 'Italy', p. 93.     [22] Laché, 'La politica ferroviaria', p. 7.

[23] For the Mediterranean and Meridionali it was around 87 per cent but for the Sicilian Railway Company it was around 93 per cent; E. Jovinelli, *Il problema ferroviario. L'ordinamento delle strade ferrate e le convenzioni* (Florence, 1904), pp. 20–1.

The inability of railway companies to handle through traffic was another matter which obstructed traffic flows and frustrated railway customers. Frequently, two different railway administrations, whether Italian or foreign, could not come to an agreement on a common rate for charging through traffic, and consequently movement was slowed down by complicated procedures and the need to change trains or buy extra tickets.

On some railway lines many of these factors coincided and caused severe traffic bottlenecks. Accordingly, traffic flows in the Italian network suffered from grave imbalances to which the railway companies were not in a position to respond. Given the low average density of traffic in Italy and its uneven distribution, it is understandable that the majority of Italian railway companies were not able to work their lines profitably.

## IV  INTERNATIONAL LINES

The amount of traffic on Italy's cross-border railway lines depended not only on the quality and costs of transport, but also on the opportunities and terms of trade between Italy and its neighbouring countries.[24] Trade policy was therefore just as important as transport rate in influencing the size and composition of international railway goods flows. After 1870, Italy began to follow a more protectionist policy, and in 1878 introduced its first tariff, which protected agricultural products and some industries. In 1888, an even more protectionist tariff was instituted, which caused a trade war with France. The 1878 tariff, on the other hand, had not provoked retaliatory measures from France, but had led to a perceptible decrease in trade between the two countries. As a consequence of this row with France over trade, after 1878 Italy tried to develop its trade relations with other neighbours to make up for the loss.[25]

One element of this trade policy was to try to reach international agreement on railway rates with Austria and Switzerland.[26] Italy therefore tried to revise the old international railway rate agreement and organized an international conference in Florence with the aim of

---

[24] *Atti Commissione Baccarini*, part 2, vol. II, p. 631. Regrettably, the railway traffic statistics cannot be compared with the more sophisticated international trade statistics because of the differences in the classification systems of the goods.

[25] Luzzatto, *L'economia italiana*, pp. 115–6, 186–98.

[26] The minutes of the railway conferences held to this end in Florence and Milan are feared to have been lost.

lowering international rates.[27] In some cases the rate system of 1872, contrary to the aim of internationally agreed rates, had in fact made the internal railway rates lower than the international ones. In order to correct this and to favour national industries, the minister had obliged the companies to apply the lowest rates for all traffic on lines where international traffic took place. This measure provoked resistance from those Italian industries which were not located along lines on which international traffic passed, and was insufficient for countering foreign competition.[28] To ship a tonne of coffee, for instance, from Genoa to Brissago (a small town near Como) a rate of 0.06 lire per kilometre for 229 km would be applied, which together with charges for unloading would result in a total cost of 17.79 lire. If, however, that same tonne of coffee were shipped to Cannobio (another small town near Como), which was not situated on an international line but was about the same distance from Genoa, a rate of 0.14 lire per TK would be applied for 223 km, which would make transportation costs including charges for unloading 35.57 lire.[29] Evidently, the resulting difference in the price of a *cappuccino* between Cannobio and Brissago could not but provoke the fiercest opposition. The Upper Italy Railway Company consequently proposed putting the international rate at a similar level to the differential rate it applied internally, but for reasons left unclear the minister refused this suggestion.

It is impossible to assess in a comprehensive way the effects of these international discount rates, but certainly the industries located along the international lines were favoured by the system. The Railway Enquiry Commission recommended a system whereby Italy could remain neutral as to the Alpine route to be followed. It also urged a reversal of the policy of applying the lowest tariff in order to stop favouring those industries situated along international lines. Whether it was the interests of foreign companies or the existence of many special tariffs that were to blame, but a general and rational system for international railway traffic never came into existence before 1885 and even then there continued to be many imperfections in the rate system.[30]

A strategic problem of the northern Italian railway system was the impossibility of competing with foreign companies for international through traffic. The railways therefore did not help to promote the international importance of the ports of Genoa and Venice by extending their hinterlands across Italy's borders. Although the volume of traffic directly from the ports to foreign destinations was

[27] *Atti Commissione Baccarini*, part 2, vol. ii, p. 907.
[28] *Ibid.*, pp. 610–37, 904–22.          [29] *Ibid.*, p. 840.
[30] Ministero di Lavori Pubblici, *Risposte*, p. 90.

only a relatively small part of the total import and export flows by rail, this flow was important for the international competitiveness of the Italian ports. The geographical position of the ports close to Italy's borders made it impossible for Italian railways to compete effectively with the Austrian or the French railway companies for international through traffic to northern Europe by lowering transport rates. A discount on transport rates on the Italian section for goods travelling from Trieste to Munich, for instance, barely altered total transportation costs at all, because the distance travelled over Italian territory was so short. Italy thus found itself in the position of not being able to develop international through traffic from its ports on the newly opened links with Austria, because of the Südbahn Railway Company's policies of undercutting any reduction made on the Italian section. If a unified railway administration had continued to exist and if the Upper Italy Railway Company had not been purchased by the Italian state in 1875, this problem would have been less severe. Italian complaints about this practice are somewhat hypocritical, however, since Italy did not eschew similar nationalistic practices itself.

In order to help the ports of Genoa and Venice, international through traffic had to be attracted to the northern Italian network, bringing goods from the ports directly to their Swiss or southern German destinations. The competition from the French railway companies and the port of Marseilles on the one hand, and the Austrian railway companies and the port of Trieste on the other prevented this. Although until 1878 the Upper Italy Railway Company and the Austrian Südbahn Railway Company were in reality one and the same company, Austrian policy continued to favour Trieste over Venice.[31]

A closer look at the conditions of transport over the Alpine routes reveals the great differences existing between them. From 1867, all traffic from Trieste and Venice to Germany and Switzerland travelled on the Cormons–Peri line. In February 1874, the line through the Pustertal, outside Italian territory, was opened, connecting the port of Trieste with southern Germany without crossing Italy. Although the distance from the Adriatic port of Trieste to Munich was about 24 km shorter via the Brenner line than via the Pustertal line, the longer line began taking over the traffic. When in 1878 the line to Austria over the Tarvis pass opened, many Italian writers hoped that Italy would get back some of this traffic from Trieste to southern Germany and Switzerland, as the pass shortened the distance by some 65 km. Nothing of the kind happened, however, for several reasons. First and

---

[31] *Atti Commissione Baccarini*, part 2. vol II, pp. 610–37, 904–22.

most important was the fact that the Austrian Südbahn Railway Company kept transport costs on the Pustertal line below those in Italy. The Südbahn Railway Company and the Austrian government cooperated in trying to prevent this traffic passing through Italy. This explains why the rates were kept high on the Austrian part of the Brenner line, and especially on the Peri–Kufstein section. Second, traffic moved more quickly over the Pustertal line because there were no customs. Third, it was a means for the Südbahn Railway Company to favour Trieste, in which it had invested heavily, over Venice. Fourth, Italian policy actually worsened the situation, since from July 1874 onwards the Italian government instituted two new taxes: one of 2 per cent on all goods traffic and another of around 6 to 10 lire per wagon. Although the second tax was revoked soon afterwards, traffic on this line decreased by 150 thousand tonnes in September of that year.[32] There is no reason to assume, therefore, that the opening of railway lines across the Alps diverted traffic towards the smaller Italian economy. Economic forces and the transport policies of France and Austria-Hungary prevented such a shift of traffic in favour of Italy.

For analogous reasons the lines to France through Ventimiglia and Modane suffered from competition with the Paris-Lyon-Méditerranée Railway Company (PLM). After 1875, the companies either refused an agreement on tariffs, or circumvented its provisions by reducing their tariffs. Only on lines where both the PLM and the Südbahn Railway Company shared the same interests as the Upper Italy Railway Company could competitive rates be offered.[33]

More than the changes in international trade flows, the opening of a new line or the lowering of a rate frequently altered the balance of railway traffic flows. Competition from French and Austrian railway companies and limited trading opportunities explain why some of these international lines never developed a significant amount of traffic. The relatively low levels of traffic on the Brenner and Tarvis lines, for example, and the abundance of transport of cheap goods, on which low rates were applied, are remarkable during the whole period (see table 29). As a consequence of hostile trade policies and competition among Italian and foreign railway companies the ports of Genoa and Venice could not develop as European ports, but remained merely the suppliers of their immediate Italian hinterland. The creation of special international rates, which were intended to facilitate

---

[32] Ministero di Lavori Pubblici, *Risposte*, p. 137.

[33] For a more in-depth discussion we refer to Michèle Merger, 'Mutations techniques et commerciales. Les relations ferroviaires entre l'Italie et l'Europe occidental de 1867 au début du XXème siècle', *RHCF* (1992), pp. 211–52.

export and import flows could therefore not be effective and merely increased imbalances by giving provinces lying along lines used for international traffic a greater advantage over others.

## V THE ROLE OF PORTS

As regards the role of Italy's major Mediterranean ports, Genoa, Leghorn, Civitavecchia, Naples, Messina and Palermo, the official port statistics do not show the true economic differences in their importance, since they do not register the amounts or values of goods handled in one year, but only the tonnage of the ships arriving and departing. For the Adriatic ports of Trieste, Venice, Ancona, Bari and Brindisi the same holds true. Although several local studies exist, a comprehensive analysis of all Italian ports and their commercial activity is still awaited. In the 1870s and 1880s Trieste's infrastructure was superior to that of Genoa or Venice, as it was the only major port of the Austro-Hungarian Empire and benefited from substantial Austrian investment in port as well as railway infrastructure. After Trieste, Genoa on the Mediterranean and Venice on the Adriatic coast were probably the best equipped ports, although their infrastructure remained below the standards of the time.

At first sight, Genoa's geographical position does not seem favourable for the development of a large, industrial port: the city lies on a thin stretch of land and is separated from its hinterland, Piedmont, by the Maritime Alps. Up to the coming of the railways the only means of communication was by a steep road, crossing a pass at an altitude of around 700 m. In earlier centuries the city's isolation, combined with the relative political freedom of the Genoese Republic, provided the conditions for its commercial success, but in the nineteenth century Genoa's geographical position proved to be a handicap for its development

The railway traffic patterns which materialized in the 1870s and the 1880s clearly show the dominance of the Genoa–Turin line over all other lines (see map 2) and the importance of the stations of Genoa, Turin and Milan (see map 3). Obviously, the port of Genoa supplied not only Piedmont but also parts of Lombardy with goods. Historically, before unification, Lombardy never looked to Venice for its supplies, since the tolls on the river Po were considerable and the import duties in Venice higher than in Genoa.[34] After unification this

---

[34] Franco Borlandi, *Il problema delle communicazioni nel secolo XVIII nei suoi rapporti col Risorgimento italiano* (Pavia, 1932), pp. 76–88.

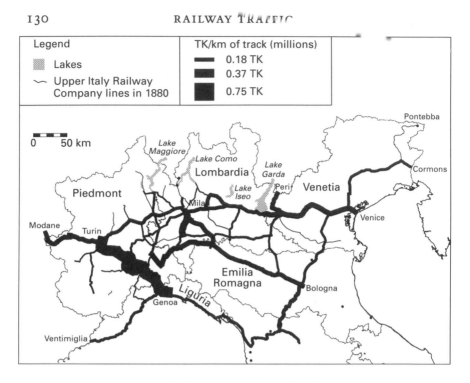

Map 2   Traffic density on northern Italian lines, 1880

pattern changed only slightly, because Venice's infrastructure was improved very little and very slowly whereas in Genoa major improvements were made.[35]

Despite the high volume of railway traffic on the Genoa–Turin line, there are reasons to believe that traffic did not develop to its full potential, because of Genoa's problems in handling both sea cargo and railway goods. Ships had to anchor in the middle of the port and had to be unloaded by smaller boats, since the length of the quays was insufficient to accommodate all ships. In 1876, for example, the port of Marseilles, a serious competitor, had a quay length about three times that of Genoa (3,800 m and 12,606 m respectively) and possessed 20 km of railway track compared to Genoa's 2 km. It is no wonder then that the average unloading time in Genoa was between three and four weeks, whereas in Marseilles it was only three days. Even after 1889, when quay lengths were increased by 70 per cent to 6,456 m, the same unloading boats were kept in use. Moreover, the railway facilities for providing a smooth sea–land transfer were inadequate.[36]

---

[35] Petri, 'Autarchia, guerra e zone industriali', pp. 73–5.
[36] Bianchi Tonizzi, 'Il porto di Genova', p. 732.

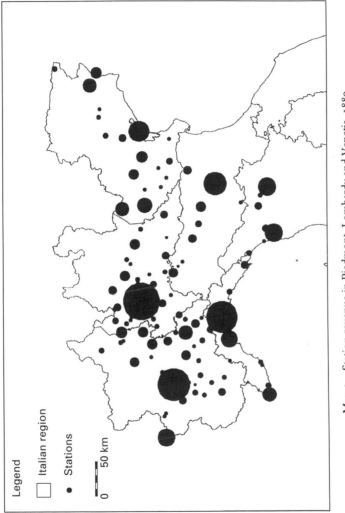

Map 3   Station revenue in Piedmont, Lombardy and Venetia, 1880

Legend

☐ Italian region

• Stations

0   50 km

The degree of traffic congestion in the port has been estimated as follows: the average unloading capacity per quay-metre grew slowly, by about 40 per cent from 336 tonnes per quay-metre per year in 1861 to 477 tonnes per quay-metre per year in 1888, whereas annual imports in the same period increased by 300 per cent. Clearly, in order to handle this cargo, working hours at the port must have increased considerably.[37] In the 1880s some alleviation of the situation was provided by the port of Savona, around 40 km west of Genoa, which began to process some traffic, particularly bulky goods such as coal.

Improvement in Genoa's port infrastructure was constantly needed, but the Italian state reacted too slowly. In 1876, it was a private citizen who provided the necessary capital for the most urgent modifications to the port. At the time of completion of these works in 1888, however, more investment was already required.[38] Improvement of the railway infrastructure progressed sluggishly, since the work could only be carried out after the modifications to the port were completed. Railway traffic between Genoa and Turin was continuously hampered by the insufficient capacity of the line. Only the electrification of the line in 1911 and the construction of a third and fourth tunnel in 1923 solved these problems.

Despite its congestion problems, therefore, Genoa and not Venice continued to be the port which contributed most to the industrialization of the northern Italian economy. Coal imports through Genoa, for instance, accounted for around 30 per cent of total Italian imports in the years 1872–5. These coal imports constituted around 40 per cent of the port's total international traffic during that period.[39] From other sources it can be concluded that during the years 1872–5 Venice's total shipping volume was only around 50 per cent that of Genoa and 40 per cent that of Trieste.[40]

A more detailed analysis of the land-side trade of the ports in relation to railway traffic statistics reveals the problems of handling goods within ports which were old historic cities. In any port traffic analysis sea-side must be distinguished from land-side commerce. Subsequently, the proportion of land-side commerce carried by rail can be estimated from the railway traffic statistics. For 1911, Fenoaltea estimates that 22 million tonnes of goods were unloaded at Italian

---

[37] *Ibid.*, p. 768.      [38] *Ibid.*, pp. 721, 743.

[39] Giorgio Doria, 'La place du système portuaire ligure dans le développement industriel des régions du Triangle', in Louis Bergeron (ed.), *La croissance régionale dans l'Europe méditerranéenne, 19–20 siècles* (Paris, 1992), p. 117.

[40] Errera, *Saggio di statistica*, p. 20.

ports of which 11 million tonnes were transported by rail.[41] In the case of Genoa the role of the railway line was crucial, since no alternative transport of comparable quality existed. One estimate suggests that from 60 to 80 per cent of goods arriving at the port were transported inland by rail.[42] Railway transport therefore dominated the land-side trade of the port of Genoa and the Genoa–Turin line continued to have the highest traffic density in Italy. The importance of these facts for the industrialization of northern Italy cannot easily be under-estimated. For Venice the percentage of goods carried by rail to its hinterland was somewhat less because of the existence of strong competition from canal and river transport. The statistics on the value and quantity of land-side trade combined with traffic statistics give some indication of the influence of the port on its hinterland and the role of railways. It is not, after all, the importance of the international role of the port or the benefits to a few merchant families that are important, but how much of the wealth generated in the port penetrated into the region.[43]

A hypothesis for the declining importance in Venice's land-side trade after 1866 has been put forward. Giorgio Roverato writes, for example: 'The union with Italy led to the almost total disappearance of what was left of the trade with Austria and was not compensated for by visible signs of new interaction with the new Italian state.'[44] This assertion, however, seems to be a bit too rash and does not find a solid basis in the port statistics.

In figure 5 the values of land-side trade compared to sea trade for Venice are given. The land trade value includes those goods transported by rail. Land-side trade diminished between 1860 and 1862, probably because of the lower volume of trade with Austria's port of Trieste. In fact, during this period the movement in the sea-trade level seems to have been mainly determined by the trade with Austria, as can be seen by the parallel between trade with Austria and total sea trade.[45]

---

[41] Fenoaltea, 'Italy', p. 77.          [42] Doria, 'La place', p. 115.

[43] All data were derived from Venice, Camera Provinciale di Commercio ed Industria, *Navigazione e commercio di Venezia negli anni 1860–1890. Prospetti statistici a cura di camera di commercio ed arti* (Venice, 1861–91). The existing studies of the ports of Genoa and Trieste do not contain any information on land-side trade. For the other ports no reliable data are known to exist; see G. Felloni, 'I prezzi nel portofranco e nella borsa merci di Genova nel 1828 al 1890', in Carlo Cipolla (ed.), *Archivio Economico dell'Unificazione Italiana* 6, series 1 (Rome, 1957); D. Beltrami, *I prezzi nel portofranco e nella borsa merci di Trieste dal 1825 al 1890* (Turin, 1964).

[44] Giogio Roverato, 'La terza regione industriale', in *Storia d'Italia. Il Veneto* (Turin, 1984), p. 167.

[45] The data from 1860 to 1865 were converted from gulden to lire using the exchange rate given by Beltrami, *I prezzi*.

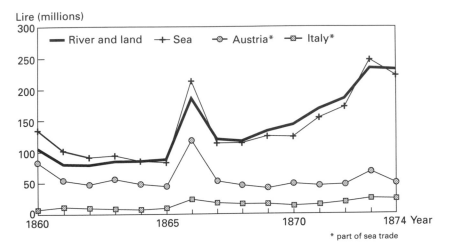

Figure 5   Venice's land and sea trade

Between 1860 to 1865, Venice's sea trade too underwent a slight depression caused by the declining trade with Austria. Nonetheless, after 1865 there seems to be no convincing basis for arguing that Venice was undergoing a general crisis caused by this loss of trade. This argument over-emphasizes the magnitude of trade with Austria in this period. On the other hand, the growth in the value of sea trade does not seem to have suffered from the stationary value of Austrian trade. Venice thus compensated by trading with the rest of the world and recovered rapidly and completely after the crisis of the early 1860s.

With regard to the impact of the general decline in trade in the early 1860s on the economy on the mainland it can be seen from figure 5 that the value of trade from the city to the mainland follows the value of sea trade quite closely. The value of exports from the mainland to the city gives another indication of the impact of the crisis of the 1860s. It is remarkable that the assumed crisis is hardly visible in the data on exports to Venice from the mainland which in fact show an upward trend throughout the period. In view of the steady increase in the value of exports from the mainland to Venice and the quick recovery of the value of sea-side trade after 1866, the impact of the depression between 1860 and 1866 of the trade of Venice on Venetia must have been less severe than usually assumed in the literature.

The problem of assessing the importance of railways for the land-side trade of Venice is that the port statistics are divided into different categories from the railway traffic statistics and therefore it is almost impossible to harmonize them. Moreover, some of the port categories

Thousands of tonnes

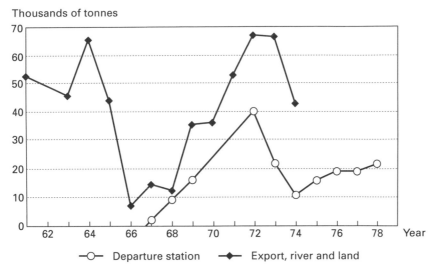

—O— Departure station     —◆— Export, river and land

Figure 6    The amount of wood and coal transported from Venice

are given in quantity and not in weight units, unlike those of the
railway company. Because of the problems with the units of measurement, no total tonnage figure can be derived from the trade statistics
for comparison with the tonnage given in the railway statistics. The
amount of coal transported by rail from the port of Venice to the
mainland for the years 1865–74 show a great variation in the percentage transported by rail. It can be seen that the role of traditional
carriers remained important, contrary to what some have concluded
from the early date of the rail connection between Venice and the
mainland (1847). The precise role of the railways in this trade cannot
be determined with great precision, but for many bulky goods the
railways must have transported around half the material (see figure 6).

The Railway Enquiry Commission revealed some particular
problems concerning Venice's railway stations. In 1879, for instance,
Emmanuel Jaurnig, Venice's station master for almost forty years,
declared that Venice's station was too small. Moreover, the station was
designed for the Südbahn Railway Company whose trains travelled on
the right but after Venetia's inclusion into the Italian railway system in
1866 trains kept to the left and therefore had to change tracks before
entering the station. This created many inconveniences and a substantial risk of accidents. In another declaration, the president of the
Venetian Chamber of Commerce, Blumenthal, complained that the
Upper Italy Railway Company did not unload its coal at the maritime
station, which hindered other operations at the main Santa Lucia

Figure 7    Venice's railway station in the early 1900s

station. Moreover, he proposed that private industry should deliver goods, since this was cheaper and quicker than the service offered by the Upper Italy Railway Company.[46] This problem was not peculiar to Venice, although the many historical monuments and the technical difficulties of building in a city with so many canals, made it more difficult to arrive at a solution. Even at the beginning of the twentieth century, smaller boats or gondolas were still used to transfer goods from sea-going ships to goods wagons (see figure 7). In any case, the Italian state reacted very slowly to complaints about its ports and it was only in the twentieth century during the fascist period that major sums were assigned for port improvements.

## VI  RAILWAY TRAFFIC BETWEEN NORTHERN AND SOUTHERN ITALY

Vera Zamagni has pointed out that there was little scope for trade between northern and southern Italy because there was no complementarity between the goods produced. Historically, trade between the pre-unification states was low and comprised at most 20 per cent of total trade.[47] Zamagni maintains that trade and traffic between the northern and southern regions did not increase substantially during the whole of the nineteenth century, since although production for the market increased, consumption diminished. Only for 1911 are there

---

[46] *Atti Commissione Baccarini,* risposte orali, p. 444.

[47] Vera Zamagni used data from various studies on trade in the pre-unification states published in the *Archivio Economico dell'Unificazione Italiana;* see Zamagni, 'Ferrovie e integrazione', p. 1641.

reliable data available which show a similar low level of inter-regional trade as that of the pre-unification period, with the difference that several goods in the food category produced in the south were directly exported to northern Europe.

It has often been deplored that after unification no precise idea of inter-regional trade can be obtained, but the detailed railway traffic statistics can shed some light on the matter. Total output in TK and PK for the various railway companies up until 1885 clearly demonstrates the differences between the north and south of Italy (tables 23 and 24).[48] Roughly 60 per cent of all Italian traffic was on the northern Italian network. Since gross revenue per kilometre of track was substantially higher and the Upper Italy Railway Company's operating ratio was lower, the company's opportunities to make profits were consequently larger.

Traffic flows from northern to southern Italy by rail were insignificant in 1867 but grew to around 200,000 tonnes in 1884 (see table 25). Imports by rail from southern Italy were relatively less important than those through the border stations and declined in relative terms to 13 per cent in 1884. In absolute numbers, however, they continued to grow. The flows of traffic in 1877 show an asymmetric pattern, with the south exporting more than the north. The railway data show that northern goods were not yet carried by rail to southern markets.

The role of the railways in facilitating this trade should not be under-estimated and traffic flows can be compared with the internal and cross-border traffic, in order to assess their significance properly. Examining the composition of goods traffic to and from southern Italy in 1884, the variety of goods transported is greater than that from foreign countries, especially for imports (see table 27). In- and outgoing traffic to southern Italy falls into the same categories, which confirms the incomplementarity hypothesis. With reference to the final destination of imports from southern Italy, in the 1870s and 1880s not more than around 3 per cent was re-exported to other countries.[49] The pattern of re-exportation of goods from southern Italy, which existed in the early twentieth century and which Zamagni assumed to have existed before, cannot be observed in the 1870s and early 1880s.

The incomplementarity thesis concerning Italian north–south trade was developed in reaction to a 'meridionalistic' school of economic historians, who argued that the north exploited the south in a colonial

---

[48] Traffic data per region for the whole of Italy are not yet available.

[49] Schram, 'The Impact of Railways', p. 290.

Table 23. *Railway goods revenue of*
*Italian railway companies (lire per TK)*

| Railway company | lira per TK |
| --- | --- |
| Upper Italy | 0.071 |
| Romane | 0.071 |
| Meridionali | 0.055 |
| Average | 0.066 |

*Sources:* see table 22

Table 24. *Traffic output of Italian railway companies (TU)*

| | Upper Italy | Romane | Meridionali | Calabrio Sicule | Sardinian | Total |
| --- | --- | --- | --- | --- | --- | --- |
| 1865 | 5,975,279,101 | | | | | 1,020,228 |
| 1870 | 860,049,268 | | | | | 1,468,461 |
| 1875 | 1,220,383,844 | 382,871,284 | 385,113,636 | 78,469,037 | 1,686,368 | 2,083,701 |
| 1880 | 1,499,706,778 | 514,968,341 | 421,155,236 | 13,837,515 | 2,328,861 | 2,597,494 |

| | Mediteranean | Adriatic | Sicilian | Sardinian | |
| --- | --- | --- | --- | --- | --- |
| 1886 | 1,832,489,609 | 1,391,767,585 | 133,799,885 | 2,067,351 | 3,378,731 |
| 1890 | 1,930,304,947 | 1,719,363,551 | 150,124,812 | 213,612 | 3,821,155 |

*Sources: Annuario Statistico Italiano 1884* (Rome, 1885)
*Annuario Statistico Italiano 1897* (Rome, 1898)
Upper Italy Railway Company, *Servizio della Contabilità e della Statistica* (Milan, 1863–85)

Table 25. *North–south traffic in 1877 (tonnes)*

| North to south | | South to north | |
| --- | --- | --- | --- |
| Grain and rice | 25,000 | Wine | 50,000 |
| Wood for construction | 11,500 | Cereals | 70,000 |
| Textiles | 7,300 | Wood | 50,000 |
| Fibres | 6,300 | Sleepers | 20,000 |
| Colonial goods | 4,400 | Dyestuffs | 12,500 |
| Metals | 4,200 | Fresh fruits and vegetables | 11,700 |
| Minerals | 4,000 | Rags | 10,000 |
| Various manufactures | 3,900 | Oil | 4,000 |
| Machines | 2,200 | | |
| Butter and cheese | 2,000 | | |
| Total | 70,800 | Total | 228,200 |

*Sources: Atti Commissione Baccarini,* 1881, Rome, 1882, part 2, vol. II, pp. 832–3

Table 26. *Traffic flows to and from the northern Italian railway network (tonnes)*

| (a) Imports by rail | 1867 | | 1870 | | 1875 | | 1880 | | 1884 | |
|---|---|---|---|---|---|---|---|---|---|---|
| Southern Italy | 67,340 | 9% | 107,536 | 9% | 225,468 | 13% | 327,886 | 14% | 346,423 | 12% |
| France | | | | | 219,079 | 13% | 149,329 | 6% | 134,212 | 5% |
| Switzerland | | | | | | | | | 171,434 | 6% |
| Austria | 66,058 | 9% | 301,164 | 25% | 304,574 | 18% | 341,545 | 14% | 411,321 | 14% |
| Genoa | 539,916 | 74% | 685,105 | 56% | 756,309 | 44% | 964,845 | 41% | 957,463 | 34% |
| Savona | | | 32,727 | 3% | 98,569 | 6% | 361,774 | 15% | 479,400 | 17% |
| Venice | 56,884 | 8% | 92,447 | 8% | 124,485 | 7% | 231,770 | 10% | 344,694 | 12% |
| Total | 730,198 | 100% | 1,218,979 | 100% | 1,728,484 | 100% | 2,377,149 | 100% | 2,844,947 | 100% |
| Internal traffic (arrivals) | 1,609,895 | | 2,054,224 | | 3,208,889 | | 3,757,769 | | 5,248,747 | |

| (b) Exports by rail | 1867 | | 1870 | | 1875 | | 1880 | | 1884 | |
|---|---|---|---|---|---|---|---|---|---|---|
| Southern Italy | 121,013 | 34% | 89,927 | 21% | 144,149 | 23% | 175,550 | 25% | 202,258 | 24% |
| France | | | | | 71,543 | 12% | 148,443 | 21% | 124,321 | 15% |
| Switzerland | | | | | | | | | 142,235 | 17% |
| Austria | 56,406 | 16% | 115,759 | 27% | 138,705 | 22% | 148,259 | 21% | 103,941 | 12% |
| Genoa | 116,746 | 33% | 148,167 | 34% | 155,382 | 25% | 137,474 | 19% | 134,400 | 16% |
| Savona | 29,480 | 8% | 27,685 | 6% | 30,418 | 5% | 38,116 | 5% | 61,100 | 7% |
| Venice | 29,480 | 8% | 54,337 | 12% | 76,815 | 12% | 67,433 | 9% | 78,214 | 9% |
| Total | 353,125 | 100% | 435,875 | 100% | 617,012 | 100% | 715,275 | 100% | 846,469 | 100% |
| Internal traffic (departures) | 2,070,121 | | 2,719,719 | | 4,237,032 | | 5,267,307 | | 6,840,834 | |

*Sources:* Upper Italy Railway Company, *Servizio della Contabilità e della Statistica*

Table 27. *Composition of north–south railway traffic in 1884 (tonnes)*

| Exports | | | Imports | | |
|---|---|---|---|---|---|
| All goods | 202,034 | 100% | All goods | 346,426 | 100% |
| Marble | 35,973 | 18% | Cereals | 71,488 | 21% |
| Wood | 31,916 | 16% | Coal | 59,826 | 17% |
| Cereals | 27,311 | 14% | Drinks | 46,864 | 14% |
| Textile fibres | 10,496 | 5% | Building materials | 25,685 | 7% |
| Building materials | 10,227 | 5% | Wood | 22,367 | 6% |
| Textiles | 9,597 | 5% | Stone | 22,068 | 6% |
| Metals | 7,512 | 4% | Marble | 15,892 | 5% |
| Colonial goods | 6,650 | 3% | Textile fibres | 10,044 | 3% |
| Empty bags | 6,614 | 3% | Minerals | 8,491 | 2% |
| Stone | 5,688 | 3% | Metals | 7,872 | 2% |
| Total percentage covered | | 75% | Total percentage covered | | 84% |

*Sources:* see table 25.

manner. Zamagni shows that the flows of trade were insufficiently large for such a form of exploitation.[50] This may be true, but it does seem worthwhile examining the incomplementarity more closely.[51] The categories the railway companies used to classify goods, or for that matter the categories used in international trade statistics, are far too general to allow for the subtle differences in quality and price that foster trade flows. Although both the north and south of Italy produce olive oil, wine and a variety of fruits and vegetables, the differences in quality and harvest times make trade in agricultural commodities possible, then as much as now. Since many fruits matured months earlier in the south than in the north, where prices were still high, the railways provided a means of transporting them, thus providing a great commercial opportunity.

Despite the rather encouraging figures for north–south traffic mentioned in table 25, railway traffic between northern and southern Italy could have been much greater if a unified goods rate had been created, but the Italian state failed to force the companies to reach an agreement on this matter. This was all the more damaging because of the predominance of coastal shipping in north–south transport. The failure of railway companies to cooperate created delays in north–south traffic, as goods had to be reclassified at the transit stations of Bologna, Pisa and Florence.[52] In 1872, the Upper Italy Railway Company, and soon afterwards the Meridionali and Romane Railway Companies had in fact introduced a differential rate system giving discounts for goods travelling over long distances on their own networks.[53] The Meridionali, however, refused to apply the internationally agreed low rates between the Upper Italy Railway Company and the French Paris-Lyon-Méditerranée Company and the Austrian Südbahn Railway Company, thus creating a kind of export barrier for articles from the south.[54] As long as the Meridionali Railway Company opposed the application of differential rates for through traffic of cereals, wine and fruit, these goods, which could very well come from southern Italy, would continue to be transported from Hungary to France.[55] Although the Meridionali Railway Company is frequently cited as a financial success story, its way of operating its railway network shows a rather conservative and short-

---

[50] Vera Zamagni, 'Le radici agricole del dualismo italiano', NRS 22 (1975), p. 97.
[51] These statistics were not used by Vera Zamagni; see Zamagni, 'Ferrovie e integrazione', pp. 1638, 1643; Luzzatto, L'economia italiana, pp. 32, 186.
[52] Atti Commissione Baccarini, part 2, vol. I, p. 571.
[53] Ibid., part 2, vol. II, p. 831.
[54] Ibid., part 3, pp. 823, 854.       [55] Ibid., part 2, vol. II, p. 834.

sighted attitude.[56] Despite its low rates which stimulated local traffic, the refusal of its management to implement differential or international rates seriously limited export possibilities for southern producers. It should also be remembered that being a more 'Italian' company, it was showered with privileges and special subsidies. It can be seen, however, that the amount of north–south traffic was not small compared to the traffic flows between northern Italy and neighbouring countries, and in the 1870s railway traffic flows from southern Italy were already comparable with those to and from Venice and France and only slightly lower than those to and from Austria.

A closer examination of the traffic flow between Venetia and Lombardy also sheds some light on the role of railways in the integration of the Italian economy. The effect of the removal of the border between these regions is commented upon in the *Osservazioni generali* included in the Upper Italy Railway Company's traffic statistics for the year 1867.[57] With regard to passenger traffic, no significant increase is noted after the disappearance of the international border between Lombardy and Venetia and probably the cholera epidemic in Venetia was main cause of this. Transport in the *grande velocità* category, however, increased by about 30 per cent, compared to the levels before the war in 1866. The main contribution to this increase was the extension of the special rate for foodstuffs to the Venetian network. In the *piccola velocità* category, total traffic increased by around 50 per cent to 323,000 tonnes. The report concludes that the elimination of political and customs barriers between Lombardy and Venetia greatly contributed to this increase.[58]

If this increase in *piccola velocità* traffic is compared to traffic flows with Austria, it can be seen that, compared with Peri (65,000 tonnes) or Cormons (90,000) in the same year this was indeed considerable. Even if it is taken in consideration that traffic with Austria increased in the following years, the flows between Lombardy and Venetia in 1867 were still more important for Venetia than those with Austria. In 1870, transit traffic at Cormons increased to *circa* 150,000 tonnes, mainly through imports of wood and combustibles, and transit traffic at Peri amounted to about 156,000 tonnes, through exports of combustibles and cereals and the import of wood. As far as the connection of Venetia with Italy to the south is concerned, in 1867 the Padua–Pontelagoscuro line (crossing the river Po) carried a total of only

[56] Capodaglio, *Storia di un investimento*, pp. 67–71.
[57] It is unfortunate that for later years these *Osservazioni generali* were not included with the traffic statistics.
[58] Upper Italy Railway Company, *Osservazioni*, p. 31.

60,000 tonnes of transit traffic and in 1870 around 150,000 tonnes. It must be concluded that the removal of customs barriers between Lombardy and Venetia in 1867 created the most important flow of railway traffic for Venetia, followed by the traffic with Austria, and last with the rest of Italy to the south. It can be assumed that commercial flows between Venetia and the neighbouring provinces were distributed in roughly the same proportions, thus showing the economic dependency of Venetia upon Lombardy. From the moment of Venetia's integration, therefore, its railway connection with Lombardy played a most important role in its commercial relations.

## VII THE OPENNESS OF THE NORTHERN ITALIAN RAILWAY NETWORK

A calculation of the overall openness of the northern Italian railway network in 1884, when the Gothard line to Switzerland was opened, creates a comprehensive framework for assessing traffic on international lines, the importance of ports and the connection between north and south. A comparison of the openness of the railway network to the openness of the whole of the Italian economy gives a crude indication whether railways can be said to have played a leading role in integrating the Italian economy into the greater European economy.[59] In order to make an overall assessment of the physical volume of cross-border traffic developing on the Italian network, the total amount of traffic going in and out of the network needs to be compared with the total internal traffic. Unfortunately, railway traffic data for the major ports (Venice, Genoa and Savona) do not indicate which goods going in and out of the railway station were consumed directly in the city, since the traffic of the port and of the city are presented together.[60] Neither is it known how many of these goods originated from Italian ports, rather than foreign ones. In 1911, around 30 per cent of total shipping in all Italian ports was domestic and it was probably somewhat higher in the 1880s. With regard to direct consumption in the port city, it seems safe to assume that this was between 0 per cent and 25 per cent. A reasonable assumption in calculating a lower bound estimate of traffic between the ports and

[59] The openness of an economy is the value of all exports plus the value of imports over total GDP. Since for GDP only a rough estimate is available, the openness can only be determined by approximation too.

[60] Goods travelling at *grande velocità* rates and cattle are omitted from these calculations.

their hinterlands would be that at least 50 per cent of total railway traffic in the ports came from abroad and was directed to destinations further inland.

At transit stations, traffic statistics reflect the actual flow in and out of the network. At all other stations only arrivals and departures are indicated, so the destination or origin of the goods is not registered.[61] The figures for total internal traffic over-represent local traffic, which is caused by double-counting the arrivals and departures. When, for instance, one tonne of wood travelled between two neighbouring stations, it was registered as a departure at the first station and an arrival at the second. In the total traffic figures in tonnes this effect is noticeable, whereas in the output in TK it is not. Total internal traffic is the sum of all arrivals and departures at all stations minus the transit stations and the ports.

It was found that imports and exports by rail together accounted for 13.8 per cent of total internal traffic in 1867 and around 17.5 per cent in 1884. Considering that it is an average for all lines, it can be seen that for the major lines the openness was higher.[62]

One would also want to compare output data, that is, compare TKs of in- and out-flowing traffic with total internal traffic. For total internal traffic there would not be a big difference, as TK value is obtained by multiplying all arrivals and departures with the average distance travelled. This distance factor for all goods and all goods traffic *piccola velocità* increased by only 13 per cent between 1867 and 1884.[63] Without making an assumption about the average distance a tonne of transit goods was transported, an output estimate cannot be produced. Although these kinds of assumptions have been made in the Swiss case, the northern Italian network seems to be too large and

---

[61] The ports in northern Italy are those of Genoa, Savona and Venice. The border stations are the transit stations of Modane and Ventimiglia to France, Chiasso and Luvino to Switzerland, and Peri, Pontebba and Cormons to Austria. Transit stations to southern Italy are Bologna, Pisa and Florence.

[62] The values for the in- and out-going traffic flows were obtained in the following way. For southern Italy, the incoming traffic at the transit stations of Bologna, Pisa, Florence and Pistoia were added. For Florence and Pistoia this was done only for the years that these stations functioned as transit stations. For Austria, incoming traffic at the stations of Peri, Pontebba and Cormons was added, for France traffic at Modane and Ventimiglia was added, and for Switzerland transit traffic in Chiasso and Luvino was taken. For the ports, half of the traffic for all stations in Genoa, Savona and Venice was taken, which resulted in a value for the physical openness of the northern Italian railway network on the basis of counting 50 per cent of port traffic.

[63] For all goods it grew from 111.6 km in 1867 to 126.4 km in 1884.

Table 28. *The openness of the northern Italian railway network (%)*

|  | Imports | | | | |
|---|---|---|---|---|---|
|  | 1867 | 1870 | 1875 | 1880 | 1884 |
| Cross-border | 1.8 | 6.3 | 7.0 | 5.4 | 5.9 |
| Half of the ports' traffic | 8.1 | 8.5 | 6.6 | 8.6 | 7.4 |
| Total | 9.9 | 14.8 | 13.6 | 14.1 | 13.3 |
|  | Exports | | | | |
| Cross-border | 1.5 | 2.4 | 2.8 | 3.3 | 3.1 |
| Half of the ports' traffic | 2.4 | 2.4 | 1.8 | 1.3 | 1.1 |
| Total | 3.9 | 4.8 | 4.6 | 4.6 | 4.2 |
|  | Total | | | | |
| Cross-border | 3.3 | 8.7 | 9.9 | 8.7 | 9.0 |
| Half of the ports' traffic | 10.5 | 10.9 | 8.3 | 10.0 | 8.5 |
| Total | 13.8 | 19.6 | 18.2 | 18.7 | 17.5 |

*Sources:* see table 25.

complex to do the same.[64] An improvement to the methodology for calculating the openness of the railway network would be to calculate a value for the traffic flows. Results prove to be rather similar, however, since a number of bulk goods with rather comparable prices dominated internal railway traffic.[65]

First, the lower bound estimate of the physical openness of the railway network of 17.5 per cent in 1884 is in the same order of magnitude as the openness of the economy of almost 17 per cent in 1890.[66] When half of the port traffic is included, therefore, the railway network had a slightly greater openness than the Italian economy as a whole. This is hardly a reason to suppose that the railways played a leading role in opening up the economy.

When imports and exports, ports and cross-border traffic are considered separately, several interesting tendencies can be observed (see table 28). First, the imbalance between imports and exports can be

[64] Paul Bairoch, 'Les spécificités des chemins de fer suisses des origines à nos jours', *RSH* 39 (1989), pp. 35–57.

[65] In the calculation of physical openness the price of all goods is disregarded or set at a value of 1; see Schram, 'The Impact of Railways', pp. 292–4.

[66] Albert Carreras (ed.) *Estadísticas históricas de España. Siglos XIX y XX* (Madrid, 1989), p. 331.

clearly seen. The import function of the network is therefore apparent throughout the period, and is likely to have increased considerably. For 1911, Fenoaltea gives an import share openness of the railway network of 48 per cent, which is substantially higher than the figure for 1884.[67]

Second, the increase in both import and export shares came about mainly because of the increase in cross-border traffic, not traffic through of the ports. Imports by rail on cross-border railway lines increased from around 1.8 per cent of total internal traffic to around 5.9 per cent in 1884. Between 1875 and 1884 they dropped from 7 per cent to 5.9 per cent, reflecting the loss of traffic with France. The opening of the connection with Switzerland in 1883 promised to compensate for this loss in the following period, but no data are available after 1884. Apparently, the imports by rail through border stations started to play a more important role, and in 1884 their share was comparable to imports through the ports. With regard to the ports, even if it is assumed that all goods from the ports benefited the hinterland and that ports had only a commercial function and not an urban or industrial function, the relative importance of ports as feeders into the railway network declined slightly from 1867 to 1884 due to the relative increase of internal traffic.

As can be seen in table 26 the most important source of incoming traffic was Genoa, and the most important out-going traffic was to southern Italy. Imports and exports to Austria also continued to play an important role, but the composition of imports was mainly cheap wood from Tyrol. Traffic to and from Switzerland occupied a significant role from the beginning and the industrial nature of imports is noteworthy.

This short investigation is, of course, far from conclusive, but it has shown the relative importance of the ports and the Swiss, French, Austro-Hungarian and southern Italian railway links. The pre-eminent role of the port of Genoa is again confirmed by the data. From the beginning, the level of openness of the Italian railway network is in the same order of magnitude as that of the whole of the economy, but the interpretation of this fact is somewhat problematic. The importance of the railway links with Switzerland from the first years of operation is remarkable, both with regard to the quantity as well as the quality of goods. At this point not much can be said about the level of physical openness of the northern Italian railway network compared to other railway networks, since these studies have not yet been carried out.

[67] Fenoaltea, 'Italy', pp. 77, 82.

Table 29. *Composition of exports and imports by rail with Austria in 1884 (tonnes)*

| Exports | | | Imports | | |
|---|---|---|---|---|---|
| All goods | 103,941 | 100% | All goods | 411,321 | 100% |
| Cereals | 26,260 | 25% | Wood | 226,749 | 55% |
| Fruit | 14,836 | 14% | Coal | 62,894 | 15% |
| Textile fibres | 12,384 | 12% | Colonials | 30,027 | 7% |
| Marble | 7,526 | 7% | Cereals | 17,365 | 4% |
| Food | 7,020 | 7% | Drinks | 17,120 | 4% |
| Total percentage covered | | 65% | Total percentage covered | | 86% |

*Sources:* see table 25.

Table 30. *Composition of exports and imports by rail with France in 1884 (tonnes)*

| Exports | | | Imports | | |
|---|---|---|---|---|---|
| All goods | 124,321 | 100% | All goods | 134,212 | 100% |
| Drinks | 35,166 | 28% | Coal | 45,579 | 34% |
| Cereals | 25,060 | 20% | Cereals | 37,174 | 28% |
| Marble | 11,164 | 9% | Metal | 17,447 | 13% |
| Food | 8,764 | 7% | Minerals | 14,449 | 11% |
| Fruit | 7,924 | 6% | Glass | 12,750 | 9% |
| Total percentage covered | | 71% | Total percentage covered | | 95% |

*Sources:* see table 25.

Table 31. *Composition of exports and imports by rail with Switzerland in 1884 (tonnes)*

| Exports | | | Imports | | |
|---|---|---|---|---|---|
| All goods | 171,355 | 100% | All goods | 142,235 | 100% |
| Cereals | 55,926 | 33% | Metal | 44,539 | 31% |
| Textile fibres | 24,657 | 14% | Ore | 31,558 | 22% |
| Food | 16,435 | 10% | Coal | 27,740 | 20% |
| Drinks | 13,389 | 8% | Machines | 13,190 | 9% |
| Fruit | 7,334 | 4% | Textiles | 9,043 | 6% |
| Total percentage covered | | 69% | Total percentage covered | | 89% |

*Sources:* see table 25.

## VIII RAILWAYS AND TRADITIONAL INLAND TRANSPORT IN NORTHERN ITALY

Railway traffic is a function of the shape and growth of the railway network itself, but also of the other infrastructural facilities. The better the feeder network of roads, waterways and ports, the greater the potential for railway traffic. It has been supposed, for instance, that in the early 1860s the absence of adequate roads in southern Italy was the cause of the slow growth of railway goods traffic. One-sided government investment in railways was at the expense of an adequate road system.[68] Compared to the later periods of the 1870s and 1880s few modes of transport existed. The motor car had not yet been invented and in comparison with the 1890s the role of tramway or street-car networks for goods as well as passenger transport was negligible. Towards the end of the century extensive tramway networks around major cities like Milan and Turin, and also in provincial capitals like Verona and Padua, were carrying a substantial amount of traffic.

If the density of the road network in 1885 is compared to that of the railways, it must be asked to what degree road transport was competing with the railways. It is likely that road traffic benefited rather than harmed the growth of railway traffic. Similarly, different assumptions about the effects of railway operation for water transport can be made. On the one hand it can be assumed that in provinces which made much use of water transportation such as, for instance, Venice's hinterland, railway traffic grew more slowly. For some areas where traditional means of transport were well developed the share of goods transported by rail may have been smaller. On the other hand, local transport of goods and passengers to and from railway stations with other carriers could have benefited the growth of railway traffic.

An examination of transport rates shows the relative strengths and weakness of water and rail transport. Table 32 shows that water transport from Venice over the Po and the Mincio was cheaper than rail transport to Pavia and Pontelagoscuro. For example, to transport rice for export from Mantua to the port of Chioggia, around 40 km south of Venice, the price by boat was 1.6 lire per quintal (100 km), whereas by rail it cost 3.3 lire. Coal travelled at 1.3 lire per quintal, which was also considerably below the railway rate. The province of Ferrara also

[68] Corbino, *Annali*, p. 179.

Table 32. *Railway and water transport rates from*
*Venice (lire per tonne)*

| To | By boat | By rail |
|---|---|---|
| Padua | 3.5 | 3.6 |
| Vicenza | 6.5 | 5.7 |
| Verona | 10.0 | 8.1 |
| Pontelagoscuro | 6.0 | 8.7 |
| Pavia | 14.5 | 22.3 |
| Milan | 20.0 | 19.7 |

*Sources:* Upper Italy Railway Company, *Osservazioni*
*Generali.*

took advantage of river trade.[69] The lines in Friuli had to suffer
competition from transport on the river Tagliamento. According to
one source, the river Sile, connecting Treviso with the sea, transported
100,000 tonnes per year, which is comparable to a middle-sized
railway line.[70] The invisible factor of technological progress on the
railways, which improved the ease, quality and speed relative to traditional transport, was probably the most important force behind the
increasing share taken by rail transport. Traditional transport could
equally well have damaged or stimulated railway transport. It is even
possible that the seemingly advantageous position of rail transport for
those provinces which had the greatest number of stations and had
built their lines earliest was offset by the inadequacy of, for example,
the inland water transport network.

As regards passenger transport by road, the risks of under-estimating
total transport flows for the 1870s in Italy by only considering railway
transport are smaller than for goods traffic, since a majority of goods
probably went by rail. In the 1850s, however, the quality of passenger
transportation offered by trains and coaches was not so dissimilar.
Heinzel describes the situation regarding passenger traffic in northern
Italy in 1855, just before the railway age.[71] On the maps accompa-
nying the book, one can see that telegraph lines preceded railway
links. Thus in 1855 between Milan and Venice a telegraph line was

[69] Upper Italy Railway Company, *Osservazioni*, p. 108.
[70] Alberto Errera, *L'Italia industriale. Studi con particolare riguardo all'Adriatico superiore*
(Venice, 1873), p. 23.
[71] Ferdinand Heinzel, *Die Eisenbahnen und Dampfschifffahrten nebst des angehörtigen Post-*
*Coursen in Oesterreich, Deutschland, Italien und den angrenzenden Ländern* (Vienna,
1856).

already functioning, but the railway line had not yet been completed. In the 1850s most coach connections had a frequency of only one coach per day. Travelling time from Venice to Milan (265 km) was 13 hours in 1855 with an average speed of 20 km/hour. Comparing this with the train in 1855, we find a frequency of two trains a day and a journey time of 12 hours 35 minutes with a slightly higher average speed of 21 km/hour. In 1861, when there was a direct line from Milan to Venice, it took a train 10 hours 16 minutes, with an average speed of 25 km/hour. In 1880, we find that express trains travelled with an effective average speed of 38–45 km/hour and in 1889 the average speed was 48 km/hour. During the whole period under study, however, the frequency of passenger trains between Milan and Venice did not increase and remained two per day.[72]

Despite the rather small differences in the quality of passenger transport between rail and coach transport, the disappearance of coach services whenever railway lines were opened clearly shows the dominance of the railways. The history of the coach company Franchetti demonstrates that whenever new railway lines came into operation in northern Italy, the company suspended regular services and began to provide complementary services on routes where railways were not yet offering regular services. In 1852, the fare from Verona to Venice was 11.25 lire second class and 6.5 lire third class, whereas Franchetti charged 16 lire in 1846 and was unable to lower its rate by much.[73] Although in general the company could not compete with the railways, in the absence of railways on particular routes it continued its services. The coach service from Mantua to Modena, Cremona, Brescia and Cremona–Piacenza, for instance, continued to operate until the 1860s in the absence of a rail connection. Savarè's study makes it clear that these kinds of companies were unable to compete with railways and were therefore only able to fulfil a complementary role.

From this it should, however, not be concluded that the railways offered passenger services comparable to the standards of today. From a tourist guide of the 1880s, it can be seen that for the European standards of the time, the quality and frequency of passenger services to Venice, Florence and Rome – then as now the major destination for foreign tourists – were below average.[74] In the following years, this

[72] Ministero di Lavori Pubblici, *Risposte*, p. 148; Foxwell and Farrer, *Express Trains*, p. 95.
[73] Carla Savarè, 'Un servizio privato di trasporto su diligenza in Lombardia. L'impresa Franchetti', *SL* 52 (1990), p. 67.
[74] Foxwell and Farrer, *Express Trains*, p. 158.

situation was supposedly corrected through cooperation between the administrations of the Mediterranean (on the western side of Italy) and the Adriatic Railway Company (on the eastern side).[75]

## IX RAILWAYS AND COASTAL SHIPPING

According to Gino Luzzatto, the effect of the development of shipping on Italian trade and commerce was even greater than the effect of Italy's inclusion in the European railway network. The increasing use of steel ships and the introduction of steam engines with helical propellers made sea transport more reliable. The success of steam shipping, moreover, meant a substantial decrease in transport costs, which combined with a general decrease in price levels.[76] The impact of coastal shipping on the northern Italian railway network must be considered smaller than for the rest of Italy, as there were relatively fewer kilometres of coastline. The railway lines along the Ligurian coast, which opened in 1874, were in competition with shipping between Savona, Genoa, La Spezia and Leghorn. On the Adriatic, there was coastal shipping between Ferrara, Chioggia and Venice.

A rough estimate of output in TKs for coastal shipping for the whole of Italy can be made and compared to the output of the railways in 1881. The only justification for making such an estimate is that in the discussion on the impact of railways it has often been said that in Italy coastal shipping played a particularly important role.[77] As was pointed out in an article by John Armstrong (1987),[78] who undertook the first comparison of this kind for Great Britain in 1910, to give a definitive evaluation of the importance of coastal shipping one would need to know more about the composition of the merchandise and the average length travelled for minerals as compared to other goods.

Using the data in the *Movimento della Navigazione* for coastal shipping from 1881 and an estimate for the carrying coefficient of ships, the tonnage of goods departing from the six major Italian ports (Genoa, Leghorn, Messina, Naples, Palermo, and Venice) can be estimated. The load factor or the effective carrying coefficient

---

[75] Older transport and communication technologies were not always in competition with the newer ones. An interesting case of the assimilation of traditional technology by the railway company was the continued use of pigeons for mail purposes. It is remarkable that in 1870, for instance, as much of the Upper Italy Railway Company's revenue came from the transport of pigeons as it did from telegraphy.

[76] Luzzatto, *L'economia italiana*, p. 196.      [77] Fenoaltea, 'Italy', p. 93.

[78] John Armstrong, 'The Role of Coastal Shipping in UK Transport. An Estimate of Comparative Traffic Movements in 1910', *JTH* 8 (1987), pp. 164–8.

between registered tonnes[79] and tonnes carried was assumed to be on average around 2, a value lower than Armstrong's figure of 2.5 for British ships around 1850. Maywald gives a factor for the maximum carrying capacity for ships around 1850 of 1.8 for wooden ships, 2.2 for iron and 2.7 for steel ships.[80] The ships were, however, never filled to capacity so these factors were deflated by Armstrong using the port bills of entry. It was therefore decided to take a carrying coefficient of 2 since it had to be lower than Armstrong's figure for Great Britain in 1910 and more in agreement with what can be expected from Maywald's maximum carrying capacity.

Next, an approximation was made as to the average distance travelled for a tonne of goods on a coastal ship. This is different depending on the factor endowments, the economic structure and the geographical characteristics for each country. For Great Britain it was found that around 1910 the average distance travelled by a tonne of goods on a coaster was between five and seven times that of the railways. For Italy the average distance was probably higher than for the railways too (123 km), but a precise estimate could only be made after examination of the records of individual ports. By multiplying the tonnage carried and the average distance travelled an output estimate can be obtained.

If an effective carrying coefficient of 2 and an average distance of 100 km is taken, total output in TKs for coastal shipping in Italy would be around 869 million TKs, which is certainly too low. Compared to the figure for all Italian railways in 1880 of 1,200 million TKs, this would be 72 per cent of the total railway output. The results for the unlikely average distance of 100 km is given to obtain a first approximation. If a more probably average distance of 400 km is taken, coastal shipping output increases to 3,476 million TKs or 2.9 times railway goods output, which is a more believable figure for the minimum output of coastal shipping in 1881.

It is not easy to compare this last figure with Armstrong's contention that for Great Britain in 1910 the output for coastal shipping was more than 1.5 times higher than that of railways. In the case of Great Britain, however, the transport of coal and coke, which for Italy was international shipping, was responsible for the difference between railways and coastal shipping. If the transport of coal and coke is eliminated, rail and coastal shipping would be roughly equal. When one takes into account, however, that because of the lower level of

---

[79] One registered tonne for a ship corresponds to 100 cubic feet, which is 2.83 m2.

[80] K. Maywald, 'The Construction Costs and the Value of the British Merchant Fleet, 1850–1938', *SJPE* (1956), pp. 46–52.

technology, the role of railways in Italy in 1880 was less important than in Great Britain in 1910, the figure for Italian coastal shipping output of 2.9 times total railway output seems an acceptable first estimate. This comparison with Great Britain shows that there is some reason to state that coastal shipping for Italy was particularly important. The purpose of the estimate made here is to determine a reasonable lower bound. The result shows that coastal shipping continued to transport a large quantity of merchandise compared with railways. These figures should not be taken too seriously, however, as no upper bound can be determined without more data on coastal shipping. Hopefully, more research will provide a better estimate for the true output of Italian coastal shipping.

## X  THE ECONOMIC EFFECTS OF RAILWAYS

There is no consensus about an adequate theoretical model to measure the economic effects of a dramatic improvement in the transport network such as the railways. The assessment of these effects is, moreover, complicated by the fact that the opening of railway lines was usually preceded by the opening of a telegraph connection, which in itself had a great economic impact, for instance by improving the communication of prices between markets.

However, nobody would seriously believe that the economic effects of a railway network were negligible. Not only were transaction costs in the economy reduced by lowering transport rates, but the technological superiority of the railways over all existing means of transport implied a great improvement in the regularity, security and speed of transport.[81] When analysing the economic effects of railways, it has proved fruitful for economic historians to borrow the concepts of backward and forward linkages from Albert Hirschman's work in development economics. Although Hirschman himself never provided a formal model for his theories, or unequivocal definitions of these concepts, backward linkages can be interpreted as those forces which enable a supplying or upstream industry to be established at minimum economic scale. Forward linkages can be seen as the ability of an industry to reduce the costs of potential downstream users of its products or services and thus create a profitable new industry.[82]

With regard to the backward linkages of railway construction in Italy, during the first decades all locomotives, wagons and rails were

---

[81] K. J. Button, *Transport Economics* (Aldershot, 1986).
[82] Krugman, *Geography and Trade,* pp. 23–4.

imported from other countries. Gerschenkron's theory that in Italy the effects of railway construction on national industries were too little and too late seems to be confirmed by recent studies. After protectionism increased in 1888, production became more costly, since many steel products for the manufacture of railway materials had to be imported and were subject to import duties. Italian locomotives were therefore more than 10 per cent more expensive and the diminishing internal demand was not compensated for by orders from outside. The industry producing railway material therefore did not have the leading role it did in Germany or France.[83] Only labour, wood and some building materials were supplied locally. Railway companies brought know-how from abroad and often preferred a vertically integrated structure above relying on local supplies. The Upper Italy Railway Company, for example, built of few mortar factories in the Po valley to provide building material. Despite the 1885 Railway Act, which stipulated that preference should be given to all railway materials made in Italy if it was less than 5 per cent more expensive, and despite the efforts of the Italian government, only at the beginning of the twentieth century was a national locomotive and rail industry established. State interference could thus do nothing about the fact that most of the supply industries for the Italian railway sector were located beyond its borders.[84]

The observation that the railways did not have strong backward linkages in nineteenth-century Italy, should, however, not be taken as meaning that the railways had only insignificant effects on Italian industry. First of all, the considerable reduction in transport costs created many new possibilities for new industries and stimulated established ones. Second, Hirschman's main point in his *Strategy of Economic Development* (1958) was to draw attention to unbalanced growth or the occurrence of a particular dynamic or sequence in the periphery of the world market which did not follow the patterns of the first industrializers. In this perspective, the weakness of backward linkages in the Italian railway sector can be interpreted as an imbalance typical of the periphery.

Apart from the backward and forward linkages, railway construction meant an income effect in the economy, although the extent of this cannot easily be determined since the archives are practically silent on the number of men and women who built the railways and their wages. On a European scale it has been estimated that in the 1860s

[83] Merger, 'L'industrie italienne de locomotives', pp. 346–61.
[84] Merger, 'Chemins de fer et croissance économique', pp. 136–8; Merger, 'Les chemins de fer italiens', pp. 128–30.

around 2 million people were employed as construction workers on the railways.[85] Occasionally, it is mentioned that the presence of a railway construction site caused seasonal migration within Italy. Only for later periods, when trade unions were operating, is information on salaries, working hours and accidents available.[86]

Another question is how much the construction and the subsequent operation of railways contributed to the economic integration of Italy. Neo-classical economic thinking suggests that political unification would be followed by convergence of regional income levels.[87] The role of railways and the banking system in facilitating flows of capital and labour would play a crucial role in this process. Although at the smaller, provincial level some evidence for this effect can be found, there is no firm evidence for the nineteenth century, and twentieth-century evidence suggests divergence rather than convergence.[88]

Nonetheless, we are not left completely in the dark on the economic effects of railways. First of all, market extension as distinct from market integration certainly took place. Railways contributed to the extension of local markets within Italy and also created new export opportunities for, for example, Italian fruits and vegetables in northern Europe. Nonetheless, this does not necessarily mean that the northern European and Italian markets became integrated. Second, it is necessary to differentiate between economic integration between regions within Italy and between Italy and the neighbouring countries. The prerequisites for greater internal integration were created in the 1860s when the regional railway networks were linked. The conditions for greater European integration were present a few decades later in the 1880s, when most cross-border lines were operational. At that time, however, greater protectionism compensated for better international transport. Third, economic integration can be defined broadly or restricted to the integration of a market for a certain good.[89] Integration in the wider sense can be measured by the size of flows of capital, labour or goods between markets. Others have studied labour specialization or income levels.[90] Econometricians generally prefer the

[85] Luzzatto, *L'economia italiana*, p. 10.

[86] Giuntini, *I giganti della montagna*, pp. 250–5.

[87] In the geographic literature the opposite is sometimes maintained, without specifying economic causes; see, for instance, Brian Berry, *Economic Geography* (London, 1987).

[88] Schram, 'The Impact of Railways', pp. 296–8.

[89] Jacob Metzer, 'Railroad Development and Market Integration. The Case of Tsarist Russia', *JEH* 34 (1974), pp. 529–50.

[90] Richard Griffiths, 'The Creation of a Dutch National Economy', *TG* 95 (1982), pp. 514–15; Williamson, 'Regional Inequality', pp. 4–5.

narrower approach and measure an increase in the degree of parallelism between prices for certain goods at different locations.[91] In sum, a convergence of regional income levels can be regarded as the ultimate measure of economic integration. The occurrence of this cannot be adequately documented for nineteenth-century Italy, and the same holds true for labour specialization. What can be affirmed, however, is that railways contributed to economic integration in the wider sense, stimulating freer flows of goods and labour, and extending the market for many goods.

Another effect of the operation of railways is on the location of industries.[92] The railway allowed industries to move closer to markets and further away from their energy sources, mainly wood or water power. Moreover, industries were less dependent on water or road communications. In this context, Fenoaltea has noted correctly that the infrastructure that mattered most for Italy's industrialization in Piedmont and Lombardy was that constructed by the Piedmontese state in the 1850s.[93] The dense Piedmontese railway network which provided connections to the port of Genoa was a prerequisite for the industrial development of the northern Italian regions of Piedmont and Lombardy. Thus railways have a panoply of economic effects and any measurement is bound to be partial.

## XI CONCLUSIONS

Railway rates in Italy were to a great extent fixed by the government. This meant that the railways did not have the means to compete aggressively with traditional means of transport. Moreover, it limited the possibility of creating traffic in poorer provinces by lowering the rate in relation to income levels.

An examination of international railway traffic shows that the effects of the opening of several transalpine lines were smaller than has been thought. The Brenner and Tarvis lines in particular were relatively under-utilized because of the railway policies of the Austrian Südbahn Railway Company. In order to attract railway traffic to the ports of Venice or Genoa from southern Germany or northern Europe, the rates between the ports and the border would have to have been reduced to an unacceptable level, since the total distance travelled by these goods on the Italian railway network was too low.

[91] Marc Chevet and Pascal St Amour, 'Market Integration in France's Wheat Sector in the Nineteenth Century', *First European Analytical Economic History Conference,* Copenhagen, July 1991.
[92] Krugman, *Geography and Trade,* pp. 95–8.       [93] Fenoaltea, 'Italy', p. 96.

A detailed analysis of railway traffic to and from the ports shows that the highest traffic density in northern Italy was reached on the Genoa–Turin line. This confirms Fenoaltea's hypothesis that the Piedmontese network was a prerequisite for Italian industrialization. The Venice–Milan line, in comparison, shows a much lower density. The port of Venice suffered only slightly from the loss of Austrian traffic and instead seems to have taken advantage of the opportunities for more international and national trade after its incorporation into Italy. The port and railway statistics show that the role of traditional transport remained important for Venice.

Railway traffic between northern and southern Italy reached considerable proportions. In particular the flow of 'imports' of agricultural products from southern Italy, in those months when they were still out of season in the north is remarkable. Little of this produce was re-exported. With regard to flows between regions very few sources are available. The traffic flow between Lombardy and Venetia, for instance, was relatively large in 1867, which shows that Venetia's railways were more directly linked to Lombardy than to any other neighbouring province or country.

The total openness of the northern Italian railway network in the 1880s is comparable to the overall openness of the economy and for all years imports always outnumber exports. These data confirm Fenoaltea's remark about the role of railways in facilitating imports, but despite the opening of cross-border railway connections it cannot be concluded that railways played a leading role. With regard to the composition of goods, the high quality of merchandise transported to and from Switzerland and France are noteworthy in relation to traffic with Austria. Although international overland traffic increased, the role of ports remained dominant. An estimate of the output of coastal shipping also shows that this mode of transport remained particularly important for Italy.

# CHAPTER 5

# CONCLUSIONS

Italy's railways have enjoyed a considerable amount of attention from historians, since it was thought that there was a strong relationship between railway construction and the political and economic unification of Italy. Optimistically, most liberal historians have heralded the railways as the very symbols of Italian unity and economic progress. Several Marxist historians, more critically, have seen the building of the railways as a conspiracy on the part of the northern Italian bourgeoisie to use national tax revenues to improve infrastructure exclusively in the north. In its crude form there is little empirical evidence for this last hypothesis, since even Marxists or other defenders of the thesis that the south was exploited like a colony by the north, have had to admit that the initial construction of the railways in the north was mainly financed by private companies and that the state, particularly after 1885, favoured the south over the north with regard to the provision of infrastructure. Moreover, inter-regional trade remained at a relatively low level, which implies that the north developed using its own strengths, rather than at the expense of the south.

Also, the optimistic vision of the role of Italian railways does not easily accord with all the facts. When the statistics for construction and traffic are put in a European perspective, the performance of Italian railways is not impressive. In 1900, there were only 508 m of track for every 1,000 inhabitants in comparison with 713 m for Spain, 746 m for Austria-Hungary, 908 m for France, 922 m for Germany and 933 m for Great Britain. Traffic density figures for 1900 are equally discouraging; for every kilometre of track only 0.30 TU was produced, which is less than a third of that for Germany and less than half of that for Austria-Hungary or France. Only Spain with 0.24 TU/km of track had a lower traffic density. The very modest performance of the Italian railway sector during the nineteenth century does not provide a

solid basis for the hypothesis that railways played a particularly important role in the country's development.

The disappointing performance of the Italian railways can be
blamed, first, on the very process of political unification, second on
the misguided policies of the Italian state, and third on the under-
development of the economy, particularly in the south. To begin
with, the phenomena which accompanied Italy's political unification,
such as the changes in international borders, the wars and ensuing
financial crises, and the erratic policy changes of the first governments,
all demanded a great capacity to adapt on the part of the railway companies. After the secession of Savoy to France in 1860, for instance, the
Victor Emmanuel Railway Company preferred to exchange its
railway building concessions in Savoy for those in the south. The
Romane Railway Company, which had enjoyed favourable treatment
from the Papal government, was in continuous conflict with the
Italian state and finally sold its network in 1873. Nevertheless, the
newly born Italian state legally recognized all the agreements between
railway companies and its predecessor states, and it was not until the
Railway Act of 1865 that several smaller companies were assimilated
into bigger conglomerates. In 1865, the Piedmontese State Railways,
which had become Italian state property, were sold to the Upper Italy
Railway Company, thus transferring control over the northern Italian
railway network to one foreign company. This was a policy error of
strategic proportions, awarding the richer north with one more significant advantage in its development. This company was indeed very
successful in developing traffic, with its northern Italian network
accounting for more than half of the TUs for the whole of Italy.
Finally, the Upper Italy Railway Company, with its mainly French
capital, was repeatedly pushed by the Austrian government to separate
its Italian from its Austrian network. This pressure, combined with the
hostile attitude of the Italian state towards the company, provoked its
sale to Italy in 1875.

Together with the sale of the Piedmontese State Railways, the
acquisition of the Upper Italy Railway Company on the part of the
Italian state was one of the most dramatic moments in nineteenth-
century railway history. The first event apparently introduced a
private railway regime, but the second heralded a reversal of policy,
with the state directly owning and operating almost half of the national
network. Since this last event was accompanied by a change in the
parliamentary majority from right-wing to left-wing liberals, it is also a
milestone in Italy's parliamentary history.

Second, part of the explanation for the disappointing performance of Italian railways lies in the governments' railway policies. The precarious financial position of the Italian state meant that it could not continue to pay out the promised subsidies, and it increasingly began to see the railway companies as a source of revenue by creating several new taxes. Italian railway policy was curious indeed. On the one hand, the Italian state supposedly honoured all the obligations towards the railway companies undertaken by the pre-unification states. On the other hand, right-wing liberal governments took every measure possible to create a state railway system and declared war on foreign railway companies, in particular the Upper Italy Railway Company. However, when the left-wing liberals came to power in 1876, they did not know what to do with the state railways, to which they were, in principle, opposed. In despair, parliament instituted a Railway Enquiry Commission in 1878, which in 1881 declared itself in favour of a private railway system. Nevertheless, the 1885 Railway Act created a mixed system, with three companies which were heavily regulated by the state. The clumsy arrangements between the state and the companies with regard to the division of revenues led to a chronic under-investment in rolling stock and a lack of maintenance. Examples abound of misdirected subsidies and absurd arrangements on sharing operating revenues. Nonetheless, many branch lines were opened in the period 1885–90, even if at the same time the form of granting subsidies discouraged their use. When the companies failed to improve services towards the end of the nineteenth century, the government decided to nationalize the railways in 1905.

The contradictions between the ideologies of economic liberalism and nationalism fomented continuous debates among Italy's ruling class and even caused the fall of the right-wing liberal government of Marco Minghetti in 1876. Time and again political conflicts arose around themes such as whether state or private railways were preferable, or whether or not the inflow of foreign capital should be reduced. Then there were the inevitable local pressure groups which advocated the construction of a particular line for the benefit of local economies, to which politicians gave in all too often. Obviously, this created an insecure environment for the Italian railway companies, which needed to invest a considerable amount of capital in railway infrastructure and were thus exposed to all kinds of risks.

The 1885 Railway Act entrusted the network on the Italian peninsula to three companies which leased the state-owned track for a period of twenty years. Complicated agreements between the companies and the state were made to divide revenue and share responsibilities. From 1885 to about 1890 the construction of new lines progressed satisfactorily, but soon investment in new track and rolling stock decreased. The 1885 Act over-emphasized the necessity of building railway lines, while at the same time several provisions hampered an efficient use of the railway network and obstructed the development of traffic. The fact that the railway rates, for instance, were fixed by the government prevented the railway companies from competing effectively with traditional transport. Moreover, it meant that the rates could not be adapted to lower income levels in the south. The fruits of the extension of the network to the south could therefore not be reaped. Both the Railway Acts of 1865 and 1885 failed to create a viable private or mixed railway system. Under both regimes relations between the railway companies and the state remained tense, mainly because of the unclear provisions and the poor quality of railway legislation. The railway companies could not flourish in such an environment, and as a consequence most companies were plagued by debts and made heavy losses.

At the end of the century, a public outcry against the poor quality of services offered increased and, as a consequence, in 1905 the lease was not renewed and nationalization of the railways was decided upon. Nationalization was thus justified by the failure of regulation and the continuous need to turn to additional subsidies, and not by a coherent policy to nationalize key industries. After almost half a century of clumsy experiments it was too late to develop a more rational system of government regulation of the railways.

The political decision-making on railway issues was therefore essentially divisive and hardly produced anything positive. In the debates in parliament, the preoccupation of the parliamentarians with local issues, international financial interests, and details of existing regulation all came together in an inextricable knot. Without the 'railway question' parliament would have been able to devote more attention to useful things such as the building of roads and the improvement of ports, the setting up of education and health systems and aid to the poorer regions. Politically, therefore, the railway question contributed more to the division than to the unity of Italy.

The third reason for disappointing levels of average traffic density on the Italian railways can be found in the low levels of development. Industrialization occurred towards the end of the century almost exclusively in Liguria, Piedmont and Lombardy and it was as if the north developed as an independent small country. The southern economy, on the other hand, despite the efforts of the Italian state to provide basic infrastructure, remained too under-developed to react positively to these investments. With regard to infrastructure, the data on road length per 1,000 inhabitants in 1885, for example, do not show a clear north–south gradient, and several of the southern regions were among those with the highest road length per 1,000 inhabitants. Although the importance of roads and of an evenly distributed national road network was realized in the early 1860s and many state and provincial roads were created in the south, the investment in roads was secondary to that in railways. Moreover, although at the state and provincial levels road provision was adequate, for the whole of Italy road construction failed at the municipal level, which meant that there was no feeder network of sufficient quality for the national and provincial roads.

One of the few indicators of social and economic development that was more equally distributed after 1885 was the railways, which showed no clear north–south gradient (see table 11). Nevertheless, an examination of the regional distribution of the Italian railway network, compared to the German network, demonstrates that regional inequality was persistently greater in Italy, even when lesser weight is given to less populated regions. So, although the south was not under-endowed in railways, the overall regional differences in railway provision remained greater in Italy than those in Germany during the nineteenth century.

As regards the health of the population, a first exploration of the data shows the health of recruits born between 1843 and 1856 in the south to have been undermined by intestinal diseases related to poor water quality and low standards of hygiene, which in turn were caused by the many wetlands near the coast. Surprisingly, the percentage of recruits rejected because of sickliness and low weight was highest in central Italy and not in the south. Obviously, a sickly population cannot be as productive as a healthy one.

During the nineteenth century illiteracy rates in Italy remained among the highest compared to other countries for which such data are available, with only Spain showing higher rates. The illiteracy indicators show a clear north–south gradient and, what is worse, the greatest progress between 1871 and 1911 was made in those regions where illiteracy was lower from the start. It must, therefore, be considered a major error on the part of the Italian state to leave the financing of primary schooling to the municipalities, placing the poorer and more illiterate south in a clearly disadvantageous position. Needless to say, the south's inability to shake off this inheritance of ignorance severely limited its prospects for economic development.

With regard to the economic effects of railway construction, it must be noted that Alexander Gerschenkron's thesis that Italian industry was not able to supply the necessary inputs for railway construction has been confirmed by recent research. The two big waves of railway construction, one in the early 1860s and one in the late 1880s, came at a time when Italian industry had not yet developed sufficiently to provide the necessary materials for railway construction and consequently most material had to be imported and a high price had to be paid, with no benefit to Italian industry.

An analysis of traffic patterns during the first decades after unification confirms that one can be cautiously optimistic about the economic benefits of railways. With the introduction of railways a sort of reorientation of the transport network needed to take place, and for a long transitional period traditional means of transport co-existed with the railways. Aggressive competition from the railways with other modes of transport was not always possible, particularly after 1885 when railway rates were largely fixed by the government. In Italy, with its long coastline and a tradition of coastal shipping, traditional transport maintained a stronger position than in other countries. The railways, however, did play a modernizing role by creating export opportunities for Italian agriculture and industry and by opening up regions which previously had not even known the benefits of roads. This probably created an income effect which had a long-term positive impact on the nation's economy. Since reliable estimates of Italian economic growth until the 1890s are non-existent, let alone estimates for regional economies, this conclusion is at best tentative.

Although it has been shown that the role of the railways in promoting trade flows between northern and southern Italy in the 1880s must not to be under-estimated, it is likely that the railways were not the most important means of transport between the north and the south and therefore captured only a small portion of this trade. Traditional coastal shipping, between Venice and Apulia, for example, is likely to have been larger than north–south railway traffic.

Given its size relative to total traffic on the northern Italian network, Italy's cross-border traffic is also likely to have played a minor role until the beginning of the 1890s, when the Gothard line to Switzerland, in particular, began to be used more intensively. The openness of the northern Italian railway network was similar to the degree of openness of the whole economy, which means that most cross-border lines did not play a particularly important role in augmenting trade. The role of the ports of Venice and Genoa was severely limited, not so much by bad railway management, but by their geographical position in relation to the main foreign markets. Since the total distance from these ports to the border was small, railway rates would have to have been reduced enormously in order to lower total transportation costs and to compete with Marseilles or Trieste.

For all these reasons, the relationship between railway construction and operation and economic growth, industrialization and higher levels of development is not so strong as has often been suggested. The main question asked at the beginning of the book – how did the railways contribute to the formation of the Italian state? – receives a three-fold answer. Politically, it is quite clear that the unsolved 'railway question' continued to divide parliament during the second half of the nineteenth century. Second, in the cultural sense, the railways promoted exchanges between the inhabitants of different parts of Italy and therefore contributed to a cultural exchange. Given the great cultural differences between northern and southern Italy this is not a minor achievement. Massimo d'Azeglio's famous dictum – that now the Italian state had been created, the principal task left was to create Italians – did not spell out how long a period was needed to create unity in more than a strictly legal sense.

Finally, economically the impact of the railways was more positive, not so much by providing better services than traditional transport but by creating new possibilities for commercial exchanges that previously did not exist. Undoubtedly the efforts of the Italian state in the nineteenth century to facilitate Italy's political and economic integration into Europe, by creating a modern tax system, embracing free-trade policies, abolishing export tariffs, devising a modern education system and improving healthcare were impressive, considering its low starting point, and the construction of railways must be considered as one element of this policy. Nevertheless, considering the enduring differences in development levels between northern and southern Italy, and the massive emigration from the south starting in the 1890s, these efforts were not sufficient to eliminate widespread poverty in the south. Given the small potential benefits the railways could offer to the poor and unindustrialized south, where most population centres were well connected by coastal shipping, alternative investment in roads, schools and hospitals might have provided more effective measures for improving development levels. In particular, the fact that much of the expense of the provision of health and education services was left to the municipalities, tended to work against the development of the south, where the municipalities were unable to increase their tax revenues by much. On the whole, the state's actions in these fields were thus at best ineffective, and at worst counter-productive, and in this sense, the thesis that not enough was done to develop the south merits serious reconsideration.

It is a remarkable fact that the Italian state has taken so long to achieve some kind of political and economic unity and that regional income levels did not start to converge significantly until the 1970s. Thus, the limited concept in the nineteenth century of how the state should intervene in economic life and stimulate development postponed the geographical spread of the beneficial effects of economic growth to the south until our own days. The stress laid on the construction of a railway network in the nineteenth century therefore had a high opportunity cost, in the sense that the investments made in railways would have had a more positive impact if they had been dedicated to other areas. Moreover, since national industry did not benefit sufficiently from railway building and the clumsy regulation of the railways impeded the development of traffic, a pessimistic rather than an optimistic view of the contribution of railways to the economic growth and development of Italy as a unified state is warranted.

# BIBLIOGRAPHY

Acworth, William M. *The Elements of Railway Economics*. Oxford, 1924
  *Railway Rates and the Traders*. London, 1891
Aldcroft, Derek H. *British Transport. An Economic Survey from the Seventeenth Century to the Twentieth*. Leicester, 1969
Armstrong, John. 'The Role of Coastal Shipping in UK Transport. An Estimate of Comparative Traffic Movements in 1910', *Journal of Transport History* 8 (1987), pp. 164–78
Associazione per lo Sviluppo dell'Industria nel Mezzogiorno. *Un secolo di statistiche italiane nord e sud, 1861–1961*. Rome, 1961
Avagliano, Lucio. *Un imprenditore e una fabbrica fuori del comune: Alessandro Rossi e il lanificio di Schio*. Bologna, 1981
Bagwell, Phillip S. *The Transport Revolution*. London, 1974
Bairoch, Paul. 'Les spécificités des chemins de fer suisses des origines à nos jours', *Revue Suisse d'Histoire* 39 (1989), pp. 35–57
Barbiero, Tom P. 'A Reassessment of the Agricultural Production of Italy, 1861–1914. The Case of Lombardy', *Journal of European Economic History* 17 (1988), pp. 103–25
Bardini, Carlo. 'Ma il vapore era davvero importante? Consumo energetico e sviluppo industriale di un paese privo di carbone. Italia, 1885–1914'. Ph.D. thesis, European University Institute, Florence, 1994
Bardini, Carlo and Albert Carreras. 'The National Accounts for Italy, Spain and Portugal, 1800–1990'. Conference paper, Groningen, July 1994, pp. 1–32
Bartoccini, Fiorella and Silvana Verdini. *Sui congressi degli scienziati*. Rome, 1952
Baten, Joerg. 'Der Einflub von Regionalen Wirtschaftsstrukturen auf den Biologischen Lebensstandard. Eine Anthropometrische Studie zur Bayerischen Wirtschaftsgeschichte im frühen 19. Jahrhundert', *Vierteljahresschrift für Sozial- und Wirstschaftsgeschichte* 83 (1996), pp. 1–34
Beales, Derek. *The Risorgimento and the Unification of Italy*. London, 1971
Beltrami, D. 'I prezzi nel portofranco e nella borsa merci di Trieste dal 1825 al 1890'. In Carlo Cipolla (ed.), *Archivio Economico dell'Unificazione Italiana*. Turin, 1964

Bernardello, Adolfo. 'Una impresa ferroviaria nel Lombardo-Veneto. La
    società Ferdinandea da Milano a Venezia', *Storia in Lombardia* (1978),
    pp. 186–99
'Imprese ferroviarie e speculazione di borsa nel Lombardo-Veneto e in
    Austria, 1836–1847', *Storia in Lombardia* 49 (1987), pp. 33–102
*La prima ferrovia fra Venezia e Milano. Storia dell'imperiale regia privilegiata strada
    ferrata Ferdinandea Lombardo-Veneta.* Venice, 1996
Berry, Brian J. L. *Economic Geography.* London, 1987
Berselli, Aldo. 'La questione ferroviaria e la "rivoluzione parlamentare" del 18
    Marzo 1876', *Rivista Storica Italiana* 46 (1958), pp. 188–238
Bianchi Tonizzi, Elisabetta. 'Il porto di Genova e la donazione del duca di Gal-
    liera'. In Elisabetta Bianchi Tonizzi, *I Duchi di Galiera.* Genoa, 1991,
    pp. 721–62
Borlandi, Franco. *Il problema delle communicazioni nel secolo XVIII nei suoi rapporti
    col Risorgimento italiano.* Pavia, 1932
Bowring, Sir John. *Report on the Statistics of the Italian States. Sessional Papers
    XVI.* London, 1839
Bresciani, Costantino. *Die Eisenbahnfrage in Italien. Die Wirkungen der Betriebü-
    berlassungsverträge von 1885 un die Neuordnung des Italienischen Eisenbahnwe-
    sens.* Berlin, 1905
Briano, Livio. *Storia delle ferrovie in Italia.* Milan, 1977
Button, K. J. *Transport Economics.* Aldershot, 1986
Caizzi, Bruno. 'La crisi economica nel Lombardo-Veneto nel decennio
    1850–1859', *Nuova Rivista Storica* 42 (1958), pp. 204–22
*La tessitura a Como dall'unità alla fine del secolo.* Bologna, 1981
Cameron, Rondo. 'Problems of French Investment in Italian Railways. A
    Document of 1868', *Business History Review* 33 (1959), pp. 89–103
Candida, Luigi. *Il porto di Venezia. Con introduzione storica di Gino Luzzatto.*
    Naples, 1950
Cantarella, Elvira. 'Lo sviluppo delle ferrovie dalle origini alla statizzazione'. In
    *Storia della Società Italiana.* Milan, 1987, pp. 101–47
Capodaglio, Giulio. *Storia di un investimento di capitale. La Società Italiana per le
    Strade Ferrate Meridionali, 1862–1937.* Milan, 1939
Caron, François. *Histoire de l'exploitation d'un grand réseau. La Compagnie du
    Chemin de Fer du Nord, 1846–1937.* Paris, 1973
Carozzi, Carlo and Alberto Mioni. *Italia in formazione.* Bari, 1972
Carreras, Albert (ed.). *Estadísticas históricas de España. Siglos XIX y XX.* Madrid,
    1989
Cattaneo, Carlo. *Scritti sulla Lombardia. I profili storici–economici della Lombardia e
    di città lombarde. I Scritti Tecnici.* Milan, 1971
'Sui progetti di strade ferrate in Piemonte', *Il Politecnico* 4 (1841), pp. 143–58
Cavour, Camillo. 'Des chemins de fer en Italie' (*Revue Nouvelle*, 1 May 1847,
    pp. 446–79). In Francesco Sirugo (ed.), *Camillo Cavour. Scritti di economia.*
    Milan, 1962, pp. 225–48
Chandler, Alfred D. *The Railroads: The Nation's First Big Business. Sources and
    Readings.* New York, 1965

Chelli, Gaetano Eugenio. *Le nostre ferrovie. Origini e constituzione delle rete ferroviarie italiane.* Milan, 1889

Chevet, Marc and Pascal St Amour. 'Market Integration in France's Wheat Sector in the Nineteenth Century'. *First European Analytical Economic History Conference.* Copenhagen, July 1991

Chiarvalotti, Alessandro. *Le strade ferrate nello Stato Pontifico, 1829–1870.* Rome, 1969

Clough, Shepard B. and Carlo Livi. 'Economic Growth in Italy. An Analysis of the Uneven Development in North and South', *JEH* 19 (1959), pp. 334–49

Corbino, Epicarmo. *Annali dell'economia italiana, 1861–1870,* 5 vols: vol. I, *1861–1870*; vol. II, *1871–1880.* Città di Castello, 1931

Correnti, Cesare. *Annuario statistico italiano. Anno I: 1857–58.* Turin, 1858

Correnti, Cesare and Pietro Maestri. *Annuario statistico italiano. Anno II.* Turin, 1864

Costantini, Massimo. 'Dal porto franco al porto industriale'. In Albino Tenente and Ugo Tucci (eds.), *Storia di Venezia.* Rome, 1991, pp. 879–914

Crispo, Antonio. *Le ferrovie italiane. Storia politica ed economica.* Milan, 1940

Croce, Benedetto. *A History of Italy, 1871–1915.* Oxford, 1929

Dacoisne, Pascal. 'Utilisation de la théorie de graphes pour l'analyse des réseaux ferroviaires', *Revue d'Histoire des Chemins de Fer* 2 (1990), pp. 103–28

David, Paul. 'Clio and the Economics of QWERTY', *AEA Papers and Proceedings* 75 (1985), pp. 332–7
 *The Economics of Gateway Technologies and Network Evolution. Lessons from Electricity Supply History.* Stanford, 1987

De Biase, Corrado. *Il problema delle ferrovie nel Risorgimento italiano.* Modena, 1940

Della Peruta, Franco. 'Malattia e società nell'Italia dell'ottocento'. In *Storia della Società Italiana.* Milan, 1986, pp. 127–50

Demarco, Domenico. 'L'economia e la finanza degli stati italiani dal 1848 al 1860'. In *Nuove Questioni del Risorgimento Italiano.* Milan, 1962, pp. 765–99
 *Il tramonto dello Stato Pontificio. Il papato di Gregorio XVI.* Turin, 1949

Dematteis, Giuseppe, Gino Lusso and Giovanna Di Meglio. 'La distribuzione territoriale dell'industria nell'Italia nord-occidentale, 1887–1927', *Storia Urbana* 40 (1979), pp. 117–56

Di Dario, Vito. *Oh, mia patria! 1861 un inviato speciale nel primo anno d'Italia.* Milan, 1990

Dietrich, Herbert. 'Die Eisenbahnen in den Italienischen Besitzungen der Habsburger', *Eisenbahn* (1986), pp. 123–4, 163–5, 185–6, 203–4

Doria, Giorgio. 'La place du système portuaire ligure dans le développement industriel des régions du triangle'. In Louis Bergeron (ed.), *La croissance régionale dans l'Europe méditerranéenne, 18–20 siècles.* Paris, 1992

Drumm, Ulrich. *Ferrovie italiane. Azioni ed obbligazioni 1840, 1861, 1947.* Frankfurt, 1986

Dumke, Rolf. 'Der Deutsche Zollverein als Modell Okonomischer Integration'. In Helmut Berding (ed.), *Wirtschaftliche und Politische Integration in Europa im 19 un 20 Jahrhundert*. Göttingen, 1984, pp. 71–101

Dunant, Henry. *Un souvenir de Solférino*. Geneva, 1990

Eckhaus, Richard. 'The North–South Differential in Italian Economic Development', *Journal of Economic History* 21 (1961), pp. 285–317

Ellis, John. *The Social History of the Machine Gun*. London, 1987

Ercolani, Paolo. 'Il prodotto interno lordo dell'Italia nel lungo periodo: vecchie e nuove stime'. Working paper, University of Ancona, 1991

Errera, Alberto. *Annuario statistico industriale del Veneto pel 1869*. Venice, 1870
*Documenti alla storia e statistica delle industrie venete e accenni al loro avvenire*. Venice, 1870
*L'Italia industriale. Studi con particolare riguardo all'Adriatico superiore*. Venice, 1873
*Saggio di statistica internazionale marittima comparata a cura del Prof. A. E. con particolare riguardo all'Adriatico superiore. Regno d'Italia e Impero Austro-Ungarico, 1870*. Rome, 1873

Esposto, Alfredo G. 'Italian Industrialization and the Gerschenkronian "Great Spurt". A Regional Analysis', *Journal of Economic History* 52 (1992), pp. 353–400

Faccini, Luigi. 'L'agricoltura italiana dal 1815 al 1859'. In *Storia della Società Italiana*. Milan, 1986, pp. 89–108

Federico, Giovanni. 'Mercantilizzazione e sviluppo economico in Italia, 1860–1940', *Rivista di Storia Economica* 3 (1986), pp. 149–85
'Il valore aggiunto dell'agricoltura'. In Guido Rey (ed.), *I conti economici dell'Italia. Una stima del valore aggiunto per il 1911*. Bari, 1992, pp. 3–103

Federico, Giovanni and Gianni Toniolo. 'Italy'. In Richard Sylla, and Gianni Toniolo (eds.), *Patterns of European Industrialization. The Nineteenth Century*. London, 1991, pp. 197–217

Felloni, G. 'I prezzi nel portofranco e nella borsa merci di Genova nel 1828 al 1890'. In Carlo Cipolla (ed.), *Archivio Economico dell'Unificazione Italiana* 6, series 1. Rome, 1957

Fenoaltea, Stefano. 'Le costruzioni ferroviarie in Italia, 1861–1913', *Rivista di Storia Economica* 1 (1984), pp. 61–87
'Italy'. In Patrick O'Brien (ed.), *Railways and the Economic Development of Western Europe, 1830–1914*. Oxford, 1983, pp. 39–120
'Railroads and Italian Industrial Growth, 1861–1913', *Explorations in Economic History* 11 (1972), pp. 325–51
'Il valore aggiunto dell'industria italiana nel 1911'. In Guido Rey (ed.), *I conti economici dell'Italia. Una stima del valore aggiunto per il 1911*. Bari, 1992, pp. 105–90

Ferraris, Carlo. 'Le ferrovie'. In *Cinquant'anni di storia italiana*. Milan, 1911, pp. 3–64

Ferrovie dello Stato. *Sviluppo delle ferrovie italiane dal 1839 al 31 dicembre 1926*. Rome, 1927
*Sviluppo delle ferrovie italiane per quinquennio*. Rome, 1910

Fischer, Douglas. *The Industrial Revolution. A Macro-Economic Interpretation.* New York, 1992

Fishlow, Albert. *American Railroads and the Transformation of the Ante-Bellum Economy.* Cambridge, Mass., 1965

Fogel, Robert W. 'Notes on the Social Savings Controversy', *Journal of Economic History* 29 (1979), pp. 1–54
   *Railroads and American Economic Growth. Essays in Econometric History.* Baltimore, 1964

Fontana, Josef. *Geschichte des Landes Tirol.* Bozen, 1987

Foreman-Peck, James S. 'Railways and Late Victorian Economic Growth'. In James S. Foreman-Peck (ed.), *New Perspectives on the Late Victorian Economy. Essays in Quantitative Economic History 1860–1914.* Cambridge, 1991, pp. 73–95

Fortunato, Giustino and Giovanni Zuccino. *Discorsi parlamentari di Agostino Depretis.* Rome, 1888

Foxwell, E. and T. C. Farrer. *Express Trains English and Foreign, Being a Statistical Account of All the Express Trains of the World.* London, 1889

Fremdling, Rainier. 'British Coal on Continental Markets, 1850–1913'. In Carl-Ludwig Holtfrerich (ed.), *Interactions in the World Economy. Perspecives from International Economic History.* New York, 1989
   'Freight Rates and the State Budget: The Role of the National Prussian Railways, 1880–1913', *Journal of European Economic History* 9 (1980), pp. 21–39

Fuà, Giorgio and Mauro Gallegati. 'An Annual Chain Index of Italy's Real Product, 1861–1989'. Working paper, University of Ancona, 1994
   'Un indice a catena annuale del prodotto reale dell'Italia, 1861–1989', *Rivista di Storia Economica* 10 (1993), pp. 281–306

Gabelli, Federico. *Il riscatto delle ferrovie.* Padua, 1876

Gerschenkron, Alexander. *Economic Backwardness in Historial Perspective.* Cambridge, Mass., 1966

Giannetti, Renato. 'L'électrification des chemins de fer italiens, 1899–1940', *Histoire, Economie et Société* 11 (1992), pp. 131–44

Gille, Bertrand. 'Les investissements français en Italie, 1815–1914'. In *Archivio Economico dell'Unificazione Italiana,* 16, series 2. Turin, 1968

Girard, Louis. 'Transport'. In H. J. Habbakkuk and M. Postan (eds.), *The Cambridge Economic History of Europe,* 8 vols. Cambridge, 1966, vol. VI, pp. 212–73, 940–3

Giuntini, Andrea. *Contributo alla formazione di una bibliografia storica sulle ferrovie in Italia.* Milan, 1991
   'Le ferrovie nella storiografia italiana', *Italia Contemporanea* (1990), pp. 327–32
   *I giganti della montagna. Storia della ferrovia direttissima Bologna–Firenze, 1845–1934.* Florence, 1984
   *Leopoldo e il treno. Le ferrovie nel Granducato di Toscana, 1824–1861.* Naples, 1991
   'La linea diretta Bologna–Verona e la formazione del sistema ferroviario italiano, 1866–1911', *Padania* 4 (1990), pp. 100–13

Glazier, Ira A. 'Il commercio del regno Lombardo-Veneto dal 1815 al 1865'. In Carlo Cipolla (ed.), *Archivio Economico dell'Unificazione Italiana*. Rome, 1966

Gómez Mendoza, Antonio. *Ferrocarril y mercado interior en España, 1874–1913*. Madrid, 1984

Gourvish, T. R. *Railways and the British Economy, 1830–1914*. London, 1980
  'What Kind of Railway History Did We Get? Forty Years of Research', *Journal of Transport History* 14 (1993), pp. 111–25

Gramsci, Antonio. *Il Risorgimento*. Rome, 1975

Great Britain, Parliamentary Board of Trade. *Continental Railway Investigation. Reports to the Board of Trade on Railways in Belgium, France and Italy. Presented to Both Houses of Parliament by Command of His Majesty*. London, 1910

Great Britain, Statistical Office. *Statistical Abstract for the Principal and Other Foreign Countries in Each Year from 1868 to 1878–9*. London, 1880

Greenfield, Kent Robert. *Economics and Liberalism in the Risorgimento. A Study of Nationalism in Lombardy, 1815–1848*. Baltimore, 1934

Griffin, Appleton P. C. *Selected List of Books on Railroads in Foreign Countries*. Washington D.C., 1905

Griffiths, Richard. 'The Creation of a National Dutch Economy', *Tijdschrift voor Geschiedenis* 95 (1982), pp. 513–37

Guderzo, G. 'Per una periodizzazione della politica ferroviaria sabauda, 1826–1859', *Studi Giuridici e Sociali in Memoria di Ezio Vanoni*. Pavia, 1961

Haskell, Daniel C. *A Tentative Check-List of Early European Railway Literature, 1831–1848*. Cambridge, Mass., 1955

Hawke, Gary R. *Railways and Economic Growth in England and Wales, 1840–1870*. Oxford, 1970

Heinze, Wolfgang and Heinrich H. Kiel. 'The Development of the German Railroad System'. In Renate Mayntz and Thomas P. Hughes (eds.), *The Development of Large Technical Systems*. Frankfurt am Main, 1988, pp. 106–34

Heinzel, Ferdinand. *Die Eisenbahnen und Dampschifffahrten nebst des angehörtigen Post-Coursen in Oesterreich, Deutschland, Italien und den angrenzenden Ländern*. Vienna, 1856

Hertner, Peter. *Il capitale tedesco in Italia dall'unità alla Prima Guerra Mondiale. Banche miste e sviluppo economico italiano*. Bologna, 1984
  'Il problema dei valichi e la politica ferroviaria internazionale', *Padania* 4 (1990), pp. 28–39

Hirschman, Albert O. *The Strategy of Economic Development*. New Haven, 1958

Hole, Jan. *National Railways*. London, 1893

Hoppit, Julian. 'Counting the Industrial Revolution', *Economic History Review* 43, second series (1990), pp. 173–93

Hotelling, H. 'The General Welfare in Relation to Problems of Taxation and of Railway and Utility Rates', *Econometrica* 6 (1937), pp. 242–69

Iannattoni, Livio. *Il treno in Italia*. Rome, 1975

Ippolito, F. 'Lo stato e le ferrovie dalla unità alla caduta della destra', *Clio* (1966), pp. 314–40

Italy, Istituto Centrale di Statistica. *Annuario statistico italiano, 1878.* Rome, 1879
  *Annuario statistico italiano, 1884.* Rome, 1885
  *Annuario statistico italiano, 1897.* Rome, 1898
Italy, Istituto Italiano di Statistica. *Sommario di statistiche storiche, 1861–1965.* Rome, 1968
Italy, Ministerio di Agricoltura, Industria e Commercio. *Movimento della navigazione, 1851–1880.* Rome, 1881
Italy, Ministerio di Agricoltura, Industria e Commercio, Direzione Generale della Statistica. *Censimento della popolazione del regno d'Italia al 31 dicembre 1871 (censimento 1871).* Rome, 1872
  *Censimento della popolazione del regno d'Italia al 31 dicembre 1881 (censimento 1881).* Rome, 1882
Italy, Ministero di Lavori Pubblici. *Atti della commissione d'inchiesta sull'esercizio delle ferrovie italiane (Atti Commissione Baccarini)*, 12 vols. Rome, 1881
  *Riassunto degli atti della commissione d'inchiesta sull'esercizio delle ferrovie italiane (Atti Commissione Baccarini).* Rome, 1881
Italy, Ministero di Lavori Pubblici, Commissione d'Inchiesta sull'Esercizio delle Ferrovie Italiane. *Atti della reale commissione per lo studio di proposte intorno all'ordinamento delle strade ferrate.* Rome, January 1903
Italy, Ministero di Lavori Pubblici, Direzione Generale delle Strade Ferrate. *Risposte al questionario della commissione parlamentare d'inchiesta sull'esercizio delle strade ferrate italiane.* Rome, 1880
James, John. 'The Use of General Equilibrium Analysis in Economic History', *Explorations in Economic History* 21 (1984), pp. 231–53
Jannattoni, Livio. *Il treno in Italia.* Rome, 1980
Jovinelli, Ettore. *Il problema ferroviario. L'ordinamento delle strade ferrate e le convenzioni.* Florence, 1904
Kalla Bishop, P. M. *Italian Railroads.* New York, 1972
Kostov, Alexandre. 'Les Balkans et le réseau ferroviaire européen avant 1914'. In *European Networks, 19th and 20th Centuries. New Approaches to the Formation of a Transnational Transport and Communications System.* Eleventh International Economic History Congress, Session B8, Milan, September 1994 (ed. Paola Subacchi). Milan, 1994, pp. 93–104
Krugman, Paul. *Geography and Trade.* Cambridge, Mass., 1992
Laché, Camillo. 'La politica ferroviaria in Italia tra il 1876 e 1900', *Ingegneria Ferroviaria* (1975), pp. 1–8
  'Il valico dei Giovi', *Ingegneria Ferroviaria* (1978), pp. 1–3
Lazzarini, A. *Campagne venete ed emigrazione di massa.* Vicenza, 1981
Leoni, Leonida. *Testo-Atlante delle ferrovie e tramvie italiane e di quelle estere in contatto Francia, Svizzera ed Austria-Ungheria con un indice prontuario di tutte le linee, stazioni, fermate, scali, ecc. delle ferrovie, tramvie e laghi italiani. Prefazione dell Ing. Pietro Lanino, pres. del Collegio Nazionale degli Ingegneri Ferroviari Italiani (Testo-Atlante).* Novara, 1913
List, Friedrich. *Uber ein Sächsisches Eisenbahn-System als Grundlage eines Allgemeinen Deutschen Eisenbahn-Systems.* Leipzig, 1833
Loria, Leonardo. *Le strade ferrate.* Milan, 1890

Luzzatto, Gino. *L'economia italiana dal 1861 al 1914*. Milan, 1963

'Introduzione'. In Luigi Candida (ed.), *Il porto di Venezia*. Memorie di Geografia Economica, Naples, 1950

Luzzatti, Luigi. *L'esercizio di stato. Discorso pronunziata alla camera dei deputati nella tornata del 18/19 dicembre 1885*. Rome, 1886

Mack Smith, Dennis. *Victor Emmanuel, Cavour and the Risorgimento*. Oxford, 1971

Maddison, Angus. *Dynamic Forces in Capitalist Development. A Long-Run Comparative View*. New York, 1991

'Una revisione della crescita economica italiana, 1861–1989', *Moneta e Credito* 174 (1991), pp. 143–71

Maestri, Pietro. *Dell'industria manifatturiera in Italia*. Turin, 1858

Marcelli, Umberto. *Interpretazioni del Risorgimento*. Bologna, 1970

Marchese, Ugo. 'Il porto di Genova dal 1815 al 1891'. In Carlo Cipolla (ed.), *Archivio Economico dell'Unificazione Italiana* 9, series 1, Rome

Mariotti, F. *Discorsi parlamentari di Quintino Sella*. Rome, 1878

Marshall, Alfred. *Principles of Economics. An Introductory Volume*. London, 1920

Maturi, Walter. *Interpretazioni del Risorgimento*. Turin, 1962

Maywald, K. 'The Construction Costs and the Value of the British Merchant Fleet, 1850–1938', *Scottish Journal of Political Economy* (1956), pp. 44–66

McCarthy, Patrick. *The Crisis of the Italian State: from the Origins of the Cold War to the Fall of Berlusconi*. London, 1995

McCraw, Thomas. 'Regulation in America: A Review Article', *Business History Review* 49 (1975), pp. 158–83

Merger, Michèle. 'Chemins de fer et croissance économique en Italie au XIXème siècle et au début du XXème siècle. Etat de la question', *Histoire, Economie et Société* 3 (1984), pp. 123–44

'Les chemins de fer italiens: leur construction et leurs effets amont, 1860–1915', *Histoire, Economie et Société* 11 (1992), pp. 109–30

'L'industrie italienne de locomotives. Reflet d'une industrialisation tardive et difficile, 1850–1914', *Histoire, Economie et Société* 8 (1989), pp. 336–70

'Mutations techniques et commerciales. Les relations ferroviaires entre l'Italie et l'Europe occidentale de 1867 au début du XXème siècle', *Revue d'Histoire des Chemins de Fer* (1992), pp. 211–52

'Origini e sviluppo del management ferroviario italiano, 1850–1905', *Annali della Storia d'Impresa* 8 (1992), pp. 379–413

Metzer, Jacob. 'Railroad Development and Market Integration. The Case of Tsarist Russia', *Journal of Economic History* 34 (1974), pp. 529–50

Mitchell, Brian Redman. *European Historical Statistics. Europe, 1750–1988*. New York, 1992

Monti, Enrico. *Il primo secolo di vita delle ferrovie italiane, 1839–1849*. Florence, 1939

Negri, Pietro. 'Le ferrovie nello Stato Ponteficio, 1844–1870'. In Carlo Cipolla (ed.), *Archivio Economico dell'Unificazione Italiana* 15, series 2. Rome, 1967

Nuñez, Carla Eugenia. 'Literacy and Economic Growth in Spain, 1860–1977'.

In Gabriel Tortella (ed.), *Education and Economic Development since the Industrial Revolution*. Valencia, 1990, pp. 125–51

O'Brien, Patrick K. *The New Economic History of Railways*. London, 1977
*Railways and the Economic Development of Western Europe, 1830–1914*. Oxford, 1983

Ostuni, Nicola. *Iniziativa privata e ferrovie nel Regno delle Due Sicilie*. Naples, 1980

Papa, Antonio. *Classe politica e intervento pubblico nell'età giolittiana. La nazionalizzazione delle ferrovie*. Naples, 1973

Papal Government, Prefettura Generale delle Acque e Strade. Report 1, Thomas Waghorn to Palmerston, Rome, 19 May 1847, vol. LXXIV, folio 249

Petitti di Roreto, Carlo Illarione. *Delle strade ferrate italiane e del migliore ordinamento di esse. Cinque discorsi*. Capolago, 1845

Petri, Rolf. 'Autarchia, guerra, zone industriali. Continuità e transizione dell'intervento straordinario nell'industria italiana'. Ph.D. thesis, European University Institute, Florence, 1987

Puffert, Douglas. 'The Technical Integration of the European Railway Network'. In *European Networks, 19th and 20th Centuries. New Approaches to the Formation of a Transnational Transport and Communications System*. Eleventh International Economic History Congress, Session B8, Milan, September 1994 (ed. Paola Subacchi). Milan, 1994, pp. 129–40

Ramm, Agatha. *The Risorgimento*. London, 1962

Rey, Guido M. (ed). *I conti economici dell'Italia. Una stima del valore aggiunto per il 1911*. Bari, 1992

Röll, Victor. *Encyclopädie des gesamten Eisenbahnwesens in Alphabetische Anordnung, 1890–1895*, 7 vols. Vienna, 1890

Romano, Roberto. 'L'industria italiana dalla restaurazione all'unità, 1815–1861'. In *Storia della Società Italiana*, vol. XV. Milan, 1986, pp. 109–26

Romeo, Rosario. *Risorgimento e capitalismo*. Bari, 1963

Rossi, Alessandro. *Dell'arte della lana in Italia e all'estero giudicata alla esposizione di Parigi. Note*. Florence, 1869

Roverato, Giorgio. 'La terza regione industriale'. In *Storia d'Italia. Il Veneto*. Turin, 1984, pp. 165–232

Sandberg, Lars G. 'Ignorance, Poverty and Economic Backwardness in the Early Stages of European Industrialization. Variations on Alexander Gerschenkron's Grand Theme', *Journal of European Economic History* 11 (1982), pp. 675–98

Savarè, Carla. 'Un servizio privato di trasporto su diligenza in Lombardia. L'impresa Franchetti', *Storia in Lombardia* 52 (1990), pp. 49–73

Schram, Albert. 'The Impact of Railways. Growth and Development in the Northern Italian Economy, 1856–1884'. Ph.D. thesis, Florence, European University Institute, 1994
'L'Italie et l'Europe: une matrice du trafic ferroviaire de nord de l'Italie, 1867–1884'. In Albert Carreras, Andrea Giuntini and Michèle Merger (eds.), *Les réseaux européens transnationaux XIXe–XXe siècles. Quels enjeux?* Paris, 1995

'De Spoorwegkwestie in de Pauselijke Staten, 1844–1856; Aarzelende Prelaten en Ondernemende Prinsen' ('The Railway Question in the Papal States, 1844–1856; Hesitating Prelates and Enterprising Princes'). Master's thesis, Rijksuniversiteit Utrecht, 1988

Sella, Quintino. *Memorie*, 2 vols. Rome, 1887

Sereni, Emilio. *Capitalismo e mercato nazionale in Italia*. Rome, 1966

Sereno, M. *Storia del paesaggio agrario italiano*. Rome, 1982

Skinner, Thomas. *Stock Exchange Year Book For 1877 Containing a Careful Digest of Information Relating to the Origin, History and Present Position of Each of the Joint Stock Companies And Public Securities Known to the Markets of the United Kingdom*. London, 1878

Sormanni, Giuseppe. *Geografia nosologica dell'Italia*. Rome, 1880

Spaventa, Silvio. *Lo stato e le ferrovie*. Milan, 1876

*Sul riscatto ed esercizio*. Rome, 1876

Strach, H. *Geschichte der Eisenbahen Osterreich-Ungarns von den ersten Anfängen bis zum Jahre 1867*, 5 vols. Vienna, 1898, vol. III.

Tajani, Filippo. *Storia delle ferrovie italiane a cento anni dall'apertura della prima linea*. Milan, 1939

Tatti, Luigi. *Nota sulle ferrovie complementari del Veneto ai confini Austriaci. Estratto dalla Gazetta di Venezia 243, 246 and 247*. Milan, 1872

Tipton, Frank B. *Regional Variations in the Economic Development of Germany during the Nineteenth Century*. Middletown, Conn., 1976

Tissot, Laurent. 'Les traversées ferroviaires alpines suisses et leur rôle sur l'économie européenne, 1880–1939', *Histoire, Economie et Société* 11 (1992), pp. 91–108

Toniolo, Gianni. 'Alexander Gerschenkron in Italia. Alcune osservazioni nel decimo anniversario della morte', *Rivista di Storia Economica* 5 (1988), pp. 397–404

*An Economic History of Liberal Italy*. London, 1990

'Railways and Economic Growth in Mediterranean Countries. Some Methodological Remarks'. In Patrick O'Brien (ed.), *Railways and the Economic Developoment of Western Europe, 1830–1914*. Oxford, 1983, pp. 227–36

Tortella, Gabriel. 'La historia económica de España en el siglo XIX: un ensayo comparativo con los casos de Italia y Portugal'. In Leandro Prados de la Escosura and Vera Zamagni (eds.), *El desarrollo económico en la Europa del sud. España e Italia en perspectiva histórica*. Madrid, 1992

Uggè, Albino. 'Le entrate del Regno Lombardo-Veneto dal 1840 al 1864'. In Carlo Cipolla (ed.), *Archivio Economico dell'Unificazione Italiana* 1, series 1. Rome, 1956

Upper Italy Railway Company. *Allegati alla memoria difensiva nell'interesse dell'amministrazione generale dei lavori pubblici*. Rome, 1875

*Costituzione della Società del Sud dell'Austria e dell'Alta Italia nonche delle linee ad essa concesse od appaltate per l'esercizio e sull'organizzazione amministrativa della rete italiana. Dati raccolti e coordinati ad uso d'ufficio dal Segretario Generale del Consiglio d'amministrazione di Milano*. Milan, 1867

*Geschäfstbericht der K.K. Lombardisch Venetianischen und Zentral Italienischen Ei-senbahn Gesellschaft.* Vienna, 1857–78

*Memoria difensiva della Società Alta Italia nella causa vertente coll'amministrazione generale dei lavori pubblici.* Turin, 1875

*Osservazioni generali relative alla statistica dell'anno 1867.* Milan, 1868

*Servizio della contabilità e del controllo della statistica.* Milan, 1863

Van den Wall Bake, T. *De Italiaansche Spoorwegen.* Utrecht, 1910

Vance, James. *Capturing the Horizon. The Historical Geography of Transportation since the Sixteenth Century.* Baltimore, 1990

Venice, Camera Provinciale di Commercio ed Industria. *Navigazione e commercio di Venezia negli anni 1860–1890. Prospetti statistici a cura di camera di commercio ed arti.* Venice, 1861

Venturi, Walter. *Interpretazioni del Risorgimento.* Turin, 1962

Vidari, E. *Diritto commerciale,* 2 vols. Milan, 1900

Ville, Simon P. *Transport and the Development of the European Economy.* London, 1990

'Transport and the Industrial Revolution', *Journal of Transport History* 13 (1992), pp. 180–5

Westwood, John. *Railways at War.* London, 1980

Williamson, Jeffrey G. 'Globalization, Convergence, and History', *Journal of Economic History* 56 (1996), pp. 277–93

'Greasing the Wheels of Sputtering Export Engines: Midwestern Grains and American Growth', *Explorations in Economic History* 17 (1980), pp. 189–217

'Regional Inequality and the Process of National Development. A Description of Patterns', *Economic Development and Cultural Change* 13 (1965), pp. 4–85

Wingate, Andrew. *Railway Building in Italy before Unification.* Reading, UK, 1971

Woolf, James Stuart. *A History of Italy, 1700–1860. The Social Constraints of Political Change.* London, 1979

Zamagni, Vera. *Dalla periferia al centro. La seconda rinascita economica dell'Italia, 1861–1981.* Bologna, 1990

*An Economic History of Italy, 1860–1990.* Oxford, 1993

'Ferrovie e integrazione del mercato nazionale nell'Italia post-unitaria', *Studi in Onore di Gino Barbieri.* Salerno, 1983, pp. 1635–49

*Industrializzazione e squilibri regionali in Italia. Bilancio dell'età giolittiana.* Bologna, 1978

'Istruzione e sviluppo economico. Il caso italiano, 1861–1913'. In Gianni Toniolo (ed.), *L'economia italiana.* Bari, 1973

'Le radici agricole del dualismo italiano', *Nuova Rivista Storica* 22 (1975), pp. 55–99

*Lo stato italiano e l'economia.* Florence, 1981

Zani, Maurizio. 'Gli incassi delle stazioni ferroviarie per la ricostruzione delle gerarchie urbane, 1880–1990', *Padania* 4 (1990), pp. 166–81

'Il reticolo urbano dell'Italia settentrionale: mutamenti nel ventennio post-unitario', *Storia Urbana* 39 (1978), pp. 77–114

Zaninelli, Sergio. 'Una fonte per la storia dell'economia del Lombardo-Veneto nella prima metà del secolo XIX. Le "Tafeln zur Statistik der Oesterreichischen Monarchie"'. In Carlo Cipolla (ed.), *Archivio Economico dell'Unificazione Italiana* 12, series 1. Rome, 1963

Ziegler, Dieter. 'La constitution de réseaux de voies de communication'. In Albert Carreras, Andrea Giuntini and Michèle Merger (eds.), *Les réseaux européens transnationaux, XIXe–XXe siècles. Quels enjeux?* Paris, 1995, pp. 23–32

'Eisenbahnen und Staat im Zeitalter der Industrialisierung. Die Eisenbahnpolitik der Deutschen Staaten im Vergleich'. Ph.D. thesis, University of Bielefeld, 1994

'Particularistic Competition and the Development of German Transport Networks, 1815–1866'. In *European Networks, 19th and 20th Centuries. New Approaches to the Formation of a Transnational Transport and Communications System.* Eleventh International Economic History Congress, Session B8, Milan, September 1994 (ed. Paola Subacchi). Milan, 1994, pp. 171–87

# INDEX

CAMBRIDGE STUDIES IN ITALIAN HISTORY AND CULTURE